MAPPING
EPIDEMICS

A HISTORICAL ATLAS OF DISEASE

Brent Hoff and Carter Smith III

Charles H. Calisher, Ph.D., Consulting Editor

Franklin Watts
A Division of Grolier Publishing
New York   London   Hong Kong   Sydney
Danbury, Connecticut

Published in association with Media Projects Incorporated

Principal Writers: Brent Hoff and Carter Smith III
Consulting Editor: Charles H. Calisher, Ph.D.
Managing Editor: Carter Smith III
Associate Editor: Karen Covington
Cartographers: David Lindroth and Anthony Galante
Designers: Anthony Galante and Carter Smith III
Cover Design: Joe Borzetta, Pisaza Design

For Franklin Watts: Douglas Hill, Senior Editor

The authors and publisher of this book have made every effort to ensure that the information presented here is accurate and up-to-date. However, as advances in medical science and changes in local conditions occur every day, travelers should not rely solely on this book but, instead, consult other authorities before preparing trips to regions they suspect may pose health risks. Similarly, the treatment of disease should be pursued only in consultation with a health professional.

Library of Congress Cataloging-in-Publication Data

Hoff, Brent H.
     Mapping Epidemics: a historical atlas of disease / Charles H.
Calisher, consulting editor; Brent H. Hoff and Carter Smith III,
writers.
     p.   cm.
     Includes bibliographical references and index.
     ISBN: 0-531-11713-8   ISBN: 0-531-16487-X (pbk.)
     1. Medical geography--History Atlases. 2. Epidemiology--History
Atlases. 3. Social medicine--History Atlases. I. Smith, Carter,
1962–. II. Calisher, Charles H. III. Title.
RA792.H64   2000
614.44'2'0223--dc21   99-16502
                                         CIP

Photo credits
Front Cover: PHOTOTAKE © Dr. Dennis Kunkel/PHOTOTAKE; PHOTOTAKE © Gopal Murti/PHOTOTAKE; Rear Cover: MPI Archives; page 8: PHOTOTAKE © Dr. Dennis Kunkel/PHOTOTAKE; page 16: Mary Evans Picture Library; page 18: Library of Congress; page 19: The Geographic Journal 124 1958 page 174 (Figure1) from the paper by E.W. Gilbert entitled 'Pioneer Maps of Health and Disease in England;' page 25: National Library of Medicine; page 28: Centers for Disease Control; page 38: Ryan White Foundation; page 41: Paul Margolies, ©1996 NAMES Project Foundation; page 46: MPI Archives; page 47: Sickness Prevention Achieved through Regional Collaboration; page 49: Science, Medicine, and History Division of the National Museum of Natural History, Smithsonian Institution; page 50: original art by Rik Fitch; page 52: American Lyme Disease Foundation; page 56: MPI Archives; page 58 (all): National Archives; page 61: MPI Archives; pages 72–73: March of Dimes Birth Defects Foundation; page 74: Library of Congress (upper left corner); Hulton Getty Picture Collection (lower right corner); page 80: The Illustrated London News page 82: National Library of Medicine; page 84: (upper left) The Granger Collection, New York, (lower left) MPI Archives; page 85: (upper left) National Library of Medicine; (upper right) National Library of Medicine/Centers for Disease Control; (lower right) MPI Archives; page 86: Mary Evans Picture Library; page 89: National Archives; page 92: National Library of Medicine; page 95: National Library of Medicine; page 100: Library of Congress.

© Franklin Watts
All rights reserved.
Printed in the United States of America and Canada
1 2 3 4 5 6 7 8 9 10 R 08 07 06 05 04 03 02 01 99

The authors wish to thank all those who have assisted us in the development of this book, particularly Dr. Michael Alderman, Department of Epidemiology and Social Medicine, Albert Einstein College of Medicine; Lynn Bahta, RN, Immunization Action Coalition/Hepatitis B Coalition; and Dr. Ottorino Cosivi, Zoonotic Diseases Unit, Division of Emerging and Other Communicable Disease Surveillance and Control, World Health Organization.

Special thanks for service above and beyond the call to our consulting editor, Dr. Charles H. Calisher, formerly of the Centers for Disease Control, and since 1993, of the Arboviral and Infectious Diseases Laboratory at Colorado State University. For many years, Dr. Calisher has also served as a baseball umpire. Like all great umpires, he possesses three critical attributes—a keen eye, a deep understanding of the rules of the game, and the confidence to make accurate, informed calls in heated and often confused situations. He brings those same qualities to the field of epidemiology, and we are thankful to have had him making the calls on this project.

INTRODUCTION

The depredations of the global HIV pandemic have been a humbling experience for the scientific infectious disease community and the public health authorities. This can hardly be compared with the human suffering induced by this alien surprise, and what may still lie ahead. However, it may yet have some salutary effect if it alerts us to still further hazards that we face as a species in our competition with microbial competitors, who crowd us at the summit of the terrestrial food chain.

—Joshua B. Lederberg, Sackler Foundation Scholar, Rockefeller University

While the human race battles itself, fighting over ever more crowded turf and scarcer resources, the advantage moves to the microbes' court. They are our predators and they will be victorious if we, Homo sapiens, *do not learn how to live in a rational global village that affords the microbes few opportunities. It's either that or we brace ourselves for the coming plague.*

—Laurie Garrett, *The Coming Plague*

Almost every day, we can read in newspapers and magazines, hear on the radio, or see and hear on television that yet another infectious disease has reared its ugly head. Newly discovered viruses, well-known viruses that have jumped to new geographic areas, bacteria and parasites in our water and our food, antibiotic-resistant bacteria, ordinary bacteria that kill people who have deficient immune systems—the list of possible causes of disease is long, and frightening. What is going on here?

For as long as there have been people on Earth, there have been diseases to make them ill or to kill them and their livestock. Why, apparently all of a sudden, are we seeing an increase in these diseases? Or are we? Perhaps we have recently taken better notice, since the Information Age has provided us with the ability to disseminate medical information more rapidly than ever before. Perhaps it is more complicated than that.

The remarkable increase in the number of humans, the cutting of trees and burning of rain forests, rapid air travel between continents, the transplanting of tissue and organs (hearts, livers, lungs, kidneys, corneas) from one human to another and even from other species to humans, all of this provides opportunities for viruses, bacteria, and parasites to migrate from their natural environments, where they had been "silent."

It is not easy to recognize new viruses or viruses that have moved into geographic areas where they had been unknown. Early in 1999, a new virus, Nipah virus, was discovered in Malaysia. At first, researchers thought they were seeing cases of Japanese encephalitis in humans and pigs. However, it quickly became apparent that that was not the case. An epidemic was aborted only when hundreds of thousands of valuable pigs were killed. Nipah virus appears to be a bat virus that somehow infected a few pigs. From there it jumped from pig to pig and from pigs to humans.

In late summer 1999, several people in New York City became ill and a few died from what appears to be West Nile virus. This virus is transmitted by mosquitoes and uses birds as its primary vertebrate host. West Nile virus is relatively common in Africa and parts of Asia and has been detected in Europe as well. However, it had never been detected in the Americas, so no one suspected its presence. As with Nipah virus, another virus was at first suspected to be the cause of these illnesses. The West Nile virus story is not yet complete. Many questions remain, including the exact identity of the virus, where it came from, and whether it will cause problems in years to come. How far will it spread within the United States? Will it spread to Canada and Latin America?

The evolution of viruses and bacteria has and always will provide challenges for humankind. We already know the causes of many diseases and how to prevent and treat them. However, with lack of funding—and lack of basic attention—even preventable diseases can make a comeback. Preventable childhood diseases—

those for which there are vaccines, such as measles, rubella, chicken pox, mumps, whooping cough, and poliomyelitis—simply should not occur. But they do.

Mapping Epidemics: A Historical Atlas of Disease is intended to familiarize high school readers and others interested in infectious diseases with many of the historically important diseases, diseases that have changed human history. Infectious diseases have had significant impact on humans determining the way we think about travel, strangers, wars, and, more recently, ecosystem destruction. And they have, of course, killed countless millions—and the occassional well-placed king, whose death changed history.

> Each time we misuse antibiotics, pack more people into ever-shrinking areas, discontinue or decrease protection of our drinking water supplies, or abuse our bodies with illegal drugs or unsafe sex, we allow disease-causing microbes the opportunity to spread.

It is important to remember, too, that diseases such as typhoid, tuberculosis, leprosy, dysentery, malaria, dengue, infectious encephalitis, hepatitis, and others, including, of course, acquired immunodeficiency syndrome (AIDS), have not at all disappeared. They may not occur or they may be uncommon in the so-called developed world, but all we need to do to have them back with us is to let our guard down—to end education programs or to stop vaccinating or to stop controlling the insects that spread disease. Each time we misuse antibiotics, we allow the development of antibiotic-resistant organisms. When we pack more people into ever-shrinking areas, discontinue or decrease protection of our drinking water supplies, we put ourselves at risk. And each time we abuse our bodies with illegal drugs or unsafe sex, we allow disease-causing microbes the opportunity to spread.

In many ways it is counterproductive for government to preach about diseases. What is needed is information, not a cover of moral certainty. The authors of this book have tried to avoid preaching and to stick to presenting information. They have also recognized that this book cannot serve scientific ends. It is intended as an introduction to the complex field of microbiology. In order to obtain in-depth information, our readers will have to read more—much more. Encyclopedias are always a good place to start, but your local library, a university library, the World Wide Web, your family physician, educational television programs, and so on also make good sources of information. Learning never ends. Perhaps this book will be the beginning of a lifetime of fascination with infectious diseases and the microbes that cause them. Perhaps that fascination will lead to important contributions to medical science.

Charles H. Calisher, Ph.D.
Arthropod-borne and Infectious Diseases Laboratory
Department of Microbiology
Colorado State University

Most of the contagious diseases discussed in this book are caused by either bacteria or viruses, both of which are discussed below. The scientific and medical terms highlighted in red throughout this book are defined in the glossary on these pages.

BACTERIA AND VIRUSES

Bacillus anthracis, *the cause of anthrax*

BACTERIUM: any unicellular round, spiral, or rod-shaped microorganisms that form colonies or move by means of flagella (tentacle-like appendages). Bacteria, the most abundant form of organism on Earth, live in soil, water, or organic matter, including the bodies of plants and animals. Bacteria reproduce through a process called binary fission, in which a cell splits into two approximately equal parts. Some bacteria, such as *Bacillus anthracis,* can survive unfavorable conditions by forming highly resistant spores with thick coverings. The living material remains dormant inside until conditions improve. Some bacterial parasites can cause diseases in humans, including cholera, tuberculosis, and syphilis. Some bacteria attack tissues directly while others produce toxins. Natural defense against pathogenic bacteria is provided by antibodies. Certain bacterial diseases, such as diphtheria, can be prevented by injection of antitoxin or of a serum containing antibodies against specific bacterial antigens. Immunity to some bacterial diseases can be gained through vaccination, while certain other bacteria can be killed by antibiotics.

Ebola virus, *the cause of Ebola hemorrhagic fever*

VIRUS: a submicroscopic entity —that is, one requiring an electron microscope to be seen— made up of nucleic acid surrounded by a protein coat. Viruses can cause disease in humans, including AIDS, influenza, and smallpox. A virus can survive outside of the cells in which it is made only if the temperature remains stable, and can reproduce only with the assistance of a specific host cell. Upon making contact with such a cell, a virus attaches itself to that cell. The virus's protein coating then opens a hole in the cell and releases nucleic acid—a long threadlike molecule— through the coat and into the cell. Once in the cell, the nucleic acid alters the cells's behavior, beginning the production of more virus. Together, the host cell and the virus begin making more nucleic acid. Following the manufacture of protein for the coat, virus particles emerge from the cell. Some viruses, such as cowpox, or *vaccinia,* contain nucleic acid that does not cause disease in humans. Since these viruses contain the same coat as pathogenic viruses, such as smallpox *variola,* they stimulate production of antibodies when introduced into the body. This process is key to vaccination, one of the primary defenses against viral diseases. In some cases, a "killed-virus vaccine" can be made by inactivating the nucleic acid without irreparably damaging the protein coat.

SOME OTHER IMPORTANT TERMS

ANTIBIOTIC: any substance, such as penicillin or streptomycin, produced by or derived from a microorganism with the ability to inhibit or kill another microorganism.

ANTIBODY: any of various proteins in the blood that are generated in reaction to foreign proteins or carbohydrates, neutralize them, and thus produce immunity against certain microorganisms or their toxins.

ANTIGEN: any substance that, upon being introduced into the body, stimulates the production of antibodies.

ANTITOXIN SERUM: a serum collected from animals that have been immunized by injection of a toxin. It is administered to neutralize a specific bacterial toxin, such as diphtheria.

ARTHROPOD: an animal that has a hard jointed exoskeleton and paired, jointed legs. These include arachnids (spiders) and insects. Arthropods of many species are capable of causing disease in humans.

ATTENUATE: to weaken, as to make a pathogenic microbe less virulent.

BACILLUS: a rod-shaped bacterium.

BACTERIOPHAGE: a virus whose host is a bacterial cell.

CAUSATIVE AGENT: a virus, bacterium, parasite, or other cause of disease.

CELL: the smallest structural unit of an organism that is capable of functioning independently. It is made up of one or more nuclei, cytoplasm, organelles, and inanimate matter, all of which is surrounded by a semipermeable plasma membrane.

CEREBRAL EDEMA: a swelling of the brain caused by an excessive accumulation of watery fluids in the tissue.

CHROMOSOME: a linear or circular strand of DNA and related proteins in the nucleus of animal, plant or bacterium cells that carry genetic hereditary information.

DNA: one of several nucleic acids (*deoxyribonucleic acid*) that are in cell nuclei and are the molecular basis of heredity in organisms.

ENDEMIC: consistently present in a region.

ENZYME: any of several complex proteins that are produced by cells and trigger a specific biochemical reaction.

EPIDEMIC: the occurrence of a disease over a wide area in a specific region.

EPIDEMIOLOGY: the branch of medical science that deals with the incidence, distribution, and control of disease in a population. An epidemiologist is a person that studies epidemiology.

FILOVIRUSES: a family of RNA-containing viruses that includes Ebola virus and Marburg virus; all cause hemorrhagic fevers in one vertebrate host or another.

GENES: formed from DNA and comprising the chromosomes; they are responsible for the inherited characteristics that distinguish one individual from another.

GERM THEORY: the theory that all infections, contagious diseases, and various other conditions result from the actions of microorganisms.

GRANULOMA: a swollen lesion made up of several cells, some of which attack and some of which repair tissues.

HOST: any plant or animal that is infected by a pathogenic organism.

IMMUNE SYSTEM: the body's system of organs, tissues, cells, and cell products (such as antibodies) that neutralizes bacteria, viruses, or other substances that may cause disease.

IMMUNITY: the condition of being immune to, or protected against, an infectious disease, either by the defense of the immune system, by immunization, or by previous infection.

IMMUNIZATION: a technique used to create immune resistance to a particular disease by exposing a person to an antigen to raise antibodies to that antigen.

INCUBATION: the period of time between the infection of an individual by a pathogen and the appearance of symptoms of the disease it causes.

INFECTION: invasion of a body part by foreign microbes, possibly leading to tissue injury and disease through a variety of cellular or toxic mechanisms.

INOCULATION: the injection of a pathogen or antigen into a human or animal, usually into the skin, in order to prevent a disease.

MACROPHAGE: a round white blood cell that helps protect the body against infection and toxic substances.

MEMBRANE: a thin, soft, pliable sheet or layer, typically of animal origin.

MIASMA THEORY: a discredited idea that disease is caused by poison vapor rising from swamps or rotting matter; supplanted by the germ theory.

MICROORGANISM: an organism that can be seen only with a microscope and not with the naked eye.

MICROBE: a living, microscopic organism such as a bacterium, fungus, or protozoa; a microorganism.

MOLECULE: two or more atoms combined through chemical bonding to create the smallest particle of a substance that retains all the physical properties of that substance.

MUTATION: any alteration of the genes or chromosomes of an organism that can be inherited.

NEUROTOXIN: a poisonous substance, usually a protein, that is toxic to the nervous system.

NUCLEUS: the center of a cell that is essential to its functions.

ORGANISM: any individual living thing, either plant or animal.

PANDEMIC: a disease that occurs over a large geographic area, such as a continent, or even worldwide, and affects an exceptionally high proportion of the population.

PASTEURIZATION: a process of sterilization, developed by Louis Pasteur, by which perishable food and liquids are exposed to a specific high temperature for a period of time in order to destroy certain organisms.

PATHOGEN: any infectious agent that causes disease.

PATHOLOGIST: a scientist who studies the nature, causes, processes, development, or consequences of diseases, especially the changes in tissue and bodily fluids associated with disease.

PARASITE: an organism that lives on, with, or in another organism and obtains food and shelter from its host.

PLASMID: an extrachromosomal ring of DNA that reproduces independently in bacteria.

PRIONS: thought to be an infectious protein devoid of nucleic acid; cause a group of fatal diseases—transmissible spongiform encephalopathies—that affect humans and other mammals.

PROTEIN: a nitrogenous organic compound containing amino acids found in vegetable and animal matter as well as in viruses, bacteria, parasites, and fungi.

PROTOZOAN PARASITE: a single-celled organism that invades a host.

RED BLOOD CELLS: blood cells in vertebrates that carry oxygen to, and carbon dioxide from the tissues.

RETROVIRUS: a virus that contains RNA at its core. The RNA makes proteins, with the help of transcriptase; the reverse (retro) transcriptase used in manufacturing new DNA gives the virus its name.

RNA: one of several nucleic acids (*ribonucleic acid*) associated with cellular chemical activity.

SERUM: the clear fluid obtained when blood is separated into its solid and liquid components.

STRAIN: a group of organisms of the same species that have distinct characteristics but are not different enough to be considered separate types.

T CELLS: cells (*thymus-derived cells*) characterized by specific surface antigens whose special function is to protect against viruses and to reject foreign tissue.

TOXIN: a poison—typically a protein produced by some higher plants, certain animals, and pathogenic bacteria—that will kill or sicken an organism.

TRANSCRIPTASE: an enzyme discovered in retroviruses that changes the formation of DNA using RNA as a template.

TRANSMISSION: passage of a disease agent from one animal to another.

VACCINE: killed microorganisms administered for the prevention of the infectious disease they cause.

VECTOR: an organism (such as an insect or rodent) that transmits a pathogen.

VIRIONS: a complete virus particle that consists of an RNA or DNA core with a protein coat, sometimes with external envelopes.

WHITE BLOOD CELLS: the part of the immune system responsible for attacking foreign invaders in the body. They include T cells and macrophages.

ZOONOTIC: relating to diseases transmissible from animals to humans.

Mapping Epidemics

ANTHRAX

Global Distribution Anthrax can be found globally, but is most common in South and Central America, the Caribbean, southern and eastern Europe, Africa, and Asia.

Causative Agent Anthrax is caused by the bacterium *Bacillus anthracis.*

Transmission Transmission of anthrax can occur in three ways: 1) through skin exposure from handling infected animal products, 2) through inhalation of *Bacillus anthracis* spores that can live in soil for many years, and 3) by eating anthrax-contaminated meat.

Symptoms Symptoms depend upon how the person is infected. An infection through the skin begins with a rash with raised, itchy bumps which within two days develops into a vesicle, and then into an ulcer with a black spot in the center. Lymph glands closest to the infection may swell. Death occurs in 20 percent of untreated cases, but is rare with proper treatment. Inhalation infection initially appears as a common cold. After a few days, the symptoms may progress into severe breathing difficulty, and usually death. Symptoms of gastrointestinal infection include severe inflammation of the intestinal tract, nausea, vomiting, fever, abdominal pain, vomiting of blood, and diarrhea. Gastrointestinal anthrax results in death in 25 to 60 percent of untreated cases.

Treatment Antibiotics such as penicillin, erythromycin, tetracycline, or chloramphenicol are effective if treatment begins early.

Prevention and Control A human anthrax vaccine is licensed for use in the United States for those who come in frequent contact with animal products and are therefore at risk, and in 1998 the Department of Defense announced plans to begin vaccinating all U.S. military personnel due to the possible threat of anthrax as a biological weapon. For those traveling to countries where anthrax continues to affect livestock, particular caution should be taken in handling or eating animal products.

During World War II, Allied forces conducted anthrax weapons tests on Gruinard Island, off Scotland. The experiments ended when sheep and cattle began dying along the coast directly across from the island. Gruinard Island remains contaminated to this day.

In the mid-nineteenth century, farmers across most of the world shared the common fear of a mysterious killer that threatened their livestock. Anthrax, with its potential to claim an entire flock of sheep, could transform a healthy animal overnight into a slow-moving creature lacking energy and appetite. Within twenty-four hours, the same animal could be dead, its blood turned sickly and black. After deaths of one, two, or several animals, the shepherd, wool-sorter, or farmer might also fall sick and die.

The symptoms in humans, however, varied from case to case. Many who came in contact with sick animals or their products developed itchy, infected boils and swollen glands. Others exhibited flu-like symptoms, and ultimately succumbed to a wheezing, pneumonia-like last breath. Still others were struck with nausea, high fever, and severe diarrhea. Although many survived, some died days after the first symptoms appeared. Even more alarming, anthrax did not kill just sheep and their herders, but also any other warm-blooded animal that it came in contact with. Those working with animals were concerned not only by this apparent lack of discrimination, but also with the economic consequences of the fatal illness.

Robert Koch's Discovery

The fear of anthrax cut across class lines. No matter how large a farmer's holdings, survival depended upon a healthy stock. That the infection seemed so arbitrary was deeply disturbing. While one beautiful, green pasture produced healthy herds and flocks, the next field caused the same group of animals to fall sick and die. Farmers feared these deadly fields, and with no other reasonable answer at hand, many felt that the pastures had been cursed by God. In 1876, German doctor Robert Koch isolated *Bacillus anthracis,* living microscopic rods and threads in a pin drop of infected blood from one of the sick animals. Cattlemen and shepherds were desperate for more answers, however. Knowledge of an organism that could kill their animals meant little to them if they could not detect which pastures would wreak havoc on livestock and which would not. Koch's breakthrough, on the other hand, did create a sensation in the medical community.

Until Koch's discovery, no scientist had proved, much less believed, that a microbe could be the single cause of a deadly disease. Koch proved not only that one specific BACILLUS, or BACTERIUM, caused one specific disease, but he also discovered how these organisms survived, and moved on to infect animal after ani-

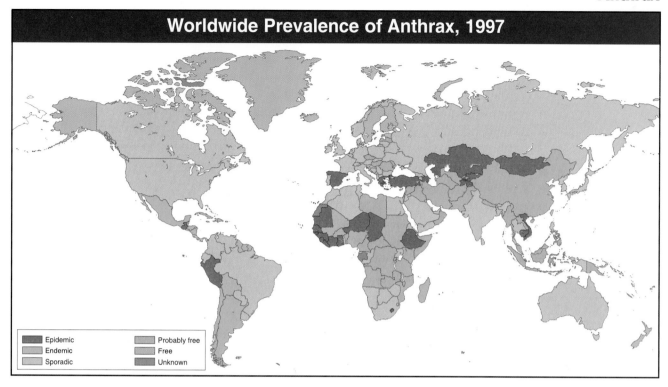

Worldwide Prevalence of Anthrax, 1997

Epidemic
Endemic
Sporadic
Probably free
Free
Unknown

mal. Koch also revealed that *B. anthracis* could survive varied weather conditions by transforming into a spore-form and living in soil, sometimes for several years. Then, once inside a living HOST, these spores became multiplying, deadly bacteria. Koch therefore advised that farmers and shepherds cremate animals that died of anthrax, so as not to infect soil. Koch's breakthrough led to a new approach to medicine, as doctors turned to the discovery and identification of disease-causing microbes in their attempt to combat epidemics.

The Threat of Biological Warfare

Although few people become infected today, anthrax still affects animals in many parts of the world, particularly in regions with poor public health systems. When individuals are infected, they will survive with immediate treatment. An anthrax VACCINE has been licensed for human use in the United States. Animal vaccines are also available.

While the annual number of human deaths from anthrax remains small in comparison with rates for other infectious diseases, the bacteria has caught the public's imagination in the past few years. In February 1998, U.S. marshals arrested two men on charges of possessing anthrax spores. One of the men had previously been convicted of illegally ordering plague bacteria through the mail. Although charges were dropped against the men, the episode alarmed the nation. That a

release of just a pound of powdered anthrax could kill thousands has not been lost on military planners. During World War II, Allied forces conducted anthrax weapons tests on Gruinard Island, off Scotland. The experiments ended when sheep and cattle began dying along the coast directly across from the island, and Gruinard Island remains contaminated to this day.

While few nations today admit to biological warfare programs, they are continuing. In 1979, an explosion at a plant in Sverdlosk, USSR, was immediately followed by an anthrax outbreak. At the time, Soviet authorities denied a connection between the two. Only in 1992, after the breakup of the Soviet Union, did Russian President Boris Yeltsin admit that anthrax research had been conducted. While Yeltsin denied that research was continuing, defectors confirm that the Russian military is carrying on that work.

Today, the anthrax risk is greater than ever. North Korea, Iran, and Iraq, all known to have links to terrorists, have also been conducting biological weapons research. Following the 1991 Persian Gulf War, United Nations weapons inspectors discovered that Iraq had been secretly growing large quantities of anthrax. Since that discovery, the U.S. military has begun vaccinating troops.

While this is a step in the direction of protection, the looming threat of biological warfare leaves us with many more safeguards to undertake.

Mapping Epidemics

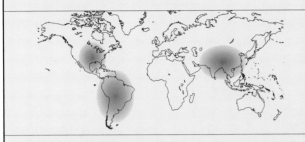

ARBOVIRAL ENCEPHALITIDES

Global Distribution Arboviral encephalitides are found worldwide, but are most prevalent in the Americas and Asia.

Causative Agent Arboviral encephalitides are caused by a range of viruses.

Transmission The word *arboviral* means viruses that are transmitted by mosquitoes and other arthropods.

Symptoms Although a number of different viruses can cause arboviral encephalitides, most cases are asymptomatic or result in a headache and flu-like symptoms. St. Louis encephalitis (SLE) can range from a mild headache to a swelling of the brain and meninges; however, the majority of cases go undiagnosed. Eastern equine encephalitis (EEE) can progress to serious symptoms such as seizures, coma, and even death. Severe cases of western equine encephalitis (WEE) may result in vomiting, anorexia, confusion, and depression. The most common form, Japanese encephalitis (JE), can result in paralysis or death.

Treatment There are no human vaccines for EEE or WEE, the major forms of arboviral encephalitides found in the United States, but Japanese encephalitis vaccines are available. Instead, medical care has centered on treating severe symptoms such as brain swelling and impaired breathing.

Prevention and Control The most effective ways to prevent arboviral encephalitides are personal cautionary measures (such as wearing long pants and using insect repellent) and insect control (such as the spraying of insecticide).

Human St. Louis Encephalitis Cases by State

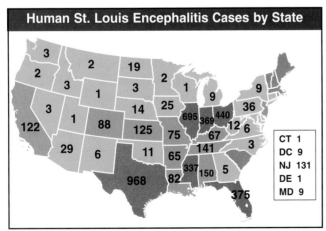

CT	1
DC	9
NJ	131
DE	1
MD	9

Since 1964, there have been approximately 4,500 confirmed cases of St. Louis encephalitis in the United States.

In August 1997, Walt Disney World went on alert. Swimming pools and water parks were closed and activities such as golf, fishing, hayrides, and campfire sing-alongs were postponed. All guests were advised to wear protective clothing after dark if they ventured outdoors. As an extra emergency measure, everyone was advised to use extra mosquito repellent.

Were these precautions and inconveniences really justified to fight off mosquitoes? Although Disney's guests were not at great risk, the company's extra measures of precaution underscore the fact that a simple mosquito bite may be fatal. Disney was responding to an Orange County, Florida, medical alert about St. Louis encephalitis, a viral infection carried by *Culex nigripalpus* mosquitoes. Seven years earlier, eleven people in the state had died from the same VIRUS

Japanese Encephalitis

Encephalitis literally means inflammation of the brain. The type of virus involved can vary widely, from polio viruses to those that cause chicken pox, measles, or rabies. Once a virus enters the blood, it can localize in the brain, causing WHITE BLOOD CELLS to invade to fight off the infection. This leads to a condition known as CEREBRAL EDEMA, or swelling of the brain tissue, followed by the destruction of nerve cells, bleeding in the brain, and consequent brain damage. When a virus is carried by ARTHROPODS such as mosquitoes or ticks, the virus is called an arbovirus ("arthropod-borne virus").

The most common mosquito-borne encephalitis is Japanese encephalitis (JE). First recognized in 1871, it killed over twelve thousand people in Japan during a twelve-year period during the 1920s and 1930s. While VACCINES now exist for JE, it remains a major threat throughout southern and eastern Asia. Today, as many as fifty thousand cases are documented each year—ten thousand of which are fatal.

One common route of JE infection is from birds to to domestic pigs, and then to humans, all via *Culex* mosquitoes. Because pools of water and soggy rice fields are the preferred breeding ground for *Culex,* most cases occur in rural areas, typically during the rainy season. In areas where irrigation allows for year-round agriculture, JE infections also occur year-round.

Studies have shown that most people living in regions where JE is ENDEMIC will be infected by the JE virus by the age of fifteen. The vast majority do not become sick. Only about one in three hundred of those infected will experience JE's typical symptoms—fever, chills, aches, and, particularly among young children, gastrointestinal pain and con-vulsions. More serious cases can lead to brain and nerve damage, coma, and death. Because no effective treatment for JE exists, vaccination pro-grams are critical to prevent even greater numbers of illness-es. Nonetheless, even in coun-tries where effective vaccina-tion programs exist, JE is still a problem.

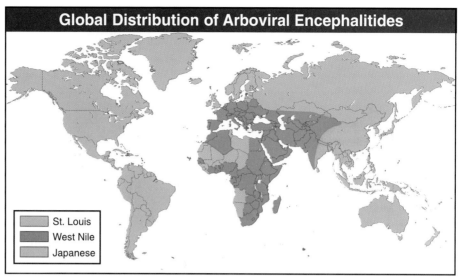

Global Distribution of Arboviral Encephalitides

- St. Louis
- West Nile
- Japanese

Prior to 1999, West Nile virus had never been found in North America. The map above shows historic ranges of West Nile, St. Louis, and Japanese encephalitis.

Arboviral Encephalitides in the United States

The first known cases of arboviral encephalitides in the United States occurred in 1933 when St. Louis encephalitis (SLE) was discovered. SLE EPIDEMICS have occurred sporadically ever since. Although the SLE virus is the most common mosquito-borne human PATHOGEN in the United States, symptoms are sometimes so minor—often no more than a headache—that less than 1 percent of cases are even identified. Nonetheless, in rare instances, the virus can be dangerous, particularly for the elderly and very young.

Two even more dangerous arboviruses in the United States—eastern equine encephalitis (EEE) and western equine encephalitis (WEE)—got their names because they attack horses as well as humans. EEE is found along the eastern seaboard, the Gulf Coast, and in some midwestern states, and is concentrated in swampy areas throughout those regions during the warmer months, although where it resides in winter is unknown. It may lie dormant in infected mosquitoes or, as some researchers have suggested, it may be spread by migrat-ing birds each spring. EEE virus can kill up to one-third of those infected by it.

The WEE virus, first found in the brain of a horse in 1930, is present throughout much of the western United States. Mosquitoes found in irrigated farmland and drainage ditches are known carriers and spread it to both mammals and birds. Human infections typically occur in midsummer and can cause fevers, headaches, nausea and vomiting, anorexia, and fatigue. While the death rate from WEE is under 5 percent, infants are at risk of permanent nerve damage.

A fourth arbovirus was discovered in LaCrosse, Wisconsin, in 1963. Most cases of LaCrosse encephali-tis (LAC) are found in the upper Midwest, but cases have been documented in mid-Atlantic states like Virginia and North Carolina, as well as in Alabama and Mississippi. In a typical year, about seventy-five LAC cases are reported to the Centers for Disease Control (CDC). Most victims are under sixteen years old.

Researchers have found that the LAC virus is passed by *Aedes triseriatus* mosquitoes to chipmunks and squirrels. *Ae. triseriatus* feeds in the daytime and lives in tree holes. Although fewer than 1 percent of vic-tims die from LAC infections, severe cases can lead to seizures, coma, paralysis, and permanent nerve damage. In most cases, symptoms are limited to fever, headaches, and nausea and vomiting.

To date, deaths in the United States from arboviral encephalitides are relatively uncommon. Even so, the potential risks are serious, particularly since no vac-cines exist for the strains most common to the United States and the far deadlier JE may be spreading in Asia. Fears of an arboviral encephalitis PANDEMIC may be unfounded, but clearly authorities—from Florida tourist meccas to Southeast Asia—must remain vigilant.

In 1999, a mosquito-borne virus killed six people in metro-politan New York. Authorities first believed the cause to be St. Louis encephalitis (SLE). However, after birds began dying in unusual numbers, scientists discovered the cause to be West Nile fever, which has symptoms almost identi-cal to those of SLE. Because West Nile virus had never been found in North America, birds in the region may have had little immunity to it.

ARENAVIRAL HEMORRHAGIC FEVERS

Global Distribution Arenaviral fevers are divided into two groups: the New World complex, which includes Argentine, Bolivian, and Venezuelan hemorrhagic fevers, and the Old World complex, which includes Lassa fever, from Africa.

Causative Agent Arenaviral hemorrhagic fevers are caused by various viruses. Junín virus, Machupo virus, and Lassa virus are three of the many.

Transmission Arenaviruses are spread by rodents through their saliva, urine, and/or feces. They can be transmitted to humans via contaminated food, through cuts in the skin, or through breathing contaminated dust.

Symptoms Typical early symptoms of arenaviral hemorrhagic fever include fever, headache, fatigue, and aching muscles. Within a week of onset patients may develop signs of hemorrhaging, including bleeding from the nose, mouth, lungs, stomach, or genitals.

Treatment The most effective treatment for arenaviral fevers is the antiviral drug ribavirin. There is presently no vaccine for Lassa virus or Machupo virus, but an effective vaccine against Junín virus has been administered to those at high risk for the virus.

Prevention and Control Rodent control, education, and better public health are necessary.

Researchers believe that the expansion of Argentina's beef industry during World War II led to the emergence of Argentine hemorrhagic fever. While many of the leading cattle producing nations were at war, Argentina took advantage of the opportunity by clearing vast areas of its dry central pampas region to create cattle grazing areas. As a result, the population of field mice carrying the Junín virus that causes the disease exploded.

Human beings do not always appreciate that nature is in fine balance. When that balance is pushed too far, nature can push back violently. Human tinkering with the environment has repeatedly led to disastrous results.

The emergence of South American arenavirus EPIDEMICS of the 1950s and 1960s demonstrate this point. In that case, encroachment into previously uncultivated lands caused radical environmental changes that led to the unfortunate emergence of new infectious diseases in humans.

Since 1953, cases of severe hemorrhagic (heavy bleeding) fevers have wreaked havoc in Argentina and Bolivia. The sources of these ailments were determined to be two previously undiscovered viruses—named the Junín and Machupo VIRUSES after rivers in Argentina and Bolivia. Because the two viruses are sandy in appearance when viewed under an electron microscope, they are known as arenaviruses, after *arena,* the Latin word for sandy.

A Consequence of War

The roots of the Junín virus epidemics can be found in World War II. During the war, Argentina stepped in to fill an agricultural vacuum that was created when the United States, Soviet Union, and other top beef and grain producers went into battle.

Through the use of new pesticides, fertilizers, and farming techniques, Argentinians created farmlands where there had never been any before—on the dry pampas, or plains. With these new farmlands, however, came a rapid increase in the number of field mice. Among these mice is *Calomys musculinus,* the carrier of Junín virus. Relatively rare to Argentina until then, the *Calomys musculinus* population exploded as new wheatfields were created.

Argentine Hemorrhagic Fever

In 1953, Argentina saw the first recorded outbreak of what was later named Argentine hemorrhagic fever (AHF). Those who ate food contaminated with virus-infested dust, as well as fieldworkers who inhaled it, soon become ill.

Symptoms included chills, fever, headaches, and nausea and vomiting. In the most severe cases, patients rapidly deteriorated further. As blood vessels ruptured, bleeding became uncontrollable, pouring from gums, and flowing through urine, feces, and vomit. The massive blood and fluid loss almost inevitably led to death.

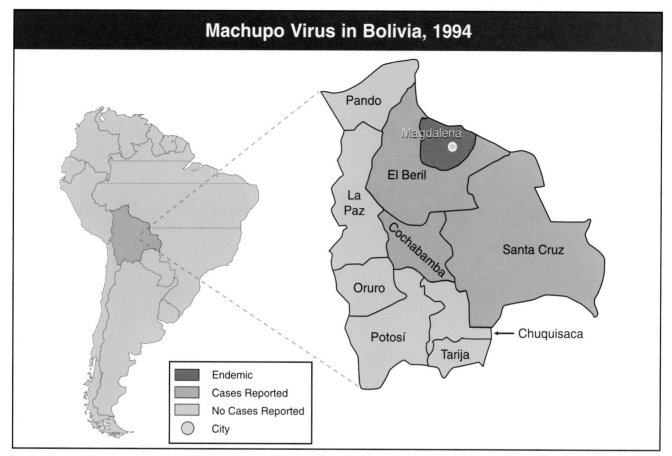

Machupo Virus in Bolivia, 1994

Pando

Magdalena

El Beril

La Paz

Cochabamba

Santa Cruz

Oruro

Potosí

← Chuquisaca

Tarija

- Endemic
- Cases Reported
- No Cases Reported
- City

Bolivian Hemorrhagic Fever

Six years later, word came from a remote region of eastern Bolivia of an epidemic with almost the same symptoms. This time, the culprit was the Machupo arenavirus, carried by *Calomys callosus,* another species of field mouse. A village near the city of San Joaquin reported the first incidence of the new ailment. Soon after, villagers in a second village, about seventy miles from San Joaquin, also became sick. One-third of all patients died, and panic spread throughout the region. After several deaths in El Mojon, villagers burned their village to the ground before abandoning it.

About fifty more people died during outbreaks in late 1962 and early 1963. The spread of the disease—by then known as Bolivian hemorrhagic fever (BHF)—was not halted until 1964. In that year, a public rodent-control campaign was launched using cats and mousetraps donated from around the world to shrink the mouse population.

Although no confirmed cases were reported between the mid-1970s and early 1990s, BHF resurfaced in July 1994, when Machupo virus attacked an extended family in the city of Magdalena in north-

In 1994, six people in the Bolivian city of Magdelena died as a result of infection with Machupo virus, the cause of Bolivian hemorrhagic fever.

eastern Bolivia, killing six. Three other cases were reported that summer. TRANSMISSION in these cases was not clear and even person-to-person airborne routes were suspected.

Lassa, Guanarito, and Sabia

In 1969, scientists isolated a new and equally deadly arenavirus in West Africa, known as Lassa. More recently, researchers have identified several other South American arenaviruses, including Guanarito virus in Venezuela and Sabia virus in Brazil. Both of these viruses have also caused hemorrhagic fevers. The ferocity of these emerging diseases has prompted increased vigilance in the scientific community. Now there is a greater understanding of the link between rapid environmental change and infectious diseases. Although a VACCINE for preventing arenaviral infections was in the testing stage as of December 1998, rodent-control measures remain the only proven method of keeping these deadly ailments in check.

CHOLERA

Global Distribution Since the nineteenth century, several cholera pandemics have spread worldwide. Recent outbreaks have been largely confined to India and other parts of Asia, Africa, and South America.

Causative Agent Cholera is caused by the bacterium *Vibrio cholerae.*

Transmission Cholera is an intestinal infection transmitted by drinking water or eating food contaminated with *Vibrio cholerae.*

Symptoms Cholera symptoms range from mild, and almost symptomless, to severe. Severe symptoms include profuse diarrhea, vomiting, and leg cramps. People with extreme symptoms must seek medical attention. Without treatment, the rapid loss of body fluids results in dehydration, shock, and ultimately death.

Treatment Immediate replacement of minerals and fluids lost through diarrhea is the best treatment. An oral rehydration solution is available in a prepackaged mix of sugar and salt to be mixed with water, or for more serious cases an intravenous fluid replacement is available. Some antibiotics such as penicillin, erythromycin, tetracycline, or chloramphenicol can reduce the duration of symptoms, but do not completely relieve them.

Prevention and Control The best way to combat cholera is through the prevention of contaminated water sources. Better sanitation and more cautious food preparation practices are also necessary. Travelers visiting areas where the disease is prevalent should heed the motto: "Boil it, cook it, peel it, or forget it."

This nineteenth-century illustration depicts one satirist's microscopic view of London's drinking water.

The stories from Europe were ominous. The enemy was on the march, and nation after nation was falling in its path. In 1830, Russia fell, and within two more years all of Europe was under attack. In Paris, over seven thousand lay dead in the streets. In January 1832, Martin Van Buren, the American secretary of state, reported from London that England too had fallen, despite a blockade of its ports enforced by heavily armed troops. Van Buren advised the U.S. government to prepare for the worst.

Although this merciless foe was not an army, military forces had spurred its worldwide assault. Instead, the invader in question was a BACTERIUM known as *Vibrio cholerae.* It was the cause of cholera, one of the deadliest diseases known to humankind.

A Passage from India

For centuries, cholera bacterium had been present in India's Ganges River delta. Descriptions of the disease written in ancient Indian Sanskrit date back to 400 B.C.E. As the holy river of the Hindu faith, the Ganges draws pilgrims from throughout southern Asia. A bath in its waters is thought to cleanse earthly sin, and every Hindu strives to visit the river at least once.

Ironically, it is because the Ganges attracts so many seeking purification in its waters that cholera—a disease carried in human feces—has flourished. Centuries before its worldwide spread, pilgrims returning from the Ganges often unknowingly carried the bacterium home with them.

Nonetheless, prior to the nineteenth century, cholera remained virtually unknown outside of India. While Europeans had established trading posts in India as early as the sixteenth century, it was not until the mid-eighteenth century that colonizers become the strongest force in India. By 1757, the British East India Company, a private trading company chartered by the British crown, had become so great a power in India that it actually commanded its own army.

In 1817, when cholera first broke out of India, doctors administered a remedy called calomel, a poisonous mercury compound. To relieve suffering from symptoms—uncontrollable diarrhea, muscle spasms and intense pain followed within days by death in as many as half of the victims—doctors also prescribed opium. Neither antidote worked.

The inability of science to combat cholera spread fear throughout India and Europe. British authorities reasoned that the disease could only be caused by con-

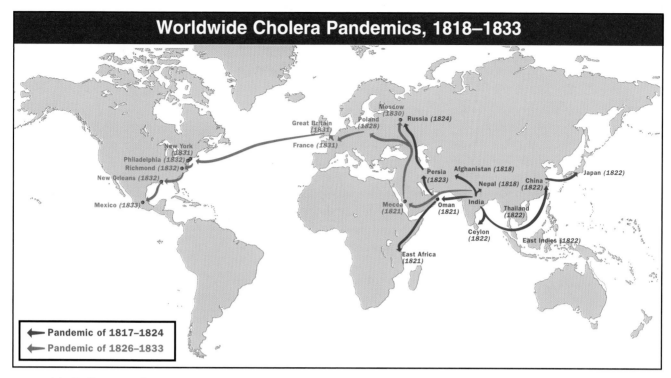

Worldwide Cholera Pandemics, 1818–1833

Legend:
← Pandemic of 1817–1824
← Pandemic of 1826–1833

tact with Indians, and encouraged colonists to avoid undue interaction with them. For their part, Indians blamed the British for this latest of outbreaks, since British commercial and military activity in India were undergoing rapid expansion at the time. As troops moved around the nation with greater frequency, cholera reached into regions it never had before. After the disease struck the state of Bengal particularly hard, local Hindus began to appeal to Ola Bibi, a new goddess known as "Lady of the Flux."

The EPIDEMIC spread deeper into central Asia when British troops skirmished with Nepalese and Afghans on India's northern frontier. Trading ships carried it in two other directions—east through Thailand, China, and Japan, and west to Arabia. In 1821, it broke out in the slave ports of Muscat of Oman, before spreading to East Africa, Persia (modern Iran), and Turkey. It then stopped short, perhaps due to the especially cold Russian winter of 1823–24.

The respite was a short one. A second, deadlier wave left India in 1826, following a path back through Arabia and into southern Russia. One city's fall would have ironic and far-reaching consequences. The bacterium reached Mecca, the birthplace of Mohammed, just as the annual pilgrimage to that Muslim holy city began. For the rest of the century, cholera would be a common feature of the Muslim pilgrimage, just as it was for Hindus bound for the Ganges. On average, cholera would surface at Mecca every other year for the next fifty years.

Troops also played a role in spreading the 1826 epidemic. During the late 1820s, Russia was at war with the Ottoman Empire in Persia and Turkey, while also engaged in putting down a revolt in Poland, which was then a Russian territory. By 1830, the epidemic reached Moscow, and the following year, the Baltic.

Cholera and the Industrial Revolution

Meanwhile, the slow death march of the disease had thrown the Europeans into a frenzy. Rumors circulated that cholera had been started as a plot to kill off the poor. In Hungary, peasants slaughtered the rich, and soldiers killed their own commanders. Even the highest

> "His face was a masterpiece of cholera symptoms. It was a *tableau vivant* depicting death and its sinuous approach. The attack had been so swift that for a moment the signs of a stupified astonishment still lingered there, childlike, but death evidently faced him at once with so horrifying a display that his cheeks lost their flesh while one watched, his lips drew back over his teeth for an eternal laugh; finally he gave a cry that put everyone to flight."
>
> —Jean Giono, *The Horseman on the Roof*

levels of government were not above pointing fingers, as Germany charged Britain with attempting to eliminate the native population of India in order to colonize the country.

French authorities, on the other hand, took the view that a disease borne in "uncivilized" India could not harm the clean and orderly state of France. Critics, however, pointed out that many Parisian neighborhoods were little cleaner than Calcutta or Delhi. Paris had undergone massive growth in the first decades of the nineteenth century, and the number of poverty-stricken neighborhoods, along with mounds of uncollected garbage, had risen as well.

By late 1831, Parisian authorities at last organized an array of last-minute commissions to plan for the disease's arrival. By late April 1832, when plans for the first mobile aid stations, known as ambulances, were finally put in place, the worst had come and gone, and laws forbidding the burial of the dead without a twenty-four-hour waiting period (to ensure victims were truly dead) left bodies piled in the streets.

The epidemic claimed its first English victim in the village of Sunderland. The response was a familiar one—first denial, and then panic. Britain's Industrial Revolution was at its height in the early nineteenth century. The country's population was growing by one hundred thousand a year, and people were flooding into urban centers such as London, Manchester, and Birmingham. Ramshackle neighborhoods sprouted up in the shadows of new mills and factories.

To cram as many workers into as little space as possible, tenement homes were built, allowing numerous families to share the same dwelling. Typically, several tenements circled a courtyard, where a common water well could be found. Often crowding the square were pigs lying in their own waste, as well as rotting food, tossed from tenement windows to feed them.

As had been the case in Paris, British preparations for the coming of cholera were hastily planned, and totally inadequate. Traditionally, responsibility for public health had fallen to local communities, with little coordination between them. Worse still, corruption was rampant, as landlords commonly paid officials to overlook what few regulations existed.

At last, in June 1831, the government established a national board of health to prepare for the worst. Local boards were established in every town or village, each charged with setting up isolation houses, where victims could be quarantined. Infected homes would be washed with lime, and windows left open to air out.

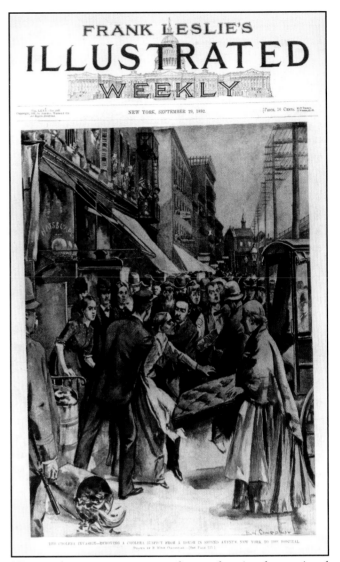

Nineteenth-century newspapers frequently printed sensational accounts of cholera's spread.

Despite these efforts, twenty-two thousand people died from cholera within two years of its arrival in England. Panic boiled over into rioting in most major cities. Parliament condemned the riots as the work of Socialist forces, failing to make the connection between slum conditions and the disease. Instead, the sick themselves were blamed, as if their illnesses were proof of low character and loose morals.

Ultimately, the riots awakened the government to the need for change. In 1834, the government commissioned William Chadwick to study the need for social reforms. Under Chadwick, an institution called the Union was borne, combining the workhouse, asylum, and orphanage under one roof. Two years later, the General Register Office, led by William Farr, began collecting data on births, marriages, and deaths. Farr was convinced that statistics could uncover patterns governing people's lives, and that once these were discovered, society could develop tools to influence them.

Chadwick, in the meantime, was following the same line of thinking. In 1842, he published a pamphlet, "The Sanitary Conditions of the Laboring Population of Great Britain," spelling out just how prevalent disease, infection, and early death were among Britain's poor. The report shocked the public by documenting the thousands of orphaned children living on the streets as beggars or prostitutes. It showed that while the average age of death among the wealthy was forty-three, it was just twenty-two among the laboring class, and that for every person dying of old age or violence, eight died of disease.

As part of his work, Farr created a document called the "English Life-Tables," which compared statistics for a particular district to those of a "healthy district," defined as one in which seventeen or fewer deaths occurred per thousand. More deaths than this, Farr reasoned, must be from "preventable causes." Where deaths existed, doctors could focus on areas where they were most needed.

A problem remained. Even by the 1830s, doctors knew nothing of bacteria. Most viewed disease as a generalized condition, caused by MIASMA, a supposed poisonous vapor emerging from the rotting corpses of the dead. Further, doctors believed that disease struck each victim in unique ways that had to do with each individual's internal makeup. Although some favored the competing view that all diseases were spread by contagion, there was no evidence that drinking water could spread them.

Farr provided some additional evidence, however. By studying the number of cholera cases in relation to proximity to London's Thames River, he found that further away from the river, fewer cases of cholera were found. Although he did not know why, he felt sure that the Thames was connected to cholera. But how?

Dr. Snow's Discovery

Dr. John Snow suspected he had the answer. In 1854, another wave of cholera was devastating Londoners. When six hundred in the Golden Square district fell ill and died, Snow mapped the location of each victim's home, and the location of area water wells. The pattern was unmistakable. Virtually all victims had been drinking from a single well on Broad Street—a well contaminated by an overflowing cesspool. Worse still, the company supplying the well had violated local ordinances by drawing water from a foul stretch of the Thames. When Snow persuaded officials to remove the Broad Street pump handle, the outbreak came to a halt.

Snow's discovery made news throughout Britain, as well as in the United States, which had seen its first cholera epidemic in 1832, when six thousand died in New Orleans. Others had died in eastern cities such as Richmond, Philadelphia, and New York. Further epidemics occurred in 1849, and again in 1866 and 1873, taking tolls along the east coast and throughout the Mississippi Valley, as river boats and wagon trains carried the bacterium throughout the heartland.

Despite Snow's work, London officials were slow to take action. Many remained convinced that as long as the disease's spread was closely tracked during any appearance in Europe, last-minute measures could be taken to prevent harm to England. Fortunately, by 1855, some in the government had had enough of a river that reeked so foully that Parliament had to suspend work. When it reconvened, lawmakers passed a bill to redevelop London's sewer system so that waste would be pumped miles downstream from the city, where it could then be swept out to sea. The project was completed and cholera never returned to London.

In the United States, Snow's work met with less resistance. During an 1866 outbreak, New York's sanitation commission was ready with an effective short-term solution. The city simply supplied clean water to infected neighborhoods and disinfected victims' homes.

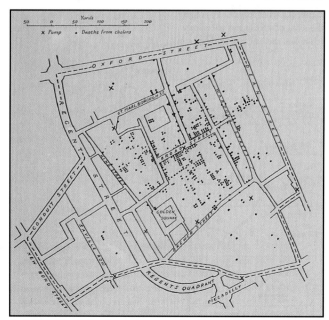

In 1854, Dr. John Snow became the first to link cholera to drinking water, when he plotted the proximity of victims' homes to drinking wells in London.

Mapping Epidemics

Despite this progress, science was still no closer to understanding the disease. An Italian named Filippo Pacini had described *Vibrio cholerae*, but no proof existed that it caused cholera. At last in 1884, Robert Koch, a German bacteriologist who had pioneered the study of anthrax *(see page 10)*, made a breakthrough. During a trip to India, he reconfirmed John Snow's earlier discovery that cholera was spread in contaminated water, on soiled clothing, and on unwashed hands.

This knowledge did not stop the bacterium from causing further havoc. As Koch was returning to Europe, another cholera wave returned, through the French ports of Toulon and Marseille. Local officials concealed the outbreak, but it soon spread to Naples, where seven thousand died, and then traveled northwards, reaching Moscow in 1891 and 1892. From there, it followed Jewish refugees fleeing Russian persecution. Koch recognized that most refugees traveled to the German port of Hamburg to board ocean liners for America or Britain. He urged that Hamburg seal its borders, but his pleas fell on deaf ears. Because Hamburg's leaders viewed the maintenance of water supplies as the duty of property owners—not governments—cholera gained safe passage through to New York.

By the turn of the century, the lessons taught by men such as Chadwick, Farr, Snow, and Koch finally began to take hold. At the same time, a new, less deadly cholera strain was isolated at Egypt's El Tor quarantine station, where pilgrims to Mecca were found with milder cases of the disease.

The Return of Cholera

Since 1950, El Tor has been the most prevalent form of cholera, breaking out wherever unsanitary conditions are present. Between 1961 and 1965, El Tor swept through Indonesia, Bangladesh, India, Iran, and Iraq. In 1970, the disease invaded West Africa, where it had not appeared for one hundred years, and is presently ENDEMIC to that continent. In 1991, it struck Peru, quickly escalating into an epidemic throughout most of Latin America.

Cholera and Climate Change

When the 1991 epidemic began, researchers noted that it appeared to have started in three separate Peruvian ports at the same time. While scientists have a clear understanding of how *V. cholerae* spreads from person to person, only recently did they learn what happens to the bacteria between epidemics. During the 1970s, Rita Colwell, a microbiologist at the University of Maryland, had isolated *V. cholerae* in Chesapeake Bay. Initially, many of her colleagues doubted her find

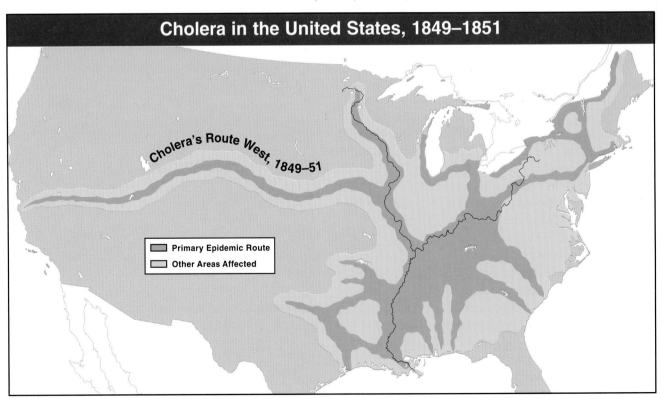

Cholera in the United States, 1849–1851

Cholera's Route West, 1849–51

Primary Epidemic Route
Other Areas Affected

Wagon trains heading west during the California Gold Rush of 1849 helped spread cholera to the Pacific.

since there had been no cholera outbreaks in the United States since 1911. Furthermore, traditional methods of detecting bacteria by growing them in laboratory petri dishes did not work when others tried to duplicate her findings.

Colwell suggested that perhaps the cholera in Chesapeake Bay was not active, but that instead it somehow went into a dormant state. She also knew that to prove her case, she would need to find new means of laboratory detection.

In the late 1970s, Colwell had her breakthrough. A Louisiana cholera outbreak was traced to several people who had eaten crab from a local bayou. After taking water samples, Colwell and her team decided to test a new detection method. They used an ANTIBODY that would latch onto the bacterium's CELL MEMBRANE. Attached to the antibody was a MOLECULE that lit up under ultraviolet light. The presence of *V. cholerae* was clear. Colwell had confirmed that the bacterium could exist naturally in the environment. Further tests uncovered *V. cholerae* in samples in Bangladesh as well.

Colwell supported the use of antibody tests by proving that she had also been right about her other theory—that *V. cholerae* goes into a dormant state when environmental conditions, such as cold water, do not allow it to replicate. Nonetheless, even in dormant states, the bacteria were still contagious, as Colwell proved when, as part of a study, volunteers were injected with samples containing dormant bacteria and became sick.

The reason that cholera outbreaks do not occur in the United States, then, was not because *V. cholerae* does not exist in American waterways, but because drinking water is filtered and chlorinated, which is often not always the case in poor regions of countries like Peru or Bangladesh. Even the simplest of filtering systems can be effective, however, as Colwell proved when she showed Bangladeshi women how to effectively filter their water by merely pouring it through a few layers of sari cloth used in their clothing.

While in that country, Colwell also discovered that *V. cholerae* has a PARASITIC relationship with plankton known as copepods. As copepods circulate with the ocean currents, *V. cholerae* travels along within them.

According to Colwell, this may explain how the Latin American epidemic started in several ports at

Cholera is still a major threat to Latin America and other impoverished regions of the world. This map traces the Latin American epidemic that began in Peru in 1991.

once. It may be that the bacteria were there all the time, waiting for the right conditions, which, she believes, are tied to the surface temperatures of the ocean. Colwell noted that a rise in temperatures in the Sea of Bengal off Bangladesh correlated directly with the a rise in the number of cholera cases seen in Bangladesh hospitals four to six weeks later. Researchers have also shown that warmer surface temperatures off the Peruvian coast following the El Niño tropical storms of 1997–98 led to an increase in nutrient levels in the water, which may have an impact on *V. cholerae*.

Colwell believes the correlation is clear. Temperatures off Latin America's Pacific coast were also warmer in 1997 and 1998, just as the number of new cholera cases skyrocketed. When Hurricane Mitch rocked Central America in 1998, all but annihilating sanitation and public health systems, the cholera epidemic spun out of control.

If sea temperatures do influence the occurrence of cholera, then one day, scientists like Colwell may be able to predict the threat of outbreaks ahead of time. Until then, wherever proper sanitation systems are not in place, *V. cholerae* bacteria will thrive.

DENGUE/DHF

Global Distribution Dengue is found in some one hundred countries in Africa, South America, the eastern Mediterranean, Southeast Asia, and the western Pacific.

Causative Agent Dengue and dengue hemorrhagic fever (DHF) are caused by four related viruses (DEN-1, DEN-2, DEN-3, and DEN-4), all of the genus flavivirus.

Transmission Dengue and dengue hemorrhagic fever are transmitted by the infected *Aedes aegypti* mosquito.

Symptoms Dengue is a severe but nonfatal flu-like illness. Infants and children experience a rash and fever, while adults may experience a mild-to-high fever, severe headache, muscle and joint aches, and rash. The symptoms of dengue hemorrhagic fever include high fever and hemorrhagic symptoms, usually with enlargement of the liver, and in severe cases, circulatory failure. Symptoms at onset are similar to those of dengue fever and may subside after a few days. In other cases, the victim's condition may quickly deteriorate to include falling body temperature and circulatory failure, followed by systemic shock and death within a day or two.

Treatment No specific treatment is recognized. Proper supervision, often including fluid volume replacement therapy, frequently saves the lives of DHF victims.

Prevention and Control Elimination of mosquito breeding grounds through community clean-up campaigns is recommended. Mosquitoes breed in stagnant water collecting in bottles, abandoned tires, cans, and other manmade objects. Emergency control techniques include immediate insecticide applications, although public health officials should closely monitor the insect's susceptibility to insecticides.

The name "dengue" comes from the Swahili phrase *Ki denga pepo,* which compares the start of dengue symptoms to being overwhelmed by an evil spirit.

For most people, mosquitoes are a price to be paid for long summer afternoon barbeques. Yet if those mosquitoes were infected with one of the four dengue VIRUSES, the result would be more than an inconvenient itch. First would come fever and an aching body. Then searing joint pain and agonizing throbbing behind the eyes, followed by weeks of depression and fatigue. And because there are four separate dengue viruses, a subsequent infection might bring on the same symptoms or a deadly version of dengue that can cause uncontrolled bleeding, circulatory failure, and death.

The Fight Against Mosquitoes

Although dengue is not well known in the United States, the world's first documented case of dengue occurred there in 1779. The next year, the disease was identified by Dr. Benjamin Rush, a Philadelphia doctor and signer of the Declaration of Independence. Rush called the disease "breakbone fever" after the joint pain it causes.

America's first serious confrontation with dengue came between 1826 and 1828, starting in Savannah, Georgia, and spread by the *Aedes aegypti* mosquito throughout the South and the Caribbean. Two more nineteenth-century EPIDEMICS followed the same pattern.

By 1900, dengue remained a threat in the southern United States and other warm regions. Nonetheless, successful mosquito-control programs in Cuba and the Panama Canal Zone had virtually rid those regions of malaria and yellow fever, and gave scientists confidence that mosquito-borne diseases would one day be eradicated. Over the next few decades, the scientific community waged war on mosquitoes, and by the 1940s, few cases of dengue were found worldwide.

A Deadly New Enemy

In 1950, just as dengue seemed headed toward extinction, a new, scarier variety appeared in the Philippines. A child hospitalized with symptoms that reminded doctors of dengue suddenly began bleeding uncontrollably.

A new disease had appeared. Its main victims were children between four and nine years old. By 1953, the disease was named dengue hemorrhagic fever (DHF) and the next year, a full-blown epidemic swept through Manila. By 1958, DHF had arrived in Thailand, where it killed almost seven hundred people over five years before spreading through South and East Asia. Along the way, the *Aedes aegypti* was joined by a second car-

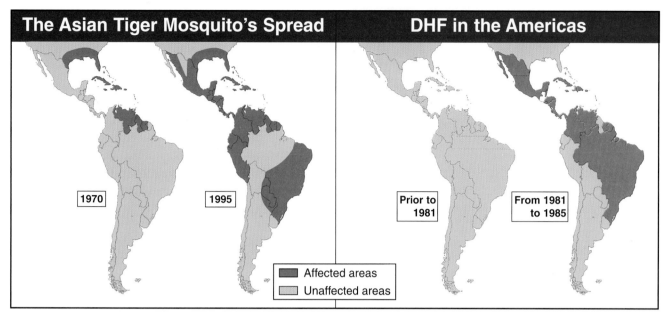

The Asian Tiger Mosquito's Spread

1970

1995

DHF in the Americas

Prior to 1981

From 1981 to 1985

Affected areas
Unaffected areas

The introduction of the Asian Tiger Mosquito to the Americas helped spread DHF throughout Latin America.

rier—the *Aedes albopictus*, or Asian tiger mosquito. Unlike *Aedes aegypti*, the Asian tiger mosquito survives by thriving not just on human blood but on that of any warm-blooded animal, allowing it to spread infection much farther.

Still, the Americas only saw intermittent dengue outbreaks during the 1950s and 1960s. Then, in 1981, a six-month epidemic hit Havana, Cuba, killing 158.

The Cuban situation rang alarms throughout the Americas. Dengue was no longer isolated to other parts of the world. Throughout the 1980s, the number of dengue cases in the Americas skyrocketed, particularly after 1985, when Asian tiger mosquitoes arrived on a Japanese freighter carrying used tires bound for Houston. By 1987, these mosquitoes had been found in seventeen U.S. cities, and throughout much of Latin America.

The Impact of World War

How did this crisis come to be? What occurred between the early 1940s, when dengue had apparently gone into submission, and 1950, when it returned, accompanied by its more virulent cousin, DHF?

During the early 1940s, most of Asia was engulfed in World War II. Before the war, single dengue serotypes could be found in many Asian cities, but rarely could more than one be found in one place. But as military planes and ships rapidly ferried troops and supplies from one part of the world to another, they also ferried viruses. Troops that liberated the Philippines, for example, had come from fighting in other parts of the Asian Pacific, where they may have been exposed to

one serotype. Once in the Philippines, they were exposed to a second serotype, after which they developed the far more deadly DHF.

Exactly how DHF emerged is a matter of considerable debate. The generally accepted view is that DHF is a complication caused by repeated infection with dengue viruses. According to estimates, roughly half of those INFECTED by one dengue serotype, and later another, will acquire DHF. In a few cases, DHF has been caused by a primary infection, or after infection by the only one serotype. For this reason, some researchers believe that DHF is caused by a new, more deadly dengue virus. That theory, however, remains unproven, since that virus has not been found.

However DHF emerged, it began spreading rapidly in the 1950s and 1960s, partly as a result of the Korean and Vietnam Wars. By 1975, DHF had become a common feature of urban Asian life. Shortly after the Vietnam War's end, the Vietnamese government launched a program of cultural, economic, and educational cooperation with Cuba, just a few short years before Havana's DHF epidemic.

Today, dengue is ENDEMIC to most of Latin America as well as Asia. As rural villagers have moved from the countryside to cities, the number of dengue strains present in each region has grown, increasing the risk of DHF. Because there is no effective treatment known for either dengue or its deadly cousin, only a new commitment to containing the VECTOR mosquitoes will prevent the situation from getting worse.

DIPHTHERIA

Global Distribution Since the 1940s, most developed countries have administered a preventive diphtheria-tetanus-pertussis (DTP) vaccine to infants, and in those countries, diphtheria is rare. In regions of the world where public heath programs are weaker, the disease remains a major cause of infant and childhood mortality.

Causative Agent Diphtheria is caused by the bacterium *Corynebacterium diphtheriae*.

Transmission Diphtheria is transmitted through the air or by touching a victim.

Symptoms The diphtheria bacteria forms an exotoxin, or poison, that can damage the heart, kidneys, and nervous system. Initial symptoms include fever, exhaustion, and a severe sore throat, followed by breathing difficulty that can lead to suffocation and death if untreated.

Treatment Infected patients should be quarantined immediately, and then treated with antitoxins and antibiotics. All items that may have been soiled by the victim should be carefully disposed of.

Prevention and Control Diphtheria can be prevented through worldwide vaccination programs.

For Addie Mehwalt, Aged 2 years, 7 months

Oh sweet be thy sleep in the land of the dead;
For our dear little angel we sorrow.
The spring shall return to thy low narrow bed,
Like the beam of the day-star tomorrow.

Oh, still we behold thee lovely in death,
Reclined on the lap of thy mother;
When the tears trickled bright, the short, stifled breath
Told how dear you were to each other.

My child, you are gone to the hole of thy rest,
Where suffering can no longer harm you;
Where the songs of the good, the hymns of the blest,
Through an endless existence shall charm you.

—*Written by Alex and Mary Mehwalt, of Santa Cruz, California, following the death of their daughter during a diphtheria epidemic in the late 1870s.*

O n January 21, 1925, terror filled the hearts of the people of Nome, Alaska. Throughout the frozen frontier village, children were suffocating to death. Parents watched helplessly as their sons and daughters gasped for breath as a mysterious gray membrane closed up their throats and their bodies filled with poisonous TOXIN from deadly diphtheria BACTERIA.

Dogs to the Rescue

Dr. Curtis Welch, Nome's only doctor, knew that without a supply of ANTITOXIN SERUM, countless children would die. The problem: he had none. Welch wired for help but learned that because of a fierce blizzard, airplanes could only carry the serum as far as Nenana, over six hundred miles away. The only way to get the serum to Nome would be for teams of dogs to carry it. On the night of January 27, a serum-filled crate was wrapped in quilts and strapped onto a sled, and the first team of dogs, driven by "Wild Bill" Shannon, set out for Nome. On February 2, the final relay team arrived with the serum. The EPIDEMIC soon was over. Today, this heroic race against time is annually commemorated by the Iditerod dog-sled race.

Early Outbreaks of Diphtheria

Although diphtheria can be traced back to ancient Greece, when cases of fatal sore throats were recorded, it was not until the sixteenth century that isolated cases turned into epidemics. In 1576, Frenchman Guillaume de Baillou provided the first detailed record of an outbreak when the disease hit Paris.

What caused this epidemic? Historians point to two trends. During the sixteenth century, European cities and towns were expanding with the flourishing of trade, arts, and scientific knowledge, all of which drew people to the cities. With this growth came the overcrowded, unsanitary conditions that fostered disease.

The epidemic also arrived at a time that Catholics and Protestants were engaged in a series of religious wars. Between 1562 and 1598, French Protestants, or Huguenots, were battling Catholics for control of France. In 1576, Catholic soldiers, many carrying diseases from the battlefield, were quartered in Paris, exposing the citizenry to INFECTION.

An epidemic struck Seville, Spain, lasting from 1583 to 1618. The Spanish called the disease *garrotillo*, after a weapon used for strangulation.

CARRIER OF DIPHTHERIA

KEEP OUT OF THIS HOUSE By Order of BOARD OF HEALTH

Any person removing this card without authority is liable to prosecution HEALTH OFFICER

A San Francisco quarantine notice, from about 1910.

Diphtheria in America

Diphtheria had arrived in America by 1695, when clergyman Cotton Mather described a "Malady of Bladders in the Windpipe." An outbreak of "throat distemper" hit New England in 1735, and spread from village to village, taking five thousand victims over two years.

In 1826, Frenchman Pierre-Fidèle Bretonneau gave the disease its current name, after *diphtheria,* Greek for a scrap of leather, referring to the telltale membrane that blocked a patient's throat. Still, it would be decades before a cure was found. Within three years of an 1855 outbreak in England, a PANDEMIC had spread across the world. By the 1870s, the disease had become every family's nightmare. In New York, diphtheria deaths rose from 325 a year in 1872 to over 2,300 by 1875. Although the *New York Times* blamed "the untidy habits of laboring men's wives . . . and pestilence-nourishing filth which is allowed to cling to floors, walls and furniture," the disease was not confined to crowded urban slums. In rural Kansas, one family lost eight children in just ten days. And in Santa Cruz County, California, at least 175 children died between late 1876 and mid-1878. Nor was the disease isolated to the lower class. In 1878, Queen Victoria of England lost both a daughter and granddaughter to the disease.

The Path to a Cure

At last, in 1883, a true advance was made. German PATHOLOGIST Edwin Klebs, isolated *Corynebacterium diphtheriae.* The following year, Friedrich Loeffler proved that the club-shaped BACILLUS was responsible for the disease. Still, it was not until 1894 that Frenchman Emile Roux, of Louis Pasteur's laboratory, would turn the tide in the diphtheria war.

An international relief effort helped to ease a diphtheria epidemic in the Ukraine during the mid-1990s.

Although Loeffler believed that the bacterium released a toxin that caused diphtheria's symptoms, Roux proved it by injecting guinea pigs with the toxin. Most, but not all, of his subjects died.

Emil Behring, like Loeffler of Robert Koch's laboratory, then isolated the antitoxin in the blood of surviving guinea pigs to create a serum. Two years later, Roux created a stronger serum from an antitoxin made in larger animals. In 1894, he announced his cure.

Diphtheria: A Renewed Risk?

Routine IMMUNIZATION programs have existed since the 1920s, greatly reducing the threat of diphtheria in much of the world. Today, most children in developed nations receive a DTP (diphtheria-tetanus-pertussis) VACCINATION. We have also continued to learn more about how the disease works. In 1951, scientists discovered that BACTERIOPHAGES, PARASITES that only infect bacteria, are the true cause of diphtheria. When certain bacteriophages infect *Corynebacterium diphtheriae,* they produce the toxins that spread throughout the body.

Despite progress, diphtheria is still a threat. Since the Soviet Union's collapse in 1990, over four thousand Russians, Ukrainians, and others have died of diphtheria. Although shortages of vaccines and clean syringes hampered initial immunization efforts, assistance from the Red Cross and other agencies helped turn the tide. In the Ukraine, almost 90 percent of the adult population was vaccinated, which helped end the epidemic. However, recent surveys have also shown the reemergence of the disease in previously vaccinated adults. Lifelong vigilance, therefore, backed by regular booster shots, is needed if humankind is to rid the world of diphtheria.

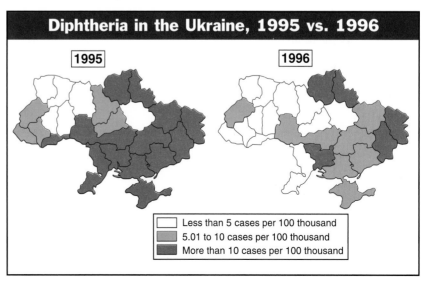

Diphtheria in the Ukraine, 1995 vs. 1996

1995   1996

☐ Less than 5 cases per 100 thousand
▨ 5.01 to 10 cases per 100 thousand
■ More than 10 cases per 100 thousand

EBOLA HEMORRHAGIC FEVER

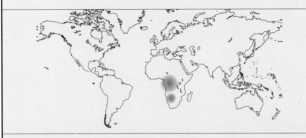

Global Distribution The Ebola virus was first identified in western Sudan and a nearby section of the Democratic Republic of the Congo. In 1979 an epidemic occurred in Sudan, and in 1995 in the Congo's Bandundu region. The most recent outbreak occurred in rural Gabon.

Causative Agent Ebola hemorrhagic fever is caused by a virus that belongs to the *Filoviridae* family.

Symptoms A sudden fever with weakness, muscle aches, headache, and sore throat followed by vomiting, diarrhea, rash, and deteriorating liver and kidney function, paired with massive internal and external bleeding through all bodily orifices, including pores of the skin.

Risk Factors The virus is passed through direct contact with blood, secretions, organs, or semen of infected people. It may also be passed by a specific species of chimpanzee from the Ivory Coast.

Treatment Although extreme cases are usually treated with intensive care to alleviate severe dehydration, there is no specific treatment or known cure for Ebola.

Prevention and Control The priority of health officials is the isolation of the victim in order to contain the spread of the disease. Hospital staff must be made aware of the extreme nature of Ebola and its means of transmission. The utmost care should be taken with high-risk procedures including the handling of blood, secretions, catheters, and suction devices, as well as with dirty linens and used syringes or needles. Any hospital staff in contact with patients should be outfitted in protective gear. Patients who die from the disease should be buried or cremated immediately.

The Ebola virus is one of the deadliest pathogens on Earth. Ironically, its virulence is also one of its weaknesses. Unlike HIV or the bacterium that causes tuberculosis, Ebola can kill so quickly that its ability to spread from host to host is more limited. Nonetheless, the virus is one international flight away from anywhere in the world, as was demonstrated in 1999 when a patient returning from Africa died of the disease in a London hospital.

Imagine a disease that can cause healthy people to spill blood from every orifice of their bodies before dying. Imagine that this disease has no cure. What you are imagining is, unfortunately, not Hollywood fantasy. It is a very real disease known as Ebola hemorrhagic fever, and it has killed hundreds of people since the 1970s.

Although there have been no confirmed cases of Ebola infection in humans outside of Africa, many fear that it is just a matter of time before the virus becomes a PANDEMIC. After all, any VIRUS on the planet is just a plane trip away. Books, movies, and television shows have made Ebola a household word.

Ebola-Sudan and Ebola-Zaire

The first reported Ebola INFECTIONS came in 1976, in the town of Nzara, Sudan. Patients first complained of fever and joint pain. Within days, these symptoms were followed by massive hemorrhaging of blood from every orifice, as well as kidney failure, seizures, shock, and finally death. The virus then spread to a hospital in a nearby town, killing numerous patients and staff members, and then relatives who had cared for the sick. Of five hundred infected victims, more than half died.

Two months later, another virus appeared five hundred miles away in Yambuku, Zaire (now the Democratic Republic of the Congo), near the Ebola River. The ghastly pattern repeated as the internal organs of victim after victim virtually disintegrated. Whatever was causing these gruesome deaths was far beyond the ability of Yambuku's Catholic mission hospital staff to control. Because Ebola viruses deprive blood of its ability to clot, each time a shot was administered, the needle hole became a new route through which blood could seep. Contact with infected blood proved deadly, and 13 of the 17 hospital staffers also died. Many surviving patients carried the disease home to their villages. Within only a few months, the virus claimed at least 318 lives, or 88 percent of its victims.

As the Zaire outbreak raged, scientists feared an EPIDEMIC virus that could kill millions. But then, just as suddenly as the deaths had started, they stopped. Apparently, the two closely related viruses now known as Ebola-Sudan and Ebola-Zaire kill so quickly that their ability to spread is limited. That has not, however, prevented further outbreaks from occurring. In 1979, a smaller outbreak occurred in Nzara, Sudan, killing 22 of 34 victims. Other isolated deaths occurred throughout the 1980s and 1990s, but none led to a major outbreak.

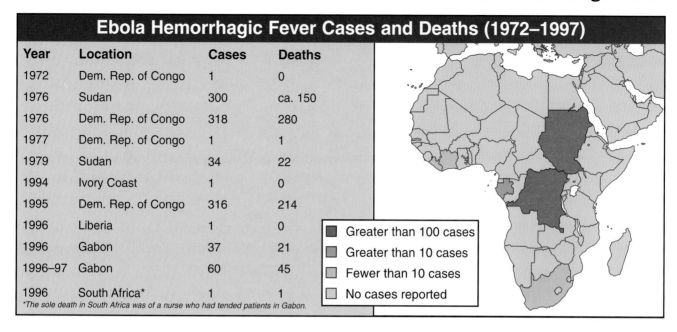

Ebola Hemorrhagic Fever Cases and Deaths (1972–1997)

Year	Location	Cases	Deaths
1972	Dem. Rep. of Congo	1	0
1976	Sudan	300	ca. 150
1976	Dem. Rep. of Congo	318	280
1977	Dem. Rep. of Congo	1	1
1979	Sudan	34	22
1994	Ivory Coast	1	0
1995	Dem. Rep. of Congo	316	214
1996	Liberia	1	0
1996	Gabon	37	21
1996–97	Gabon	60	45
1996	South Africa*	1	1

*The sole death in South Africa was of a nurse who had tended patients in Gabon.

Greater than 100 cases
Greater than 10 cases
Fewer than 10 cases
No cases reported

The Filoviruses

Scientists now know that Ebola is closely related to the extremely rare Marburg virus, which passed from infected monkeys to workers in a laboratory in Marburg, Germany, in 1967. Close comparison of the Marburg virus with the two Ebola viruses revealed that the VIRIONS, or virus particles, in all three share the same worm-like appearance, and are thus classified as FILOVIRUSES. (*Filo* means worm in Latin).

Infected monkeys may have also been behind the Ebola outbreaks. Although how and from where Ebola spread to the monkeys is still unknown, officials recognize that human behaviors helped it spread among humans. At the remote mission hospital in Yambuku, they reused hypodermic needles on numerous patients because of the difficulty of obtaining such supplies, thus spreading the virus from patient to patient.

Cultural practices also played a role in the Zaire outbreak. According to traditional burial customs, female relatives prepare the deceased for burial by removing all food and waste from the digestive tract, usually with bare hands, making transmission of the virus essentially inevitable.

A Crisis in Virginia

Prior to 1989, Ebola-Sudan, Ebola-Zaire, and Marburg were the only known filoviruses. That changed when monkeys imported to a laboratory in Reston, Virginia, began dying. Officials at the U.S. Army Medical Research Institute of Infectious Disease were called in, and found that the monkeys were dying from a new filovirus, now called Ebola-Reston. The surviving monkeys were destroyed and the laboratory facility decontaminated. Ebola-Reston turned out to be harmless to humans. In 1990 and 1996, monkeys imported from the Philippines to the United States were found to be carrying strains of the virus. Again, no humans fell ill. Incidents like these have set off alarms, particularly since they seem to illustrate that the source of Ebola many not be restricted to Africa.

While no humans have died outside of Africa from Ebola hemorrhagic fever, several new epidemics have occurred in the 1990s. In 1994, a single victim died in the Ivory Coast, but that was enough for yet another strain—Ebola-Côte d'Ivoire—to be identified. In 1995, a more serious epidemic raged through the populous Zairian city of Kikwit, killing over three hundred. In 1996 and early 1997, two separate Ebola outbreaks killed 66 in the West African nation of Gabon.

A Global Threat?

There can be no disputing that Ebola is among the most deadly of viruses. Victims of Ebola hemorrhagic fever die an unimaginably gruesome death. Still, through January 1999, only 615 people had died from it, far fewer than from the millions who have died of AIDS or even the flu. Some worry that the worldwide danger posed by Ebola has been exaggerated, distracting scientists from studies of more common diseases. Nonetheless, the nature of Ebola ensures that it will continue to fascinate scientists and nonscientists alike.

HANTAVIRUS PULMONARY SYNDROME

Global Distribution Outbreaks of hantavirus pulmonary syndrome can be found worldwide.

Causative Agent Hantavirus pulmonary syndrome is caused by one of the many hantaviruses.

Transmission Both hantavirus pulmonary syndrome (HPS) and hemorrhagic fever renal syndrome (HFRS) are transmitted through the inhalation of aerosolized urine, feces, and/or saliva from infected rodents. Various species of rodents can be carriers of hantaviruses.

Symptoms The characteristics vary depending on the kind of hantavirus. The early symptoms of hantavirus pulmonary syndrome include fatigue, fever, and achy muscles, and in some cases headaches, dizziness, chills, or vomiting; diarrhea and abdominal cramps occur. Later symptoms include shortness of breath and coughing as lungs fill with fluid. The symptoms of HFRS include severe headache, backache, fever, and chills in an initial stage, advancing to rash, and nausea and vomiting. In the most extreme cases, bleeding and acute shock can cause death.

Treatment There is no specific treatment for hantavirus infections. It is known that the earlier the virus is detected and medical attention is administered the better the chance for survival.

Prevention and Control Contact with rodent droppings should be avoided. Homes should be cleaned inside and outside if rodents are present. Public rodent extermination and control measures need to be taken in some areas.

The deer mouse is the natural reservoir of the Sin Nombre hantavirus.

In 1993, Muerto Canyon earned its name. Young, otherwise healthy Navajos living in the area were dying, struck down by the sudden onset of severe flu-like symptoms. Clearly, a frightening EPIDEMIC had surfaced among the one hundred seventy-five thousand people living in the Four Corners region of New Mexico, Utah, Arizona, and Colorado, where Muerto Canyon—Spanish for Canyon of Death—is located. The drama that ensued over the next few months led to a media frenzy, ethnic tensions, and startling discoveries using new technology.

The Sin Nombre Virus

In May 1993, an athletic young Navaho couple died within days of each other after contracting an infection. Several family members and neighbors died soon after. All victims suffered fevers and aches that rapidly progressed to respiratory illnesses. Their lungs filled with fluid and could no longer extract oxygen. Their hearts stopped.

Dr. Bruce Tempest, a physician for the Navaho Indian Health Services (IHS), realized that something serious was at work. He reported his findings to Richard Malore, New Mexico's chief medical examiner, warning him of a possible outbreak of a deadly, though still unknown, disease. Tempest then alerted the New Mexico Department of Health, and Dr. Jim Cheek, the EPIDEMIOLOGIST for the IHS, who in turn made the decision to call in the Centers for Disease Control (CDC).

While the rapid response by medical personnel and epidemiologists helped prevent a more serious spread of the outbreak, it also drew unwanted attention. The media seized on the mysterious ailment, quickly dubbing it "Navajo disease." Navajos and other indigenous peoples justifiably found the name racist and insulting. Navajos had been first to fall ill, but they were not the only racial group affected. Nonetheless, non-Navajos (including not only whites but Hopi Indians as well) began to avoid contact with Navajos and their lands. Worse still, the media attention violated Navajo cultural taboos that forbid talking of the recent dead. This clash of cultures ignited sparks of animosity and distrust that inhibited the work of epidemiologists trying to get to the bottom of the outbreak.

In an effort to cool tensions, investigators consulted with Navajo elders and asked them for any information they could provide on how the disease had spread. The elders confirmed what investigators already knew, that a 1992 drought followed by heavy snows had led to

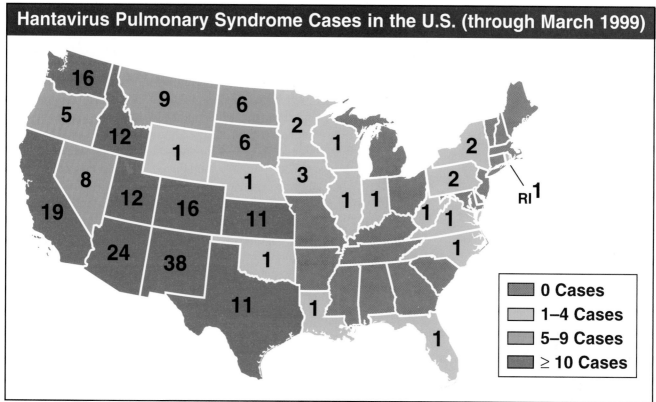

Hantavirus Pulmonary Syndrome Cases in the U.S. (through March 1999)

Legend:
- ■ 0 Cases
- □ 1–4 Cases
- ▨ 5–9 Cases
- ▩ ≥ 10 Cases

The Four Corners region of Arizona, New Mexico, Colorado and New Mexico, where the Sin Nobre virus was first identified, remains the region with the highest number of hantavirus pulmonary syndrome cases in the nation.

an increase in the mouse population. The deer mouse, *Peromyscus maniculatus,* inhabits a vast range in North America from Mexico to the Arctic Circle. The Navajos noted that according to their oral tradition similar deaths had coincided with past booms in the mouse population. In time, researchers would identify a new hantavirus and name it Sin Nombre ("without name," in English, in order to avoid any racial insensitivity).

The links between the Sin Nombre VIRUS and other hantaviruses were discovered with a relatively new medical tool: the PCR, or polymerase chain reaction, test. Developed in the late 1980s, this technology allowed scientists to quickly replicate the genetic material of a virus in order to discover its GENETIC makeup.

To scientists, hantavirus refers to at least fourteen related viruses. Because the genetic information in all of these viruses is stored as ribonucleic acid (RNA), hantaviruses are known as RNA viruses. RNA viruses are naturally susceptible to frequent genetic code MUTATIONS. In the Four Corners case, scientists realized that the Sin Nombre strain was unlike previously known hantaviruses, not only because of differences in its RNA but also because of the damage caused to the respiratory system. Half of all victims died. This syndrome is now known as hantavirus pulmonary syndrome (HPS).

A Growing Threat

Hantaviruses made their first, though far less deadly, appearance during the Korean War between 1950 and 1953. About three thousand U.S. and other UN soldiers developed a collection of symptoms, collectively known as hemorrhagic fever with renal syndrome (HFRS). Although symptoms included heavy bleeding followed by kidney failure, only about 5 percent of victims died.

The Four Corners epidemic marked a turning point in the study of hantaviruses and confirmed the fears of virologists that there are many hantaviruses out there, some posing serious health threats. In fact, HPS is even more common in Latin America, where cases have been reported in Argentina, Brazil, Chile, Costa Rica, Mexico, Paraguay, and Uruguay.

All told, more than twenty different hantaviruses have been identified worldwide. Because no effective medical treatment has been developed for the disease, rodent control remains the only effective weapon to keep hantaviruses at bay.

HEMORRHAGIC COLITIS
(*E. COLI O157:H7* INFECTION)

Global Distribution It is difficult to pinpoint the prevalence of the dangerous strain of *E. coli O157:H7* as it continues to pop up unexpectedly from various contaminated sources, particularly meat, unpasteurized milk, and in the bacteria of infected stool passed through poor hygiene habits.

Causative Agent The bacterium *Escherichia coli* causes *E. coli O157:H7*.

Transmission *E. coli O157:H7* is transmitted through contaminated food and water.

Symptoms The infection causes severe abdominal cramps and bloody diarrhea. Sometimes there is nonbloody diarrhea or no symptoms at all. The illness lasts 5 to 10 days. Particularly in children and the elderly, the infection can cause hemolytic uremia syndrome, a complication in which the red blood cells are destroyed and the kidneys fail.

Treatment Most people recover without the aid of antibiotics or any other specific treatment. In fact, there is no evidence that antibiotics help infected persons. In the case of hemolytic uremia syndrome, the infected person should be treated in an intensive care unit as blood transfusions and kidney dialysis are often necessary.

Prevention and Control Health officials advise that meats be cooked thoroughly and that only pasteurized milk and juice, or water that has been either boiled or treated with adequate levels of bacteria-killing chlorine be consumed. Infected victims should take care to thoroughly wash their hands to reduce the rate of spread.

The *E. coli* bacterium is one of the most common bacteria in the intestines, and is a major source of vitamin K. *E. coli O157:H7,* the product of a dangerous mutation, releases a toxic protein that can do severe damage to the host's intestines.

In 1993, patrons of a chain of fast-food restaurants in the state of Washington received an unwelcome surprise in their hamburgers. After a supply of contaminated undercooked beef was served at a number of the chain's locations, three people died and more than five hundred became seriously ill. The outbreak caused concern throughout the Pacific Northwest—and eventually around the entire United States. People rushed to hospitals reporting sudden and severe bloody diarrhea.

Since then a number of similar outbreaks have occurred. In 1996, a sixteen-month-old Colorado child died and forty others fell ill after drinking apple juice that had not been PASTEURIZED. The following year, twenty-five million pounds of hamburger meat sold by a commercial food processor in Nebraska were recalled after meat from the plant was found to be contaminated. And in 1999, in the largest outbreak in U.S. history, over one thousand people fell ill and a three-year-old girl died after drinking contaminated well water at the Washington County Fair in upstate New York.

The *E. coli* Bacterium

In all four of these cases, the source of contamination was the *Escherichia coli* BACTERIUM. Ironically, if not for the billions of *E. coli* bacteria that live in the intestines of all animals, humankind would be hard pressed to survive. That may seem surprising to the millions who followed the outbreaks caused by the same bacteria. However, understanding how *E. coli* can be both a critical component of human survival and a potentially deadly PATHOGEN is a key to understanding how MICROBES like *E. coli* can MUTATE over time from one form to another.

All animal fetuses are completely sterile. After birth, the infant (human or otherwise) becomes home to billions of bacteria. As a person goes through life, bacteria continually take up residence in parts of the body that have the most direct contact with the outside world. For example, bacteria can enter the digestive system through food and drink or on the things one touches, or enter the respiratory system through the air one breathes. Once nonpathogenic bacteria become absorbed into a person's system, they help provide the body with many of the vitamins it needs. The *E. coli* bacteria, for example, one of the most common bacteria in the intestines, is a major source of vitamin K as well as B-complex vitamins. Experiments have shown that animals raised under bacteria-free conditions suffer from thinner than normal intestinal walls as well as weakened hearts. What is more, they will die from vit-

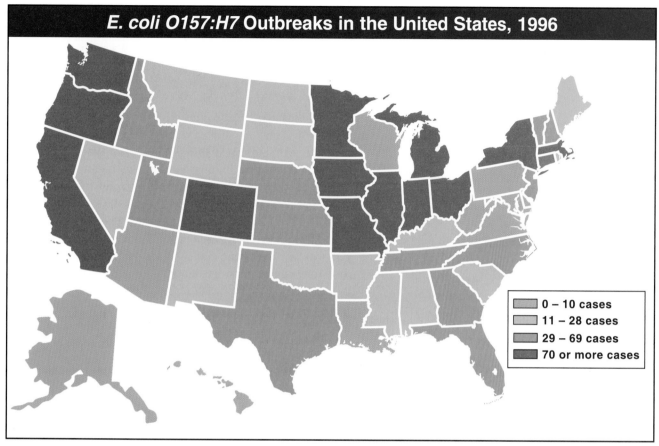

E. coli O157:H7 Outbreaks in the United States, 1996

- 0 – 10 cases
- 11 – 28 cases
- 29 – 69 cases
- 70 or more cases

The Centers for Disease Control reported a total of 2,741 cases of E. coli O157:57 *infection in 1996.*

amin deficiencies unless they are given dietary supplements to offset the absence of bacteria.

The Mutation Process

Just as animals come in constant contact with bacteria, bacteria are in constant contact with other MICROBES. One result of this interaction is that bacterial CELLS can pick up pieces of GENETIC information from those other microbes—be they viral PARASITES called BACTERIOPHAGES (also called phages), or units of DNA called PLASMIDS. In the process, a particular STRAIN of a bacterium mutates, acquiring new genetic traits that while not vital to its survival, can be beneficial—to the bacterium, if not to the HOST that it lives in.

Hemorrhagic Colitis

E. coli O157:H7 appears to be just such a strain. Researchers believe that at some point, a cell of *E. coli* bacteria became infected by a phage that inserted its own DNA into the bacterium's CHROMOSOME, thus creating a new strain. Once this process was complete, this new genetic material could then be passed on to new cells each time the now mutated cell replicated. In the case of *E. coli O157:H7,* the new information being

passed on had given the bacterium the ability to produce a toxic PROTEIN called Shiga-like TOXIN, or SLT, that causes swelling that leads to severe damage to the lining of host intestines. SLT gained its name because of its similarity to the bacterium that causes shigella dysentery *(see page 80),* another intestinal disease.

Once the intestinal lining is damaged, the body begins to lose large amounts of fluid and salt. Even more dangerous, SLT damages blood vessels, which can lead to massive blood loss, or hemorrhaging. For this reason, the most common condition caused by an *E. coli O157:H7* infection is called hemorrhagic colitis. (*Colitis* means inflammation of the intestines.) While this can be deadly for anyone, it is particularly lethal in children, whose immature immune systems cannot handle such stress.

Although hemorrhagic colitis is the most common condition caused by *E. coli O157:H7* infections, an even more dangerous syndrome is hemolytic uremia syndrome (HUS), which is characterized by kidney failure and the loss of red blood cells. Up to 10 percent of all hemorrhagic colitis cases in small children progress to HUS, which, when it does not kill, can lead to permanent liver damage.

E. Coli and Antibiotic Resistance

Since the end of World War II, hundreds of ANTIBIOTICS have come into use, leading to enormous progress in the fight against bacterial diseases. With each new antibiotic, it seemed, another of the great scourges of medical history was suddenly made treatable.

This revolution in medical care did not stop with humans. Food-processing companies noted with great interest that antibiotics were equally effective in animals. Diseases among cattle, pigs, chickens, and other animals could be routinely treated with antibiotics, saving the agricultural industry money and preventing the loss of countless animals to disease.

It was with some alarm then that when the first cases of hemorrhagic colitis and HUS occurred in 1982, doctors noted that antibiotics such as tetracycline and ampicillin, two of the bulwarks in the fight against bacterial INFECTIONS, had little effect. Researchers had seen the same kind of drug resistance during the 1970s in studies of the *Salmonella* bacterium, which had begun showing up in chicken and eggs. At that time, Dr. Stuart Levy of Tufts University had shown that feeding high amounts of antibiotics to chickens had actually weakened their ability to fight off harmful bacterial infections. Since then, he has also shown that *E. coli O157:H7* can easily be passed from livestock to the farmers that handle them.

Livestock are not the only animals that have been overtreated with antibiotics. An increasing number of

Other Causes of Food-Borne Illness

Botulism: *Clostridium botulinum* is a spore-forming MICROORGANISM that produces a strong NEUROTOXIN that causes botulism. Because botulism spores are heat-resistant, they are able to survive in poultry, livestock, or fish that has been minimally or improperly processed, as well as in horses and wild fowl. The botulism bacterium can be destroyed if properly heated to a high temperature for ten minutes or longer. Although botulism is relatively rare, it can be very deadly if not treated quickly and effectively. Symptoms occur within days of exposure to the toxin and include muscle weakness, double vision, and difficulties speaking, breathing, and swallowing. Most outbreaks in the United States are linked to home-canned goods, but some improperly processed commercial sausage, meats, canned vegetables, and seafood have also caused the disease.

Listeria: Listeriosis is an infection caused by food contaminated with the bacterium *Listeria monocytogenes*. The disease mostly affects pregnant women, newborns, and adults with weakened immune systems. If infected with *L. monocytogenes*, a person may take up to eight weeks to experience mild flu-like symptoms such as fever, chills, or upset stomach. If the infection spreads to the nervous system, headache, stiff neck, loss of balance, disorientation, and convulsions may occur. While pregnant women may only experience flu-like symptoms, the infection can pass to the fetus, risking miscarriage, stillbirth, or serious health problems. Because *L. monocytogenes* is found in soil and water, vegetables can become contaminated from contaminated soil or manure-based fertilizer. Because the bacteria can also live undetected in animals, they can pass to humans in meat and dairy products. Although listeria is killed by pasteurization and heating processes used for cold cuts, these products can become recontaminated before leaving the plant, as well as en route to the store, or at the deli counter.

Salmonella: A rod-shaped bacterium, *Salmonella* can live in water, soil, and animal feces; in meats, poultry, and seafood; and on kitchen and factory surfaces where such foods are handled. Salmonella that typically cause diarrhea in humans are *Salmonella typhimurium* and *Salmonella enteriditis*. Most infected people also develop fever and abdominal cramps within twelve to seventy-two hours after exposure, and the illness usually lasts for four to seven days. Although most recover without medical treatment, the diarrhea may be so severe that hospitalization may be necessary. In these cases the salmonella infection may spread from the intestines to the blood stream, causing death unless the person is treated immediately with antibiotics.

Trichinosis: *Trichinella spiralis,* the cause of trichinosis, is a parasitic, intestinal roundworm that can cause fever, muscle soreness, swollen eyelids, profuse sweating, thirst, chills, diarrhea, and high fever in humans. Infections occur when a person eats raw or undercooked meats (usually pork) infested with the roundworm larvae. Symptoms usually occur eight to fifteen days after exposure and can range from mild to severe. Failure to receive proper medical attention can be fatal.

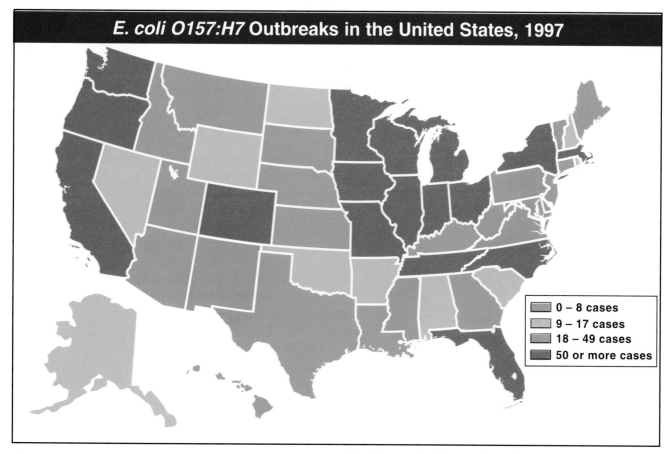

E. coli O157:H7 Outbreaks in the United States, 1997

Legend:
- 0 – 8 cases
- 9 – 17 cases
- 18 – 49 cases
- 50 or more cases

The Centers for Disease Control reported a total of 2,555 cases of E. coli O157:57 *infection in 1997.*

doctors argue that far too many people are using them as well. In some cases, the cause is patients who demand that their doctors give them *something* to ease disease symptoms, particularly when the sick person is their child.

On the other hand, some patients blame doctors for not taking the time to explain what antibiotics are used for—that they are useless against common viral infections, for example, and that every time a child takes an antibiotic unnecessarily, his or her IMMUNE SYSTEM develops greater resistance to that antibiotic. In the case of *E. coli O157:H7* infections, some evidence has shown that treatment with antibiotics can actually worsen symptoms because dying bacteria release more toxins into the system.

Danger in the Food Chain

Clearly, *E. coli O157:H7* can and has been spread by sloppy procedures in food-processing plants. In the contaminated apple juice case, inspectors found that runoff from pigstyes had gotten into water used to process the juice. Likewise, hamburger meat is particularly susceptible to contamination by *E. coli O157:H7* right in the processing plant, since bacteria can easily be

ground into the meat during processing. Nonetheless, Americans consume millions of hamburgers every year, and can continue to do so safely by making sure that the meat is cooked properly so that any bacteria are killed.

In reaction to national concerns about food safety, the Clinton administration ordered that food safety inspections be tightened. That short-term solution, however, is merely a start, most food safety authorities say, because it does not address the issue of the potential danger of overusing antibiotics. Each time humans eat meat from an animal that has been fed antibiotics, they run the risk of weakening their body's natural ability to fight off disease. It may take some years to find an antibiotic or other chemical that can be used to treat *E. coli* that are resistant to current antibiotics. The sooner the search begins, the sooner it will be successful.

Evidence suggests that using antibiotics to fight *E. coli O157:H7* infections actually makes patients sicker by causing dying bacteria to spill even more toxins into the bloodstream.

HEPATITIS

Global Distribution Hepatitis is found worldwide.

Causative Agent The many different types of hepatitis are caused by different hepatitis viruses.

Transmission Hepatitis A is spread through fecal-oral transmission, which occurs when someone puts something in his or her mouth such as food or drink that has been contaminated with feces of an infected person. Hepatitis B is spread from mothers to newborn infants through blood exposure at birth, by people sharing contaminated needles during intravenous drug use or transfusion, through sexual intercourse, or through exposure of cuts or mucous membranes to contaminated blood. Hepatitis C is transmitted in the same ways as hepatitis B.

Symptoms *Hepatitis* literally means "inflammation of the liver."

Hepatitis A (HAV) causes fever, nausea, vomiting, and diarrhea. The skin and whites of the eyes take on a yellow color. Outbreaks most commonly occur in child-care centers and restaurants.

Hepatitis B (HBV) symptoms include fatigue, loss of appetite, dark urine, nausea, vomiting, and abdominal pain. Chronic infection occurs in 5 to 10 percent of older children and adults; the rate is higher for infants and young children. If a chronic infection develops, cirrhosis or liver cancer usually occurs in 15 to 25 percent of patients.

The symptoms of hepatitis C (HCV) are similar to HBV, but many people with HCV do not experience any symptoms. Chronic infection occurs in more than 85 percent of cases; liver disease occurs in 70 percent.

Treatment There are vaccines for hepatitis A and hepatitis B. There are a few medications on the market for hepatitis C, but they are not fully effective.

Prevention and Control For hepatitis A, better sanitation education with extra hygiene measures in the child-care environment. Hepatitis B and C can be controlled with universal screening of blood and blood products, and public education about safe sex.

Every person who received a blood transfusion or organ transplant prior to 1992 is a possible carrier of hepatitis C.

In its most literal sense, *hepatitis* means "inflammation of the liver." While fatal diseases like AIDS and Ebola hemorrhagic fever have captured the public's attention, hepatitis has quietly become one of the most important public health threats worldwide. The disease, caused by either a number of VIRUSES or on occasion chemicals such as alcohol or prescription drugs, is ENDEMIC in many parts of the world.

The classic sign of hepatitis is jaundice, which indicates liver problems, and is characterized by the yellowing of the skin, eyes, and mucus MEMBRANES Jaundice warns that the liver is no longer cleansing the blood properly and that an excess of bile has entered the bloodstream. The first known case of jaundice was described in the fifth century B.C.E. by the ancient Greek physician Hippocrates. Medical historians now believe the patient may have been suffering from hepatitis caused by a virus.

Jaundice and War

Throughout history, jaundice has been connected with warfare. Crowded, unsanitary military encampments gave "campaign jaundice," as it was called, the ideal environment in which to spread. During the American Civil War (1861–65) more than seventy thousand Union troops were felled by the condition.

Despite the frequent occurrence of jaundice outbreaks, physicians had little understanding of it until the mid-twentieth century. During World War II, jaundice swept through U.S. forces, and doctors ultimately linked the outbreak to a human SERUM used in the VACCINE that had been administered to prevent yellow fever *(see page 100).*

In 1947, two years after the war's end, British doctors G. M. Findlay and F. O. MacCallum announced a discovery that helped explain how the wartime epidemic had occurred. Although it was already known that a hepatitis INFECTION could be passed via unsanitary conditions, Findlay and MacCallum also identified a second hepatitis virus, TRANSMITTED in human blood serum. It was that virus that had been spread in the yellow fever vaccine. Today, our ability—or inability—to properly screen blood for all forms of hepatitis remains an issue of great concern. In fact, not until 1992 were all of the viruses causing the disease even traceable to blood.

Hepatitis A

Findlay and MacCallum were the first to distinguish between what they called infectious hepatitis, or

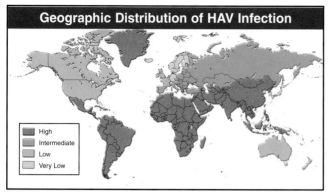

Geographic Distribution of HAV Infection

High
Intermediate
Low
Very Low

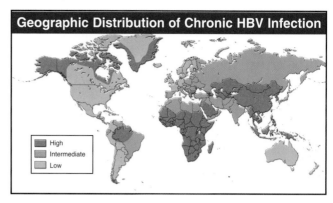

Geographic Distribution of Chronic HBV Infection

High
Intermediate
Low

hepatitis A (HAV), and the second form, which they called serum hepatitis, or hepatitis B (HBV).

Hepatitis A is the least threatening form of hepatitis but it is also the easiest to transmit. Medical historians believe that most jaundice epidemics in history were caused by HAV. HAV is transmitted through water or food that is contaminated by human feces, and is therefore common in regions with poor sanitation.

On occasion, HAV is spread to youngsters in child-care centers. Children generally show only mild symptoms of the disease, if any, but can easily transmit the virus to adults. In addition to jaundice, adult HAV infections can also cause diarrhea, nausea, fever, and fatigue. The Centers for Disease Control (CDC) estimates that there are between 125,000 and 200,000 infections a year in the United States alone, although only about 80,000 to 130,000 of these cases exhibit symptoms. Death from HAV is rare, with about 100 a year in the United States. Once a person is infected, he or she will develop a lifetime IMMUNITY to the virus.

As mild as an HAV infection usually is, it is also entirely preventable through vaccination. On February 22, 1999, an advisory committee to the CDC recommended that the eleven states with the highest incidence of hepatitis A add vaccination to their routine childhood vaccination schedules and require those vaccinations for admission to day-care centers or school.

Hepatitis B

A more complex and potentially harmful virus than the HAV virus, the HBV virus is primarily transmitted in blood serum. It can also be passed though other bodily fluids, including saliva, semen, and mucus. For this reason, those most vulnerable to HBV infection are people having unprotected sex, as well as intravenous drug users sharing unsanitary needles.

Hepatitis B is extremely contagious, in part because it remains infectious even when it has been outside the body for as long as a week, making seemingly innocent actions like using a borrowed razor a dangerous proposition. There are now an estimated 350 million carriers of HBV globally.

Because it can take up to six months for hepatitis B symptoms to appear, newly infected persons can unknowingly spread the disease to others before they learn they are infected. And unlike HAV, once HBV is in the body it can remain there for life.

Roughly half of all adults and about 10 percent of all children who become infected with HBV will develop symptoms such as fever, diarrhea, jaundice, and fatigue, which can last for a few weeks or even months before disappearing. However, 70 to 90 percent of all infected infants, up to 25 percent of infected children between the ages of one and four, and 5 to 10 percent of older children and adults develop chronic hepatitis, in which HBV persists in the body indefinitely, most often for the person's lifetime. Repeated attacks on the liver leave scars and fibrous tissue that replace healthy CELLS. Destruction of the cells damages the normal functions of the liver, including blood detoxification, causing cirrhosis. If the damage continues, victims can suffer liver failure and require a transplant in order to survive, or they may develop liver cancer. HBV-associated liver cancer is particularly prevalent in Africa and Asia, where the rate of HBV infection is high. The availability of a vaccine gives hope that there will be fewer HBV-related liver cancer cases in the future, both in the developing world and the developed world.

The Politics of Mandatory Vaccination

With the availability of an effective vaccine, worldwide prevention of HBV has become a major priority for international health organizations. In the United States, childhood vaccination for the hepatitis B virus is mandatory in forty-one states and the District of Columbia. Unfortunately, a number of obstacles make reaching the goal of hepatitis eradication difficult to obtain. First, there is the question of access. Although many of the world's wealthier nations have national hepatitis vaccination programs either in place or in the planning stages, a great number of developing countries do not. The expense of not only orchestrating a national program, but obtaining vaccines from manufacturers in the United States and elsewhere is often well beyond the means of many developing nations.

In the United States, other hurdles exist. People have objected to the idea of mandatory vaccination, including some parents who are concerned that since HBV is primarily transmitted through blood or unprotected sex, the laws target the wrong population. Concerns are underscored by theories that the vaccine may trigger immune and neurological disorders. On the other hand, groups ranging from the CDC to the American Academy of Pediatrics argue that there is no confirmed evidence that the vaccine can cause these chronic illnesses.

Nonetheless, the controversy has led to increased efforts to change the way public vaccination programs are carried out. France recently ended its school-based vaccination program in order to give parents access to more information about the vaccine. Advocates of mandatory vaccination argue that because HBV is a preventable disease, doing all that we can to reduce the risk of HBV's spread is the only responsible choice.

Hepatitis C

While the debate over mandatory HBV vaccination shows no signs of ending, advocates on both sides of that debate feel assured that vaccination is at least an option. There is no such option for those infected with hepatitis C (HCV), the most deadly form of viral hepatitis.

"The Silent Epidemic," "The Quiet Stalker," and "The Hidden Epidemic" are all used to describe HCV. While HIV *(see page 38)* has garnered far more attention in the last twenty years, HCV has spread around the globe just as quickly. With one hundred seventy million people infected worldwide and no effective treatment available, some fear that the annual death rate in the United States alone could reach thirty thousand in the next decade.

It was not until 1975 that researchers surmised that a third type of hepatitis existed, which they named non-A, non-B hepatitis (NANB). Further studies revealed some alarming news: about 65 percent of hepatitis cases found to be associated with blood transfusions were caused by NANB, and NANB-related infections had been occurring ever since blood transfusions were first

Hepatitis D, E, F, and G

In addition to hepatitis A, B, and C, four other forms of the disease, known as hepatitis D, E, F, and G, have been identified. A summary of each is outlined below:

Hepatitis D virus (HDV) The hepatitis D virus (HDV), first isolated in 1978, is unique among all animal viruses, for it relies on HBV for survival. HDV covers itself in the PROTEIN shell that surrounds HBV. When hepatitis B is compounded with an HDV infection, it can kill as many as 20 percent of its victims. Still, so little is known about HDV that its long-term impact is unclear. Researchers believe that HDV epidemics may have struck indigenous populations in Venezuela, Colombia, Brazil, and Peru, and that the virus may have been present in South America for some time.

Hepatitis E virus (HEV) In 1955 and 1956, a hepatitis epidemic struck Delhi, India, after sewage contaminated drinking-water supplies. At the time, officials believed the epidemic was caused by HAV. In 1980, however, a study of samples from that epidemic identified a new form of hepatitis virus, now known as hepatitis E (HEV). HEV is spread, like HBV, through the fecal-oral route. While there is no vaccine for hepatitis E currently available, it does not appear to be a chronic liver disease and is only fatal 1 to 3 percent of the time. No HEV outbreaks have been reported in the United States, but it is known to be endemic in Mexico, parts of Africa, and areas in South and Southeast Asia.

In the last few years, a number of hepatitis cases have been documented that do not appear to be caused by A, B, C, D, or E types. In 1991 and 1992, investigators in Japan reported the discovery of what they called **hepatitis F virus (HFV)**. Since then, some studies have suggested that HFV may be a mutant form of HBV, but that has yet to be verified. The newest hepatitis viruses were identified in 1995 and 1996, and because both share a very similar structure, they are now jointly known as **hepatitis G virus (HGV)**. Preliminary studies indicate that between nine hundred and two thousand infections occur per year in the United States, mostly without symptoms. HGV is thought to be blood-borne. Further study of the causes, routes of transmission, and symptoms is needed to establish HGV as a distinct virus.

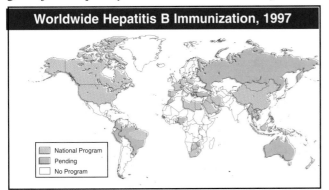

Worldwide Hepatitis B Immunization, 1997

National Program
Pending
No Program

administered in the 1940s. Finally, in 1989, the specific virus causing NANB hepatitis was identified, and named hepatitis C (HCV). Three years later, it was detected in blood samples.

HCV enters its HOSTS in a variety of ways: through tainted blood, contaminated needles, unprotected sex, and, in rare instances, from mother to newborn. It then harbors itself in the liver, causing continuous damage. Those infected by HCV can then unknowingly spread it to others. Most ominously, because there was no test to detect HCV in blood prior to 1992, every person to have received a blood transfusion or organ transplant prior to 1992 needs to be tested to determine whether they were infected by HCV during that procedure.

The challenges that this HCV crisis present to public health officials are enormous. In 1998, six years after scientists first gained the ability to screen for HCV in the blood supply, Dr. David Satcher, the surgeon general of the United States, announced a plan to send a mass mailing to all those who may have received blood tainted by the HCV virus. Although the goal of this program was to ensure that infected victims be made aware of their status as potential carriers, the fact remains that no vaccine or effective treatment exists for the illness.

Tainted Blood and Medical Ethics

The transfusion of blood tainted with HCV prior to 1992 has led to several multimillion-dollar lawsuits. In January 1999, a suit was brought against two U.S. companies and the U.S. government by four hundred Canadians who believe they were infected with HCV-tainted blood taken from prisoners in Arkansas jails in the 1980s, at a time when all other U.S. states had ended the practice. According to the plaintiffs, the FDA knew the risks inherent in allowing the sale of blood drawn from prisoners. The presence of HIV and HBV in prisoner blood samples had been clearly documented since 1986, when the medical community first gained the ability to screen for those viruses. Therefore, although HCV was not detectable prior to 1992, its presence during that time might reasonably have been suspected. The same group of Canadians has already won a lawsuit for 1.1 billion Canadian dollars against Canada's federal and provincial governments.

The Silent Epidemic

The potential cost of an HCV PANDEMIC is alarming. According to a leading blood specialist, the growing number of HCV-infected patients is "an iceberg problem. We see only a small part of the problem now—the tip, those ill or needing liver transplants—and that's very frightening." It is estimated that four million Americans have HCV. Eight to ten thousand HCV patients die each year in the United States alone.

As of 1999, two drugs—interferon and ribavirin—were in use on HCV patients. Neither has proven very effective and both have caused serious side effects in some patients. Until researchers better understand this "quiet stalker," millions worldwide will struggle with the disease.

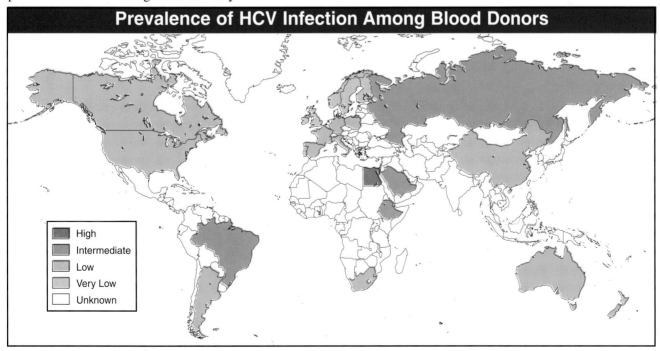

Prevalence of HCV Infection Among Blood Donors

- High
- Intermediate
- Low
- Very Low
- Unknown

HIV/AIDS

Global Distribution AIDS is found worldwide.

Causative Agent AIDS is caused by HIV (human immun-odeficiency virus).

Transmission HIV is transmitted through the exchange of bodily fluids, including blood, semen, and breast milk. The risk of contracting the disease is particularly high in unpro-tected sexual intercourse, sharing infected needles, and mother-to-infant transmission.

Symptoms AIDS patients lose their ability to fight infec-tions. Bacteria that normally pose no threat become poten-tially lethal. AIDS patients are particularly susceptible to pneumonia, liver disease, and skin cancer. People who are HIV-positive are at high risk for developing AIDS; however, this may take many years, if it happens at all. Initial symp-toms of HIV infection are fever, fatigue, weight loss, sore throat, rash, and gastrointestinal distress.

Treatment Since HIV/AIDS was recognized, the scientific community has struggled with ways to treat this mysterious disease. The most recent practices include immediate treat-ment after the earliest detection possible.

Prevention and Control Until a cure for AIDS is developed, prevention will remain the most effective way to battle HIV. Worldwide HIV education programs must continue to be supported. Many health authorities advise that safe-sex practices, particularly the use of latex condoms, should be taught as early as possible, and that abstinence should be encouraged. Although controversial, needle exchange pro-grams, which provide clean hypodermic needles to interve-nous drug users, have helped prevent the spread as well.

Ryan White, infected with HIV at age thir-teen after receiving a contaminated blood transfusion, faced enormous prejudice during his short life. Children ran from him, bullets were fired into his home, and parents demanded that he be banned from school. In response, he sued in court, won, and returned to school. After his court vic-tory, Ryan continued to speak out. "I've seen how people with HIV/AIDS are treated, and I don't want others to be treated like I was," he once said. Ryan died of AIDS in 1990. His mother, Jeanne, has continued to help peo-ple deal with issues related to HIV and AIDS through the Ryan White Foundation.

In 1988, seven hundred top health delegates from 148 nations around the world gathered in London at the request of the World Health Organization (WHO) to discuss an emerging disease. The World Summit of Ministers of Health on Programmes for AIDS Prevention had been organized by WHO's Global Programme on AIDS, headed by American Jonathan Mann. The conference was attended by the top health minister of almost every nation, with the exception of the United States. The administration of President Ronald Reagan sent the country's third-ranking health official, Dr. Robert Windom, instead of Surgeon General C. Everett Koop.

Although Mann and others had begun predicting that AIDS (or *a*cquired *i*mmuno*d*eficiency *s*yndrome) would erupt into a global PANDEMIC shortly after it was first identified in 1981, these fears were not shared by all of Mann's colleagues. Officials from other WHO divisions saw the attention on AIDS as misplaced. After all, they argued, malaria *(see page 56)* and tuberculosis *(see page 92)*, the world's first and second most fatal diseases, killed millions each year, yet neither had ever gathered such media attention. Despite the debate, many felt the conference marked a new era of coopera-tion and commitment to world health. And indeed, at that time there was much to be optimistic about.

"Winning the War Against Disease"

In 1977, WHO officials announced the defeat of the smallpox virus *(see page 82)*. For the first time, a dead-ly VIRUS had been eradicated from the globe. Prior to this victory, the world had often faced pandemics—such as bubonic plague *(see page 68)* or cholera *(see page 16)*—with a mixture of panic and finger-pointing. These responses had often been complicated by period-ic economic turmoil and warfare, making international cooperation all too rare.

During the fight against smallpox, however, WHO had not only effectively distributed the resources need-ed to mobilize global VACCINATION programs, but had done so in war-torn, poverty-stricken regions of the world, regions almost completely lacking in health-care infrastructures.

Given this success, optimism about the fight against AIDS was high when health officials met at the London conference. While there was no known cure for AIDS, fewer than one hundred thousand cases had been reported worldwide. In addition, the main methods of AIDS TRANSMISSION were known. Surely, predictions of a new "Black Death" were overblown.

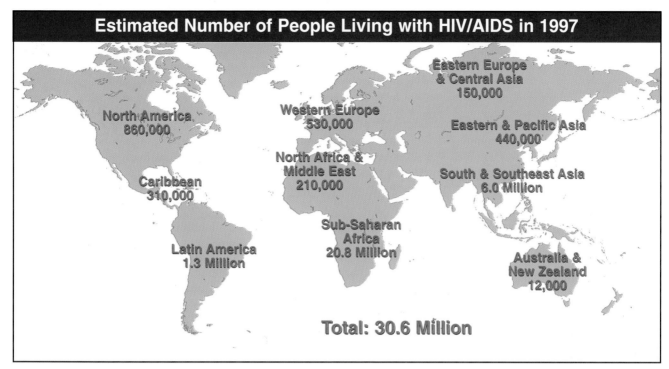

Estimated Number of People Living with HIV/AIDS in 1997

Eastern Europe
& Central Asia
150,000

Western Europe
530,000

North America
860,000

Eastern & Pacific Asia
440,000

North Africa &
Middle East
210,000

South & Southeast Asia
6.0 Million

Caribbean
310,000

Latin America
1.3 Million

Sub-Saharan
Africa
20.8 Million

Australia &
New Zealand
12,000

Total: 30.6 Million

Almost two-thirds of all adults and children living with HIV/AIDS are Africans. In some countries, over 25 percent of the population is HIV-positive.

What the optimists had not counted on was that AIDS was like no disease ever faced before. AIDS is a slow killer, typically taking eight to ten years to claim its victims. This long INCUBATION period would dramatically aid the spread of INFECTION. What is more, HIV, the virus that causes AIDS, has confounded researchers with its ability to adapt, changing genetically to protect itself against each new form of treatment. Finally, the early history of the disease, beginning with the discovery of the first cases in the gay communities of New York, Los Angeles, and San Francisco, has ensured that the search for a cure has been inextricably bound up in a web of both personal and public politics and morality.

The Early Years of An Epidemic

In July 1980, doctors in Los Angeles diagnosed a thirty-three-year-old male patient with PCP (*Pneumocystis carinii* pneumonia), a form of pneumonia that typically attacks infants, the elderly, or those with weakened immune systems. Blood tests revealed that the patient's blood contained very few T CELLS. T cells (short for *t*hymus-derived *cells*) protect the body from infection by recognizing invading MICROBES and triggering the IMMUNE SYSTEM to respond. Without T cells to perform this crucial function, even relatively benign organisms can do great harm to an otherwise healthy adult. Within a year the patient was dead. That same year, five similar cases were diagnosed in Los Angeles.

Kaposi's Sarcoma

Meanwhile, doctors in New York and San Francisco had started seeing patients with equally unusual infections. One was a condition known as Kaposi's sarcoma, a skin cancer that is ordinarily extremely rare in the United States. One New York dermatologist soon recognized a similarity between the PCP and Kaposi's sarcoma patients. They were all homosexual males averaging thirty-nine years of age, and all had contracted various sexually transmitted diseases. Because homosexual behavior seemed to link the patients, the first surveys released by the Centers for Disease Control (CDC) identified the disease as gay-related immunodeficiency disease, or GRID.

Concerned that promiscuous sexual behavior might cause GRID to spread to other cities, researchers sought out additional federal funding to further their investigations. As Surgeon General Koop would later explain, however, the Reagan administration was "predisposed to antipathy toward the homosexual community." The CDC's requests for additional funding were ignored.

In mid-1982, when intravenous drug users also began contracting GRID, the response was the same. The administration had taken a strong stance against drug abuse, and had little interest in spending tax dollars to cure those breaking the laws. Even when a num-

WILDERMUTH

ber of heterosexual Haitian immigrants were diagnosed in July 1982 with what the press had begun calling "Gay Plague," the government remained silent.

GRID and Hemophilia

That same year, GRID began showing up among people suffering from hemophilia, a disorder that prevents blood from clotting. Hemophiliacs often require transfusions of blood to survive. When three heterosexual hemophiliacs were diagnosed with GRID in 1982, CDC researchers realized that it was not just sexual behavior that transmitted GRID. Clearly, whatever was causing the disease was being passed through infected blood. That meant that anyone was susceptible to infection. The disease's name was officially changed to acquired immunodeficiency syndrome, or AIDS.

Ironically, before safer blood screening techniques were put in place, it was common practice for intravenous drug addicts to sell their blood to support their habits. Since hemophiliacs were contracting GRID, it seemed undeniable that the nation's blood supply had been tainted.

The CDC immediately alerted representatives from the National Hemophilia Foundation (NHF). That fall, the NHF met repeatedly with executives from the blood industry to try to persuade them to ensure the safety of the nation's blood supply, but to no avail. The following January, the CDC convened a meeting with representatives of the four U.S. companies that controlled nearly 60 percent of the world's blood supply. At the meeting, the blood-bank representatives disputed the CDC's claims of a tainted supply, citing a lack of hard evidence. No action was taken and the meeting dissolved. Before 1983 was out, the Food and Drug Administration would cut the number of its blood-quality-control inspections in half. In the meantime, hemophiliacs as young as seven years old continued to die from tainted blood.

HIV is Discovered

Not all the news was bad in 1983, however. That year, American and French researchers finally solved one of the greatest riddles about AIDS—its cause. While researchers at the CDC were studying a Florida AIDS outbreak, which had raised fears that mosquitoes might be capable of spreading the disease, the human immunodeficiency virus (HIV) was discovered.

HIV is a RETROVIRUS. The first retroviruses were discovered in 1970 but not cultured in laboratories until 1978. Retroviruses pose especially difficult challenges

to researchers because their genetic structures and means of reproduction are unlike those of any other virus. In cells and in certain viruses, deoxyribonucleic acid (DNA) contains the information necessary for proteins to be synthesized and for the DNA molecules to replicate. PROTEIN is synthesized when a DNA MOLECULE separates into two strands. Then a process called transcription occurs, as a new strand of nucleic acid called messenger ribonucleic acid (mRNA) is produced. The mRNA then carries the DNA's information to ribosomes, where proteins, including an ENZYME called TRANSCRIPTASE, are manufactured.

Retroviruses, including HIV, are composed of an envelope that is derived from the outer membrane of the host's CELL. From this viral membrane protrude proteins that bind to target host cells. Within the envelope are two strands of RNA. These enter the target cell MEMBRANE, whereupon viral nucleic acid is reproduced and inserted into the HOST cell's DNA. From then on, whenever that host cell reproduces, it also reproduces the HIV RNA. The HIV, in turn, begins killing off cells called CD-T-lymphocytes, paralyzing the immune system, which eventually brings about the onset of AIDS.

The Politics of AIDS

The scientific hurdles facing AIDS researchers were daunting in 1983. Unfortunately, the stumbling blocks outside the laboratory remained daunting as well. Because only a small minority of the U.S. population suffers from hemophilia, most Americans felt little personal threat from AIDS. While scientific evidence had proven otherwise, the popular perception remained that AIDS was a disease caused by, and confined to, homosexuals and drug addicts.

This perception was strengthened by activists in the gay community who lobbied vocally for increased research funding. Since gays were the first to be affected by the epidemic in America, some conservative leaders saw the disease as a direct result of homosexual behavior. In 1983, television evangelist Jerry Falwell preached that "AIDS is God's punishment, the scripture is clear: we do reap it in our flesh when we violate the laws of God." Clearly the debate on how best to approach AIDS had sparked a political tinderbox.

A Strategy of Isolation

Five years later, the aftermath of the 1988 AIDS conference in London reflected this conflict. Many governments were still unwilling to admit that AIDS posed a threat within their borders, and suggested that any rise in infections would be caused by foreigners. Following the conference, eighty-one nations passed laws that denied visa permits to HIV-positive foreigners. In China, the government made having sex with a foreigner a crime. In Cuba, when 174 soldiers returning from war in Angola were found to be infected, they were placed under a lifetime quarantine. In the United States, the government pushed for mandatory testing of all immigrants, even as it discouraged Surgeon General Koop from discussing AIDS in public. Critics of government policies such as these argued that attempts to deny or isolate victims would only drive them underground, making the disease harder to understand and harder to control.

Slim Disease

One mystery that long puzzled AIDS researchers was the question of where HIV originated. In 1984, Harvard University researcher Max Essex found evidence of AIDS-like viruses in African monkeys. (His theory was confirmed in 1999 by Dr. Beatrice Hahn of the University of Alabama, who traced HIV to a subspecies of African chimpanzee.) Ironically, at virtually the same time that the first cases of GRID were diagnosed in the United States, similar illnesses were beginning to appear in Africa. Among Africans, the disease had become known as "slim disease," due to the tell-tale weight loss of victims. Starting in 1982, doctors in Zambia and Uganda began seeing numerous cases of

In 1996, the Names Project displayed a tapestry of quilts representing the names of thousands of AIDS victims on the Mall in Washington, D.C.

Kaposi's sarcoma. As early as 1977, a Danish surgeon who had worked in Zaire (now the Democratic Republic of the Congo) later identified the disease as AIDS. In 1981, several African travelers to Europe were diagnosed with the disease, and clinical records suggest that there may have been AIDS cases in Africa as early as the 1950s or 1960s.

When "slim disease" emerged, in the early 1980s, local doctors first thought it could be any number of diseases that are ENDEMIC to Africa. In Tanzania and Uganda, where a fierce war between the two countries had raged since the 1970s, medical officials had another theory—that they were seeing some form of sexually transmitted disease (STD), as STD outbreaks frequently follow the paths of armies. However, when some of the sores associated with diseases like herpes failed to heal, they realized that something new was at work.

Searching for an answer, Dr. Clint Nyamuryekunge traveled to the Tanzanian city of Dar es Salaam with blood samples from some of his patients. When tests proved inconclusive, Nyamuryekunge found a report about the PCP cases from Los Angeles. He was immediately struck by the similarity of the symptoms. However, he could not fail to note one troubling difference between his cases and those that he read about: none of his patients fit what seemed to be the four H's of the AIDS profile—homosexuals, heroin addicts, hemophiliacs, or Haitians.

By 1984, several researchers at the CDC had also come to believe that "slim disease" and AIDS were connected. The next year, researchers in western Uganda confirmed the belief when they found that all twenty-nine "slim" victims tested positive for HIV.

The connection between AIDS and "slim disease" helped lead to the First International Conference on AIDS, held in Atlanta in 1985. It also helped lead to a rift in the international medical and political communities when an ill-intentioned member of the media posed the following question to an African health expert: "We have all heard what Max Essex said here about AIDS originating as an African monkey disease. Tell me, Doctor, is it true that Africans have sex with monkeys?" The comment highlighted what struck many as blatant racism. "African AIDS reports are a new form of hate campaign," Kenyan president Daniel arap Moi proclaimed, seizing on the remark as evidence that Africans were being used as scapegoats for

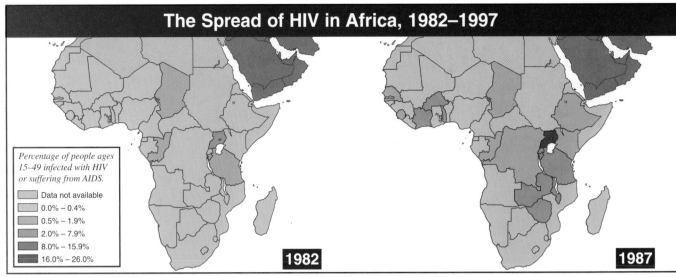

The Spread of HIV in Africa, 1982–1997

Percentage of people ages 15–49 infected with HIV or suffering from AIDS.

- Data not available
- 0.0% – 0.4%
- 0.5% – 1.9%
- 2.0% – 7.9%
- 8.0% – 15.9%
- 16.0% – 26.0%

1982

1987

The dramatic spread of HIV in Africa since 1982 is illustrated on the four maps above.

AIDS. Sadly, the comment also allowed Moi to deny the seriousness of the threat to his continent.

The AIDS Highway

Much of sub-Saharan Africa was desperately poor in the early 1980s, and remains so today. In Uganda, only one out of every 830 people owns a telephone. In Tanzania, just half the population has access to safe water. And in Mozambique, just 39 percent of the population can get even the minimum necessary level of health care.

Sadly, fighting between Tanzania and Uganda in the 1970s was far from the only violence the region has seen in recent decades. Virtually every nation south of the Sahara has been involved in either an internal or external conflict in the past twenty years. This almost constant warfare has wreaked havoc on local economies and helped perpetuate the region's deep poverty.

As armies have traveled through small rural villages in central and southern Africa, they have spread HIV. From there HIV has traveled along international highways, striking hardest in the border truckstop towns where drivers wait out customs clearances. Villagers that have become infected with the virus take it with them as they travel to larger cities in search of work, and then back to villages once more. This pattern has become so prevalent that the long east-to-west highway from Kinshasa in the Democratic Republic of the Congo to Mombassa in Kenya is known as "the AIDS Highway."

The Cost of War

The many wars fought in sub-Saharan Africa have also brought an enormous rise in the number of refugees fleeing their homelands. Since 1984, Africa's refugee problem has exploded. That year, Africa was also hit by its worst drought in a century. By 1985, thirty million refugees were spread throughout the continent.

Because no AIDS vaccine exists, health officials have stressed prevention and control as the only way to contain the disease. Public education programs focusing on the importance of safe sex and the use of latex condoms have met with some success, though enormous hurdles remain. In some traditional African societies, when a husband dies, his wife marries his brother. If the husband had died of AIDS, the wife may infect her new husband, or she may be infected by him. In refugee centers, the problems faced by AIDS educators are even more daunting. Many refugees have watched as their entire families were murdered in front of them. Many have been raped by invading soldiers. In such an environment, educators have great difficulty convincing people to worry about a disease that may kill them ten years later. Lastly, there is the question of money. Education programs cost money, and during wartime, government funding for public health all but disappears.

Today in Africa, an entire generation is in danger of being wiped out. Over twenty-one million out of the thirty million people worldwide that are infected with HIV are Africans. In several nations, as many as one in four are infected with HIV. Even in relatively wealthy nations that are not at war, the virus is spreading at an alarming rate. In Nigeria, for instance, where the government has earned millions selling off the rights to valuable natural resources, money is still in short supply

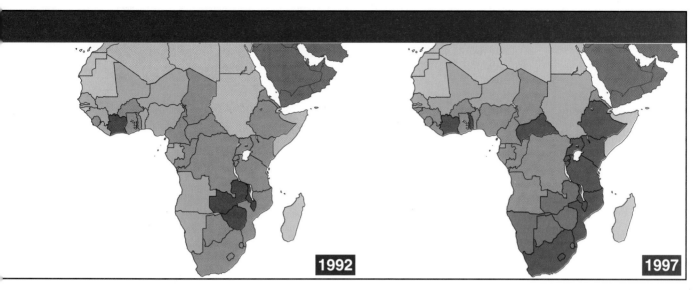

1992

1997

for health research or even basic medicine. Doctors in Mozambique are often lucky if they can provide aspirin to their suffering AIDS patients. Under these conditions, tuberculosis, malaria, and other normally treatable STDs become lethal assistants to HIV. Today, 80 percent of African AIDS patients die within two years of becoming infected with HIV.

New Hope for the Fortunate

Although AIDS patients in the West continue to die as well, there is new hope for those who can afford it. In the United States, AIDS-related deaths dropped by two-thirds between 1997 and 1999, largely due to a number of new drug therapies known as protease inhibitors that have shown great promise. Major American drug companies have invested hundreds of millions of dollars in new research. Experimental vaccines have also been manufactured using less harmful viruses to transport "live" or "killed" HIV DNA to the cells.

Yet even these advances have proved controversial. Evidence suggests that a new multidrug-resistant HIV STRAIN may be appearing. Another troubling issue is that of availability. The new therapies are extremely expensive. Only about 10 percent of all HIV-infected Americans have access to the new protease inhibitors. Even in the United States, HIV is threatening to become a disease of the poor. Recent statistics show that poor, urban blacks are eight times as likely to contract HIV as whites, so the economic questions are troubling.

The Research Gap

Manufacturers who have invested heavily in research and development argue that high prices are necessary if they are to recoup their investments, and many compa-nies have taken out patents on products to protect them as intellectual property. Critics argue that drug companies should be able to provide greater access to their products and still be profitable. Regarding the patenting of drug products, many have quoted the late Jonas Salk, creator of the polio vaccine *(see page 72)*, who once said, "To patent the vaccine . . . would be like patenting the sun."

Drug companies have also been criticized for their focus on HIV strains prevalent in the developed world. Little research has been done using the strains most common in Africa, India, and Southeast Asia. At the 1998 International AIDS Conference in Abidjan, Ivory Coast, WHO experts once again called on the world to make health a human right. A step in the right direction may be WHO's plan to provide a three-week regimen of azidothymidine, or AZT, a medicine that can slow the progress of AIDS, to HIV-infected pregnant women in a dozen developing countries. While this regimen is far shorter than that available to HIV patients in the West, there is evidence that the program will reduce the risk of mother-to-child transmission. Concerns remain, however, that a lack of funding will mean that the treatments will stop after babies are born.

Today, the AIDS story continues to be shaped by political, economic, and cultural battles. In 1998, 2.8 million more people became infected with HIV. Each minute, eleven more are infected. HIV's ability to adapt raises what is perhaps the greatest fear held by AIDS researchers—that the virus will MUTATE again, into a form that can be transmitted in the minute liquid particles released into the air during breathing. Studies suggest this is unlikely to occur. One can only hope that they are right.

INFLUENZA

Global Distribution Influenza is found worldwide.

Causative Agent Influenza is caused by various strains of the influenza virus, including type A, type B, and type C.

Transmission Flu viruses are transmitted from person to person very easily, particularly through coughing and sneezing. People can also pass the virus through mucous membranes of the eyes, nose, and mouth.

Symptoms There are several types of influenza that circulate and mutate constantly. In humans the symptoms of influenza virus infection can range from mild to deadly. Usual initial symptoms include fever, cough, and chills.

Treatment There is no real treatment for the flu except plenty of bed rest and drinking lots of fluids. The drug rimantadine may be used to treat influenza type A only and must be taken within forty-eight hours of onset of symptoms to be effective.

Prevention and Control There is a vaccine for the flu, but it must be taken six to eight weeks before the typical flu season begins, because it takes the immune system some time to respond to the vaccination. Also, rimantadine can be used in a preventive form by children over age one and by healthy adults. The drug must be taken for about six weeks during the flu season.

I had a little bird
And its name was Enza
I opened the window
And influenza.

–A popular children's rhyme during the fall of 1918.

arch 9, 1918, began like many others at the U.S. Army base at Camp Funston in Fort Riley, Kansas—with a dust storm. But it was not the bitter wind that troubled company cook Albert Gitchell when he reported to the camp infirmary before breakfast complaining of cold symptoms. Gitchell was soon joined by Corporal Lee W. Drake, who felt almost the same way. By lunch, the infirmary had filled with 100 men, all suffering from the same illness—later identified as Spanish flu. A week later the number had climbed to five hundred. The first wave of the most deadly disease PANDEMIC in human history had begun. Within a year, virtually every member of the human race had been infected by the influenza VIRUS, and at least thirty million people were dead.

An Ancient Illness

Influenza has followed humankind for centuries, making mostly minor, though occasionally disastrous, appearances around the globe each year. Historians speculate that the first outbreak may have occurred as early as 2000 B.C.E. Nonetheless, the virus had only a limited chance to spread since humans could not then travel the great distances in short periods of time they can today.

Although there are accounts of an influenza epidemic in 1510, there is little thorough documentation of outbreaks before the eighteenth century, when there were at least three, and perhaps as many as five, pandemics. The worst occurred in 1781, when the virus spread from Russia and eastern Asia to infect most of Europe before crossing the Atlantic to the Americas. Tens of millions were infected, many of whom died.

Because this pandemic began in Russia, a common name for it was *la Russe*. The word *influenza* itself was also coined during this time, in Italy. Many believed that since the disease seemed to afflict virtually everyone, it must be caused by the universal influence, or *influenza,* of the stars.

While some looked to the heavens for answers, the causes of the 1781 spread were actually more down-to-earth. The late eighteenth century was a period of both great population growth and rapidly increasing migration, two factors that go hand in hand with the spread of disease.

Although the 1781 epidemic swept through much of the world, it struck the elderly and those who were already sick hardest. Perhaps this explains why the pandemic did not inspire the panic that other widespread diseases have. A second factor may have to do with the

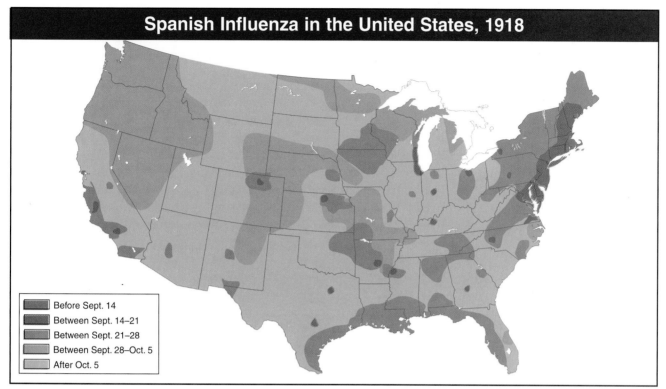

Spanish Influenza in the United States, 1918

Legend:
- Before Sept. 14
- Between Sept. 14–21
- Between Sept. 21–28
- Between Sept. 28–Oct. 5
- After Oct. 5

nature of disease itself: even widespread influenza outbreaks last just a few months, and then disappear as quickly as they came.

Influenza in the Nineteenth Century

In 1833, influenza again emerged out of Asia, infecting up to half of the citizens of some European cities. And again, the elderly and others with weakened IMMUNE SYSTEMS were the most common victims. Physicians blamed MIASMA, or "bad air," a commonly invoked yet unfounded explanation for disease prior to the late nineteenth century. In 1890, another EPIDEMIC struck down 250,000 people in Europe before wreaking similar havoc in North America. This era, however, was a period of enormous scientific breakthroughs. Researchers such as Robert Koch and Louis Pasteur were in the process of revolutionizing medicine. The GERM THEORY, the idea that diseases are caused by specific MICROORGANISMS passed to humans through water, food, or air, was at last gaining acceptance, and social reformers were using these new ideas to push for improved sanitation and living conditions. The era seemed to hold great promise, and many came to believe that infectious disease would soon be a thing of the past. By the turn of the twentieth century, numerous victories were being won. Malaria *(see page 56)* and yellow fever *(see page 100)* were being all but eradicated in the Caribbean and Panama Canal Zone. And even

In August 1918, the influenza pandemic that had begun the previous spring appears to have taken on a new virulence. In the United States, Boston and other port cities were struck hardest and earliest, but by early October, the virus had spread not only nationwide but worldwide.

in an era in which worldwide transportation had increased to new heights, the annual influenza outbreaks remained minor.

History's Deadliest Epidemic

Two months after the March 1918 outbreak of Spanish flu at Camp Funston, in Kansas, more than five hundred inmates at San Quentin prison in California came down with the same illness, as did people at several other army bases around the country. Nonetheless, in the spring of 1918, the United States had its attention focused elsewhere.

In 1914, World War I had broken out in Europe, and for three years President Woodrow Wilson had managed to keep the nation out of the conflict. In 1917, however, German aggression against American ships and the publication of a secret telegram from Germany to the government of Mexico promising support for a direct attack on the United States at last pushed Wilson into declaring war. The first U.S. troops shipped out in June of that year.

Just as the influenza wave was hitting Camp Funston, another two hundred thousand troops were preparing to ship out for Europe. Little did they know, but along with their guns and ammunition many also carried with them a deadly STRAIN of the influenza virus. Before their ship even reached Europe, thirty-six members of the Fifteenth U.S. Calvary fell ill; six of them died. Shortly thereafter, the virus began taking its toll in Europe. In June 1918, thirty-one thousand cases were reported in Great Britain alone.

In July, the first concerted efforts to alert the public were made. Philadelphia health authorities issued a bulletin regarding what they called "the Spanish flu" due to inaccurate reports about the virus's place of origin.

By August, however, new, far more serious cases were being reported not just in one place but in several, all of them seaports—in Boston, Massachusetts; in Freeport, Sierra Leone (in West Africa); and in the coastal port of Brest in Brittany, France. While the three ports were far from each other, doctors noted that they did have one thing in common. They were all actively involved in transporting men and arms to the battlefields of Europe.

By September, the virus took on a new, more deadly force. Infections were often accompanied by pneumonia or other secondary infections. When Dr. Victor Vaughn, the acting surgeon general of the U.S. Army, visited Fort Devens outside Boston, he saw hundreds of previously healthy young men filling the infirmary. On

the very day he arrived, sixty-three patients died. By winter, nations around the world were facing disaster.

The 1918–19 outbreak remains quite possibly the single worst PANDEMIC in human history. All told, it killed an estimated thirty million people worldwide, nearly twenty million in India and five hundred thousand in America alone. The 1918 outbreak took more lives in one year than the Great Plague of 1348 took in four.

Because the epidemic came in the midst of a world war, popular speculation raged that Germany was using germ warfare against the Allies, speculation that ended when Germans also began falling to the disease. In New York City, where twenty thousand died in fewer than four months, there were reports of the virus killing at an amazing speed. Some reports claimed that passengers who had felt the first pangs of illness while boarding a subway on Long Island were dead by the time the train reached Columbus Circle in Manhattan. With so many sick and dead, social mechanisms virtually disintegrated.

As the death toll mounted, mass graves were dug and talk of divine or cosmic influence rose again. Others suggested that unclean pajamas, nudity, or race mingling were responsible. Obviously, this was hysteria, not fact.

The Swine Flu Connection

When the pandemic finally abated in the winter of 1919, more people had died of influenza than had died in four years of world war. Nonetheless, scientists were no closer to understanding why this was than they had been before the pandemic began.

In the early twentieth century, medical investigations were severely handicapped. Every effort to identify the cause of the disease failed. It was not until 1932 that the true cause of influenza was revealed.

That year, American doctor Richard Shope proved that infected pigs could transmit the virus through nasal secretions by their rubbing against the nostrils of other pigs. This discovery earned the influenza virus the additional name "swine flu." Shope later established that people who had lived through the 1918 epidemic were resistant to swine flu, showing that they had ANTIBODIES to the 1918 virus. When he showed that the survivors indeed possessed such antibodies, it provided further evidence that swine flu was in fact the cause of the 1918 pandemic.

In 1933, a British team finally isolated what is now known as one of the three major strains of the virus, "influenza A." Of these three strains, A, B, and C, it is A that is the most deadly.

A Philadelphia newspaper reports the deadly death toll during the 1918 Spanish flu pandemic.

SPARC, a regional health program in northwest Connecticut, has been cited by the CDC for its pioneering work in preventive medicine.

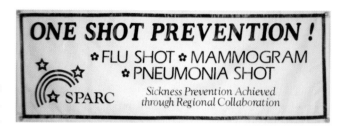

No one has conclusively proven where the virus responsible for the 1918 epidemic came from. The initial outbreaks in humans that spring were followed only later by outbreaks among pigs. Then, later that year, it returned to humans in deadly form.

Viral Drifts and Shifts

Influenza virus is spread through the air via coughing, sneezing, or contact with an infected person's breath or mucus. The virus normally infects the respiratory system, causing fever, aches, coughing, and other signs and symptoms. INFECTION is usually contained in the respiratory tract, but occasionally the virus manages to escape the system. Each time influenza A virus makes its annual appearance, it has changed slightly. Minor MUTATIONS, typically genetic changes that manifest themselves in the surface PROTEINS of the virus, are called "drifts." Even these can make the work of the immune system's antibodies more difficult.

The greater danger comes when influenza virus "shifts." That occurs with a large change in the GENE order or when two different flu viruses join to create a new one. Shifts disguise flu viruses, allowing them to fool the body's defenses and perhaps leave the respiratory system to attack other organs. When that happens, pneumonia, hemorrhaging, and other secondary infections can result, leading to death. Because the virus can mutate in this way means new VACCINES must be continually developed to protect against them.

The Swine Flu Scare

In 1976, several hundred cadets at Fort Dix, New Jersey, were hospitalized with flu symptoms. Because some of the cadets had antibodies against Shope's swine flu strain, doctors feared that the virus that had caused the 1918 pandemic had returned. Millions of dollars were poured into developing a vaccine. Although an anticipated epidemic never emerged, the research proved invaluable as new insight into the transmission of flu viruses was revealed.

The Latest Discoveries

Scientists believe influenza A virus originates in birds and spreads directly to humans when infected birds come in contact with otherwise healthy people. In 1997, when a flu virus originating in chickens killed six people in Hong Kong, authorities responded by killing most of the territory's fowl, including millions of chickens and ducks. More often, the virus passes from birds to pigs, where it takes on characteristics that are easier to pass to humans.

Ever since the 1918 pandemic ended, scientists have wondered why it was so much more deadly than any other before or since. At the time, not many authorities thought to preserve tissue or blood samples from victims for future study. Ever since, investigators have been searching for viable samples of the 1918 strain, but have always come up short.

In 1998, there was finally a breakthrough. A team from the Armed Forces Institute of Pathology lead by Dr. Jeffrey K. Taubenberger used tissue samples acquired from a researcher named Johan Hultan to identify the 1918 strain. Forty-seven years earlier, Hultan had taken lung tissue samples from the body of an Alaskan Inuit buried in permafrost in hopes of finding a preserved version of the 1918 virus, but he had had little luck. Taubenberger's team however used a technique that allowed the extraction of genetic information from poorly preserved tissue. This enabled them to map, or sequence, the hemagglutinin (HA) gene of influenza. The virus uses this gene to infect CELLS, and it is HA that researchers look for first to identify the virus. Severe influenza epidemics occur when a virus with a mutated gene, one producing a different, even slightly different HA protein appears. That information has helped change the way researchers understand the virus. Thanks to Taubenberger's work, scientists now also know that the deadly 1918 virus was closely related to the classic swine flu strain, A/Sw/Iowa/30. Further, their research indicates that the 1918 virus was of mammal rather than bird origin. With this knowledge, researchers are now one step closer to understanding the cause of the 1918 pandemic.

LEGIONNAIRE'S DISEASE

Global Distribution The prevalence of Legionnaire's disease is sporadic, but has been isolated in areas that are air-conditioned, as well as in hot tubs and showers. The disease effects middle-aged or older men most, particularly if they are smokers.

Causative Agent Legionnaire's disease is caused by the bacterium *Legionella pneumophila*.

Transmission The disease can occur when tiny droplets that carry the *Legionellae* bacteria are inhaled.

Symptoms The first symptoms of Legionnaire's disease are muscle aches, loss of appetite, fatigue, dry cough, and headache. These symptoms are often followed by diarrhea, chills, and a high fever. Legionnaire's disease can range from a mild illness to pneumonia and death.

Treatment Legionnaire's disease is treated with antibiotics.

Prevention and Control *Legionellae* bacteria are naturally occurring in the environment, making the disease difficult to prevent. However, precautionary measures may be taken by cleaning and draining cooling towers and by using biocides that prevent the growth of organisms in air-conditioning systems.

Although Legionnaire's Disease was not identified until 1976, the researchers at the Centers for Disease Control estimate that two to six thousand people have died of the disease each year since World War II.

In July 1976, the United States was proudly enjoying its two hundredth birthday, the bicentennial anniversary of the signing of the Declaration of Independence. Among the celebrants were several thousand convention participants, members of the American Legion, one of the nation's leading veterans' organizations. The legionnaires had gathered in Philadelphia, where the declaration had been signed, to commemorate the events of 1776 and to visit such sights as Independence Hall and the Liberty Bell. Several weeks later, twenty-nine legionnaires, many of whom had survived enemy fire three decades earlier during World War II, were dead, and nobody knew why.

A few hundred legionnaires—and all of the dead—had been staying at the Bellevue-Stratford, a large, stately hotel in the center of town. On the convention's second day, dozens of veterans began suffering from fever, chills, dry cough, and other flu-like symptoms. Within a few days, several had developed acute pneumonia and had to be hospitalized. Given that the victims were generally in their mid-fifties and older, and that they had been celebrating for several days, the doctors who treated them saw little reason to be concerned. But then, once victims began dying, one after the other, medical authorities realized something serious was occurring.

As news spread of the initial deaths, the remaining legionnaires and other guests at the Stratford fled the hotel in a panic. Soon, EPIDEMIOLOGISTS were dispatched from the Centers for Disease Control (CDC) to investigate the outbreak. They tested the hotel's food, air, and water supply but couldn't establish a link among the victims. Furthermore, because no relatives of the victims had contracted the mystery illness, it did not appear to be passed though human contact. In September, the outbreak subsided, just as mysteriously as it had arrived. Yet the public's fears remained.

Swine Flu or Microbes from Space?

Before the mysterious Philadelphia outbreak, federal health officials had warned the public about a possible EPIDEMIC of swine flu *(see page 44)*, the same deadly VIRAL disease that killed more than half a million Americans and thirty million people worldwide in 1919. Even though autopsies of the dead legionnaires revealed in August that swine flu was not responsible, intense media attention on both the legionnaire deaths and on swine flu had nonetheless left the public convinced of a connection. Before long, even more outlandish theories began circulating. Some suggested the disease was caused by biological weapons tests performed by the Central Intelligence Agency. Others decided that American astronauts had accidentally carried back killer MICROBES from outer space.

The Legionella Bacterium

In January 1977 hard scientific fact at last prevailed. CDC researchers announced that they had isolated a previously unknown BACTERIUM from a victim's blood. The germ, dubbed *Legionella pneumophila,* had been difficult to find. However, once researchers found their culprit, they knew they had made a major discovery. By analyzing further blood samples, scientists found that Legionnaire's disease had also been responsible for unexplained cases of fatal pneumonia outbreaks as far back as 1947.

Over the next several months, the CDC continued its investigation, even as new cases of "killer pneumonia" were reported around the world. The only connection seemed to be that the outbreaks generally occurred in hotels, hospitals, and workplaces. It was as if the buildings themselves were breeding the germs.

Authorities finally realized that was exactly what was happening. The bacteria that had proved so elusive in sanitized laboratories were found growing abundantly in the stagnant water stored in the Philadelphia hotel's cooling tower. The same cooling tower provided water for the building's air-conditioning system, which in turn had distributed bacteria throughout the hotel.

The discovery at the Bellevue-Stratford helped explain the other outbreaks as well. Before long, *Legionella* was being found in other air conditioners and cooling towers, as well as in humidifiers, hot tubs, grocery store vegetable misters, and even in shower heads.

Since that first outbreak in America's bicentennial year, scientists have established that *Legionellae* bacteria are common in lakes and ponds worldwide and anywhere else that there is stagnant, mineral-rich water. However, in order for the bacterium to make people sick, it has to be spread into the air in large quantities, which almost always requires man-made devices like

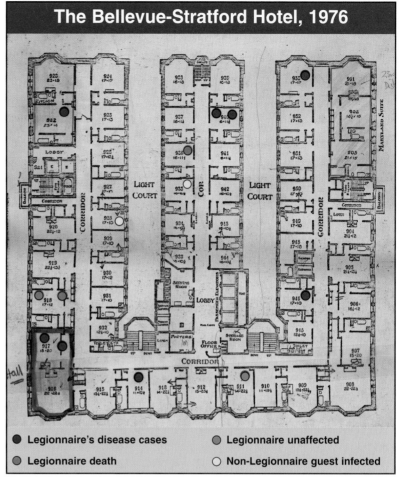

The Bellevue-Stratford Hotel, 1976

● Legionnaire's disease cases   ● Legionnaire unaffected
● Legionnaire death   ○ Non-Legionnaire guest infected

Following the outbreak of an unknown form of pneumonia at Philadelphia's Bellevue-Stratford Hotel in 1976, epidemiologists discovered that the bacteria responsible for the illnesses could be traced to the hotel air-conditioning system. Most victims had contracted the infection in the hotel's hospitality suites.

air conditioners that exist mostly in the world's wealthier countries. Difficult to kill with ANTIBIOTICS, *Legionella* is particularly deadly to cigarette smokers, asthma sufferers, and the elderly and other people with weakened IMMUNE SYSTEMS. The CDC estimates that since World War II, two thousand to six thousand people have died of the disease each year. In 1994, tourists on a cruise ship contracted the disease from an onboard hot tub. Another outbreak occurred at a 1999 Dutch flower show. New cases continue to be identified around the world.

Most cases of Legionnaire's disease remain unreported, and after a brief illness, the victim recovers. Since the 1976 outbreak in Philadelphia, however, scientists have warned that there are likely numerous and possibly more deadly, as yet unidentified, bacterial ORGANISMS in the earth's soil and water supplies awaiting the right circumstances to spread to humans.

LEPROSY

Global Distribution Leprosy is most common in India, Indonesia, and Myanmar, but is also endemic in other areas of Asia, Africa, and Latin America, particularly Brazil.

Causative Agent There are two types of leprosy; both are caused by the bacillus *Mycobacterium leprae.*

Transmission Leprosy is an infectious disease, passed from person to person, but is very difficult to transmit. Frequent physical exposure to an existing case must occur over a long period of time.

Symptoms Both types of leprosy affect the skin, nerves, and mucous membranes. Victims of the first type, paucibacillary (PB), have far fewer bacteria in their bodies than the more serious multibacillary cases, which can have more than a billion bacilli in one gram of skin tissue. Although the disease can take years to manifest itself, it does eventually cause serious disfiguration of the body. The classic characteristics are swelling of the face, sores on the skin, mutilated fingers and toes, and paralysis.

Treatment The most current treatment involves a multidrug therapy (MDT) combining three drugs, dapsone, rifampicin, and clofazimine.

Prevention and Control The Global Strategy for the Elimination of Leprosy bases its work on the need to detect and treat all remaining cases of leprosy in the world with the MDT. After leprosy patients have been treated with MDT they need to be monitored to ensure that they have been thoroughly treated.

Father Damien de Veuster (right) is shown tending to a fellow member of the leper colony at Molokai, Hawaii.

With black lava cliffs rising four thousand feet out of the Pacific, the tiny volcanic island of Molokai sits between the Hawaiian islands of Oahu and Maui. Present-day visitors would be hard pressed to imagine that from 1866 to 1940 this beautiful paradise was a harsh prison. Although its inmates had committed no crime, they were nonetheless abandoned to fend for themselves, with no housing, no clean water, no hospitals, no government, and no escape. The reason for this cruel sentence was simple: leprosy.

The Molokai leper colony came into being in 1865, after the Hawaiian government purchased the land as a way of controlling an EPIDEMIC of the disease that had struck the islands several years beforehand. Since Hawaii's board of health reasoned that containing the disease was far more important than caring for those already stricken, little thought was given to the fate of those condemned. In 1873, however, word of the colony reached a Belgian priest named Father Damien de Veuster. Father Damien immediately set out for Molokai, and upon reaching it, he began administering both medical care and spiritual comfort to the afflicted, continuing this work until 1889, when the disease claimed his own life.

Leprosy's Double Identity

The isolation suffered by the lepers of Molokai is not surprising, based on firmly held and long-standing popular beliefs regarding the disease. The divide between the disease that can be identified by science and the disease of popular imagination is enormous. Historians who have attempted to trace the earliest appearances of leprosy have found their task complicated by the fact that although leprosy is mentioned frequently in the Bible, the symptoms described sound nothing like the disease that we know as leprosy today. In fact, the word *leprosy* is from *lepra,* a Greek mistranslation of the Hebrew *tsara'at,* which refers to the banishment of the unclean, as described in the Old Testament Book of Leviticus, a virtual handbook for the treatment of lepers. Hippocrates, the fourth-century Greek physician, used *lepra* to describe a scaly, flaking skin ailment that some have suggested may have been nothing more than the skin condition psoriasis.

On the other hand, fifth-century B.C.E. Indian and Chinese medical texts describe "the big disease," with symptoms almost identical to leprosy, and some evidence suggests that *Mycobacterium leprae,* the BACTERIUM that causes leprosy, may have spread out of Egypt in about 150 C.E., carried with Roman soldiers

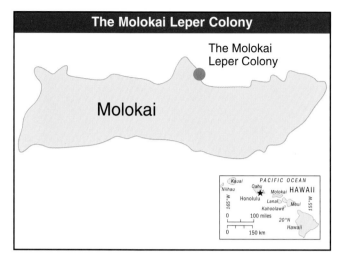

The Molokai Leper Colony

The Molokai
Leper Colony

Molokai

PACIFIC OCEAN
Kauai
Niihau   Oahu
Molokai HAWAII
Honolulu Lanai
Kahoolawe   Maui
20°N
Hawaii
0   100 miles
0   150 km

The leper colony at Molokai, Hawaii, was situated on an isolated peninsula.

returning from battle. Ironically, this would have occurred just as Christianity was also spreading throughout Europe from the Middle East. Although there is no scientific proof of this theory, whenever and wherever the disease originated, Biblical references to ailments called leprosy had a profound impact on how the real disease was viewed.

Leprosy and Sin

To theologians, leprosy as it was described in the Bible provided a powerful example of the consequences of sin. The mandates set forth in Leviticus found a wide audience in early Christian Europe, although they were frequently paired with New Testament ideals. Roman emperor Constantine the Great, for example, ordered that lepers be quarantined from larger society, although he also assigned ministers to tend to them.

By the eleventh and twelfth centuries, this ideal of Christian charity led to the establishment of hundreds of asylums, or leprasariums, throughout Europe, which were specifically opened to care for those lepers who could afford them. In fact, opening a leprasarium was often seen as a means of achieving salvation.

Nonetheless, the Old Testament view governed most policy. In 1179, Pope Alexander III established a number of rules regarding the disease. Lepers were forced to wear oversized tunics, often emblazoned with a large red L on the back. In addition, lepers were banned from touching or even looking directly at a non-leper, and were forced to use a bell or wooden clapper to warn others of their approach.

The stigma attached to lepers often made them convenient scapegoats for society's ills. In 1320, King

Philip V of France accused them of plotting with Jews and Muslims to destroy Christianity by poisoning water wells with the disease. In panic, the public lashed out, destroying hospitals and burning lepers at the stake. England's King Edward I took the more charitable approach by ordering that lepers be given funeral rites, after which they would be buried alive.

Christians were not the only people to fear lepers. Hindu poetry dating back to 2400 B.C.E. states, "Let us drive him from our village with stones and cover him who is himself a living excrement, with ordure."

Hansen's Discovery

Medical authorities of the Middle Ages were divided about how best to treat leprosy. Jordan de Turre, a fourteenth-century doctor who wrote several studies of the disease, advocated "superfluous exercise" and "frequent coitus." Meanwhile others urged abstaining from all exercise, including sex.

In 1873, a cruel experiment finally helped shed some light on the illness. By taking an unwilling woman and scratching her eye with a needle covered in pus from a leper's lesion, the Dutch doctor G. Armauer Hansen isolated *M. leprae* by proving that a substance in the pus caused leprosy to spread. *M. leprae* thus became the first bacterium ever recognized as the cause of human disease, and helped diminish the perception that leprosy was a punishment for immorality.

Since the 1940s, leprosy, now known as Hansen's Disease, has been treatable. While there is no true VACCINATION against the disease, there are new multidrug therapies (MDT) that have proven effective. By 1996, there were fewer than one million cases worldwide. Organizations like the Leprosy Mission International and the World Health Organization (WHO) have maintained an effective campaign of pressure on governments to ensure the free availability of these new medicines for patients.

WHO has targeted the year 2000 for the eradication of leprosy worldwide. (According to WHO planners, eradication does not mean the complete elimination of the disease, but rather a reduction to no more than one case per ten thousand people.)

Although the total number of cases has declined, the number of new cases has remained constant at around six hundred thousand, largely in Asia, Africa, and South America. There have even been cases in Texas and Puerto Rico. These patients are no longer viewed as sinners to be cast out from society, but there is work to be done to ensure that lepers are not left to fend for themselves.

LYME DISEASE

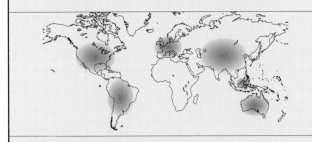

Global Distribution Lyme disease has been reported in Japan, China, and South America, but the highest number of cases have been in the United States and Europe.

Causative Agent Lyme disease is caused by the *Borrelia burgdorferi* bacterium.

Transmission The disease is transmitted to humans by a particular type of tick, the *Ixodes scapularis*, which usually infests deer and rodents. The tick carries the organism that causes the disease and passes it on to humans. The tick must feed on the human for some time (several hours) for the organism to be transmitted.

Symptoms Lyme disease will usually begin with a circular red rash around the area where the tick fed. Fever, fatigue, and a headache also occur at this time followed after a few weeks by heart and joint problems. Symptoms usually begin within a month of becoming infected.

Treatment Lyme disease is treated with antibiotics.

Prevention and Control Authorities advise individuals to take protective measures before and after venturing into wooded areas or other likely tick habitats. Such measures include wearing (and tucking in) long sleeves and long pants, followed by thorough checks of the body for ticks.

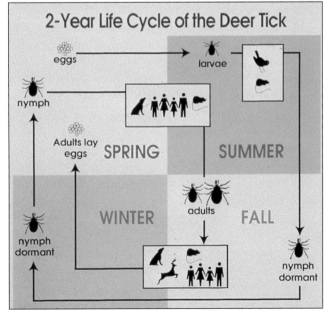

Most cases of Lyme disease are transmitted to humans at the end of the tick's two-year life cycle.

During the summer of 1975, two young boys in suburban Old Lyme, Connecticut, fell ill with fevers that would not go away. Both also suffered from painful, aching joints. Doctors diagnosed the boys with juvenile rheumatoid arthritis (JRA), an extremely rare condition that tricks the IMMUNE SYSTEM into attacking the body's joints as if they were invading ORGANISMS.

Shortly thereafter, the boys' mothers learned that other area children had come down with similar symptoms. Alarmed, they quickly contacted the Connecticut health department. Because JRA is not contagious, state health officials also grew concerned after hearing the mothers' stories. To investigate further, a research team headed by Dr. Allen Steere of Yale University traveled to Old Lyme. Steere found that nearly forty more people had come down with the same symptoms, all within the previous few years. Many reported that the illness had coincided with a red-to-pink bull's-eye rash, which, some remembered, developed after being bitten by a tick. In a stroke of luck for Steere's team, one victim had saved the culprit.

The Deer Tick

The tick was identified as *Ixodes scapularis*. Its common name, the deer tick, is somewhat misleading, since the deer actually plays a role only at the end of the tick's two-year life cycle. During its first summer, the tick larva feeds primarily on the white-footed mouse, from which it acquires the MICROBE that causes Lyme disease. By fall, the larva passes into its nymph stage, and after remaining dormant in the winter, emerges in its second spring still capable of passing the microbe on to whatever warm-blooded HOST it can find, including humans. By the end of the second summer, the tick undergoes its metamorphosis from nymph to adult, and it is at this stage—when the adult tick attaches to a deer, where it finds another tick, and mates with it before gorging itself on blood for its final meal—that most cases of Lyme disease are transmitted.

A New Bacterium

For years after the outbreak in Old Lyme, researchers had not identified what kind of microbe caused the disease. Then, in 1981, deer ticks collected in Long Island, New York, during an outbreak of Rocky Mountain spotted fever (another tick-borne disease) were sent to Dr. Willy Burgdorfer at the National Institute of Health in Hamilton, Montana. In one of the ticks, Burgdorfer found a corkscrew-shaped BACTERIUM, which he injected into several rabbits. The rabbits developed the same rash as found in Lyme disease patients. When Allen Steere and his staff isolated the same bacterium in the blood of one of their patients, the medical community had its confirmation. A new bacterium, known as *Borrelia burgdorferi,* was identified as the cause of Lyme disease.

Even though Burgdorfer had identified its cause, Lyme disease remains very difficult to detect. For one, the bull's-eye rash appears in only about half the victims. Second, more universal symptoms, such as fatigue, aching joints, and headaches, are symptoms of many other ailments, includ-

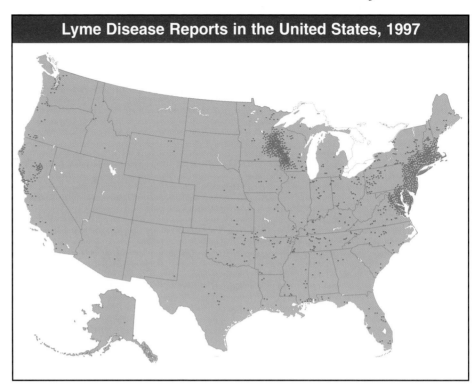

Lyme Disease Reports in the United States, 1997

Lyme disease cases are concentrated in the Northeast and upper Midwest.

ing the common cold. Worse still, laboratory tests for Lyme bacteria are extremly unreliable. And finally, symptoms seem to come and go—disappearing for up to twenty years at a time in some people, while progressing to constant and chronic symptoms in others, including impaired memory, meningitis or paralysis.

The difficulty of detecting the disease, and the ease with which it can be misdiagnosed, have alarmed health officials and concerned citizens alike. In the Northeast and upper Midwest, where rates of infection have been highest, some alarmed parents have kept their children inside in summer for fear of infection. Despite these measures, the number of reported Lyme disease cases skyrocketed during the 1980s and 1990s.

A Changing Habitat

Although the sudden rise in Lyme disease cases is a new phenomenon, scientists doubt that it is truly a new disease. When Burgdorfer identified the Lyme bacterium, he remembered hearing of a similar tick-borne illness that struck Germany in 1883 and Sweden in 1910. Traces of the bacteria have also shown up in ticks collected on Long Island in the 1940s.

Scientists have thus concluded that it is not the ticks that have changed, but the environment they inhabit. Any time the ecological balance between species shifts,

there are consequences. One hundred years ago, the eastern United States had far fewer woods than it does today. Early European settlers had cleared much of the growth for agriculture. Deer were almost extinct. During the nineteenth century, settlers moved westward, clearing new lands for farming. Meanwhile, as easterners began moving to the cities, the amount of farmland shrank once again. Gradually new growth forests reclaimed the edges of settlements. Wildlife—deer and ticks included—reclaimed their habitats.

By the mid-twentieth century, another environmental change had begun. Humans, who had left the countryside for the city, left the cities once more—for the suburbs. The same land that had had few trees a century before now grew thick with second and third growth woodlands. And the wildlife living in those woods—whether mice, deer, ticks, or other creatures—were flourishing. Today, many suburban homeowners wake up to find deer grazing on their front lawns, as new suburban developments sprout right along the edge of the forest.

To the relief of many, a promising new Lyme disease VACCINE was developed in 1998. However, the fact remains: Lyme and other tick-borne diseases have increased because human contact with ticks has increased.

MAD COW DISEASE

Global Distribution More than 99 percent of all cases have occurred in Great Britain.

Causative Agent Mad cow disease and other transmissible spongiform encephalopathies are suspected to be caused by a rare protein called a prion.

Transmission The outbreak of bovine spongiform encephalopathy (BSE) is believed to have occurred through contaminated sheep or cattle meat and bonemeal that was fed to cattle. Evidence also shows that the situation was made worse by giving recycled infected bovine (cow) meat and bonemeal back to the cattle for food.

Symptoms The brain and spinal cord of cows affected by BSE develop brain lesions characterized by a sponge-like appearance when viewed under a microscope. The outward symptoms of the disease are dementia; the cow literally appears "mad"—it is nervous, has a heightened sensitivity to external stimuli, and has difficulty moving, often exhibited by stumbling. BSE usually manifests itself in cows between four and five years of age and is fatal to cows within a few weeks to a month of its onset. BSE is related to other forms of spongiform encephalopathy, including similar mink, cat, deer, elk, and human (Creutzfeldt-Jakob disease) versions, among others.

Treatment There is no known treatment for BSE. All cattle in the United Kingdom suspected of being infected with BSE have been slaughtered, many before they were old enough to exhibit any signs of the disease.

Prevention and Control In 1988, Britain banned the use of sheep- and cattle-derived offal in animal feed. Since that time, the number of BSE cases has declined.

Bovine spongiform encephalopathy (BSE),

popularly known as mad cow disease,

has been linked to the use of offal in cattle feed

by British ranchers. Offal is made up of excess

parts of other cows, including brain,

spinal cord, spleen, eyes, intestines,

and other organs.

One evening in November 1986 in Surrey, England, a rancher discovered several of his cows acting strangely. They staggered as if drunk, a few behaved aggressively, and by the next morning one had died. An autopsy of the animal revealed that its brain was riddled with tiny sponge-like holes. Those holes—which scientists believe were caused by unusual PROTEINS called PRIONS—suggested that the animal had contracted a type of transmissible spongiform encephalopathy, or TSE. TSE diseases, which cause fatal damage to the nervous system, include among others scrapie, a disease found in sheep; Creutzfeldt-Jakob disease (CJD), a rare human disease; and Kuru, also formerly found in humans, but only among tribal people from Papua-New Guinea who practiced cannibalism. Authorities named the cattle disease bovine spongiform encephalopathy (BSE). The press, on the other hand, called it "mad cow disease." Since that first death in 1986, more than 175,000 cases of BSE have been identified, with over 99 percent of them in Great Britain.

Danger in the Feed Chain

Scientists investigating BSE first concentrated on two critical questions: "How is it spread?" and "Can it jump from cows to humans?" In November 1987, as new cases were being reported throughout Britain, researchers concluded that BSE was linked to the use of sheep- and cow-derived meat and bonemeal used by British ranchers in cattle feed. This offal, as it is known, often includes brain, spinal cord, spleen, eyes, intestines, and other organs.

A few months before, the researchers had also confirmed that BSE could be TRANSMITTED to mice. The question of whether humans were also at risk would remain at center stage not just for scientists but for politicians and the public as well.

In June 1988, the British government took its first major step against BSE, banning the use of sheep offal in cattle feed. Later that summer, Parliament also ordered the destruction of all cattle suspected of carrying the disease. For every slaughtered cow with a confirmed case of BSE, the government would pay 50 percent of market value. For any cow slaughtered that proved to be healthy, on the other hand, the ranchers would receive full value. (Due to protests from ranchers, payments were later increased to full value for all cattle.)

Outside of Britain, the news of the BSE EPIDEMIC was greeted with alarm. In fact, British ranchers could not even give their beef away. An emergency donation of meat to Russia during a food shortage was returned untouched. In 1989, the United States announced it would no longer accept imported cows, sheep, or goats from Britain or any other country with confirmed cases of BSE. The same year, the European Community (EC), the organization that sets international trade policy for its member countries, ordered the first of several progressively more restrictive bans on British meat.

Containing the Damage

For British ranchers, the consequences were severe. In protest, they blocked roadways and demanded the government appeal to the EC for financial relief. For its part, the British government waged a futile campaign to assure the public that the food supply was safe. In 1990, John Gummer, the minister of agriculture, publicly urged his own daughter to eat a hamburger in front of the Parliament building. As television cameras recorded the moment, the girl refused.

For the next two years, British authorities continued to assert that the BSE epidemic posed no threat to humans, even as they closely monitored the incidence of CJD. Then in 1993, as the number of new BSE cases

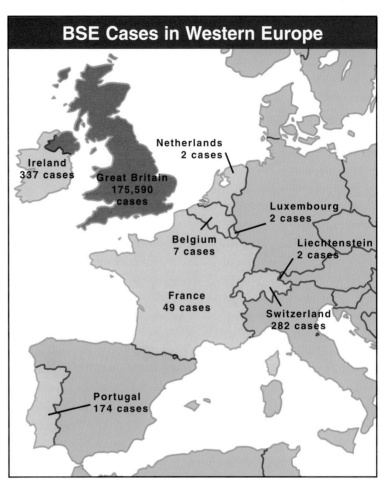

BSE has remained rare outside of Great Britain.

reached as many as eight hundred reported in a single week, two farmers with BSE-infected cattle died from CJD. The next year a sixteen-year-old girl from North Wales also contracted CJD, reportedly after eating BSE-infected meat a decade earlier. In early 1996, ten more people died, all of them at a far younger age than is typical with classic CJD. The government announced that the victims had died from a new variety of CJD (nvCJD). More significantly, it also declared for the first time that nvCJD was probably caused by the transmission of BSE to humans.

Oprah and the Cattlemen

Since the first BSE cases occurred in Britain, scattered cases have been confirmed in thirteen other countries, though none in the United States. Nonetheless, Americans have watched the crisis in Britain with alarm. In 1996, several guests on the *Oprah Winfrey Show* suggested that CJD had the potential to become more devastating than AIDS. Winfrey remarked that she would "never eat a hamburger again." The price of cat-

tle futures on the commodities exchange plummeted. In response, a Texas cattlemen's association filed an unsuccessful libel suit against Winfrey under Texas' food disparagement laws. These laws allow food-processing companies to sue those who publicly "state or imply that a perishable food product is not safe for consumption by the public."

In 1997, the U.S. Department of Agriculture banned the use of offal in cattle feed. At the same time, it ruled that offal could be used in feeds for other livestock. Further, the ban does not prevent cattle offal from being fed to chickens and pigs who are then slaughtered and fed back to cattle.

It is impossible to know how many people may have been INFECTED with CJD in Britain. In 1998, British authorities proclaimed that the BSE epidemic had been halted, and that no new cases would occur after 2002. Other scientists are not convinced. Some estimate that before 1996, more than 750,000 infected animals may have entered the food chain. Although the worst is probably over, only time will tell for certain.

MALARIA

Global Distribution Malaria is endemic to Latin America, Africa, and Asia.

Causative Agent Malaria is caused by any of four types of parasites called plasmodia.

Transmission Malaria is passed to humans through the bite of an infected female *Anopheles* mosquito.

Symptoms Symptoms include fever, chills, muscle aches, and headache, recurring in cycles every one to three days. Malaria can also cause vomiting, diarrhea, coughing, and yellowing (jaundice) of the skin and whites of the eyes. In severe cases, victims can develop bleeding problems, shock, kidney or liver failure, central nervous problems, and coma. The period between initial infection and onset of symptoms is usually seven to twenty-one days.

Treatment Treatment options vary since some malaria strains are resistant to certain vaccines. If a person is infected with *falciparum* malaria he or she must receive immediate medical attention due to the severity of this type.

Prevention and Control All travelers to regions where malaria is endemic should be given antimalarial drugs. The World Health Organization's malaria control strategy includes four elements: 1) early prevention and immediate treatment; 2) mosquito control; 3) early detection and prevention of epidemics; and 4) a strengthening of basic and applied research in order to regularly assess local ecological, social, economic, or other factors that may contribute to the disease.

West Africans were kidnapped and taken to the New World on slave ships like this one partly because they had a high resistance to malaria. Native American populations quickly succumbed to the disease when made to work in the fields.

For at least thirty million years, humans and mosquitoes have had a shared history, much of it defined by disease. Malaria, a mosquito-borne disease, has likely killed more people over time than any other in history. It has weakened empires, turned back invasions, and spurred the growth of human slavery. And while humans briefly held malaria in check just decades ago, they did so only with toxic chemicals that did almost as much harm as good. Today, malaria continues to plague humankind, killing millions worldwide each year.

The Plasmodium Life Cycle

Malaria is caused by any of four types of tiny PARASITES called plasmodia that infected mosquitoes pass from one infected host to another. One of the most common forms is *Plasmodium vivax*, which though not usually deadly can severely incapacitate victims with freezing chills, followed by severe fevers reaching as high as 106 degrees F. This freezing to feverish cycle repeats itself for several days before subsiding. The other main form of malaria—known as *P. falciparum*—is even worse, and is usually fatal.

Living in the gut of a female *Anopheles* mosquito, plasmodia move from HOST to host through the mosquito's saliva glands each time it bites a new victim. Once in the new host's bloodstream, the plasmodia head directly for the victim's liver, where they reproduce and then return to the bloodstream. They then multiply again within RED BLOOD CELLS, causing them to burst, thereby creating malaria's awful symptoms. When another female *Anopheles* bites the newly infected victim, the cycle repeats in another unlucky human.

The Mother of Fevers

The earliest written record of the fight against malaria can be traced back thousands of years to Chinese medical texts. The classic *Nie Ching,* written in 2700 B.C.E., describes some of the disease's symptoms—the enlarged spleen, recurring high fevers, and crushing headaches. The disease, which the Chinese knew as "The Mother of Fevers," was believed to be the work of three demons, one responsible for each symptom. To treat the disease, the Chinese used "Quinghuasu," an effective remedy made from the wormwood plant.

Malaria was also well known to the ancient Greeks and Romans. In the fifth century B.C.E., the Greek physician Hippocrates became the first to relate the occurrence of the disease with the time of the year and

Malaria's Worldwide Distribution in 1850

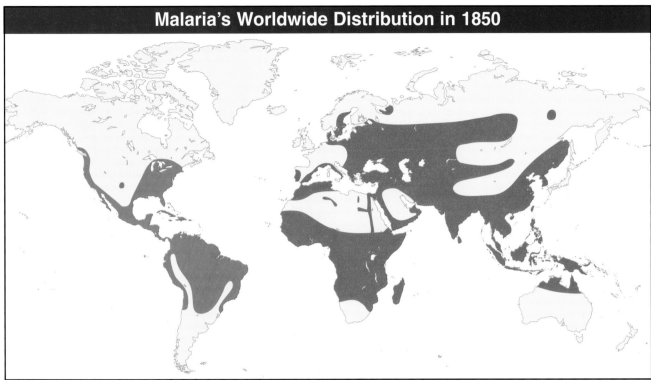

Prior to the discovery that malaria is spread by mosquitoes, the disease was common in both the Northern and Southern hemispheres, spread by wars, international trade, and other causes of large scale population movements.

where victims lived. Having done so, he declared malaria to be caused by drinking stagnant water. While no one considered that the culprit was the mosquitoes that lived near stagnant water rather than the water itself, Hippocrates's methodical study of environmental factors and their relationship to illness would become a cornerstone of developing medicine. Despite this advance, one hundred years later, Macedonian king Alexander the Great, creator of an empire that stretched from Greece to the Indus Valley, succumbed to malaria. Upon his death, his territories crumbled into warring factions.

Roman Fever

Throughout the Mediterranean, malaria was so common that it eventually became known as "Roman fever." Beginning in 95 B.C.E., it was recognized that malaria was ENDEMIC to the swampy farmland outside of Rome. The disease raged for the next five hundred years. By 395 C.E., malaria had become so prevalent in the farmland that fed Rome that the farmers had to take the lands out of cultivation. The farmers then moved to the city, bringing malaria with them. From then on malaria deaths caused Rome's population to fall even at a time when the population elsewhere in the empire was rising dramatically.

The curse of malaria *did* have a silver lining for Rome, however. Romans and other Mediterranean peoples may have developed more tolerance for the disease

than did outsiders. In 410, soon after the Teutonic chieftain Alaric captured Rome, he died of malaria.

Although the Romans were the first to attempt to intervene against malaria by draining swamps, their efforts had little long-term effect. One reason the residence of the pope was briefly moved to southern France during the fourteenth century may have been because foreign dignitaries calling on the pope found themselves constantly threatened by the disease while in Rome. The word *malaria,* which means "bad air," refers to the air around swamps.

Malaria in the Age of Exploration

With the start of Portuguese exploration of the West African coast in the mid-fifteenth century, a new era in malaria's history began. Europeans were constantly felled by malaria in Africa, and their inability to cope with it delayed exploration of the African interior for centuries.

Explorers in the Americas had no such delays. There is little evidence that malaria-like disease even existed in the Western Hemisphere before Europeans arrived. Upon arriving in Latin America and the Caribbean, Spanish and Portuguese colonizers began

Mapping Epidemics

These posters were published by the U.S. government during World War II to educate its troops about the dangers of malaria. The anti-Japanese sentiment of the middle poster is seen on the mosquito's wings: they are colored like the Japanese flag.

enslaving the natives they encountered, killing off those who resisted. Ironically, weapons were not required for most of the deaths. Millions were killed by malaria and other diseases carried by Europeans. The death toll was so high that by 1503 the Spanish looked back across the Atlantic for a new slave-labor source—to Africa. Although African slaves still died in very great numbers in the New World—especially in the Caribbean and in the Latin American tropics—they proved less vulnerable to malaria. This was due in part to a condition known as the sickle-cell trait, which is most common in Africans. When malaria-carrying mosquitoes feed on sickle-shaped red blood cells, the victims suffer lighter INFECTIONS with fewer symptoms.

Jesuit's Bark

Ironically, the first effective malaria treatment used by Europeans came from the Indians they were destroying. During the seventeenth century, Jesuit priests returning to Spain from the New World reported that Peruvians used an extract from a certain tree bark to treat the disease. In 1642, Spanish doctor Pedro Barba became the first European to try the treatment on a patient when he administered it to the countess of Chinchon. Before long, Jesuits were traveling through Europe popularizing the new treatment that they called chinchona bark.

Not all Europeans, however, were convinced that chinchona bark really worked. Not only doctors were skeptical. When Oliver Cromwell, who led Puritan forces to victory over the Catholic King Charles I in the English Civil War, acquired malaria in 1658, he refused to take what he called "Jesuits' Bark" since, in his view, it was a Catholic remedy. Ironically, when Cromwell died soon thereafter, his death paved the way for Charles II, a Catholic like his father, to reclaim the throne. The usefulness of chinchona bark, of course, had nothing to do with religion. In 1820, the active ingredient in the bark was isolated and named quinine.

Laveran's Discovery

While quinine gave Europeans a relatively effective treatment for malaria, scientists were not much closer to understanding malaria's origins than they had been in Hippocrates' time. His theory, that the disease was caused by drinking stagnant water, was still the commonly accepted view. Even in 1880, when Charles-Louis-Alphonse Laveran, a Frenchman stationed in colonial Algeria, announced that he had identified plasmodia as the cause of malaria, the medical community resisted letting go of Hippocrates' theory. Unfortunately, Laveran's experiments, which called for fresh, live-blood samples, were hard to reproduce. At last, in 1897, Ronald Ross, a British doctor in India, showed that the *Anopheles* mosquito was spreading malaria from bird to bird. A year later, Italian scientists proved that mosquitoes also spread the disease to and among humans.

DDT and Mosquito Control

Once public health officials understood that mosquitoes were responsible for malaria's spread, they put their knowledge to work. By destroying mosquito breeding grounds, supplying workers with protective

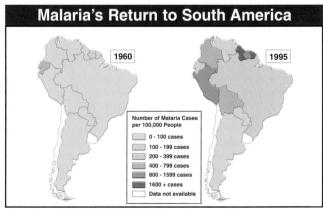

A weakening of mosquito control programs has helped lead to an increase in the number of malaria cases in South America since 1960.

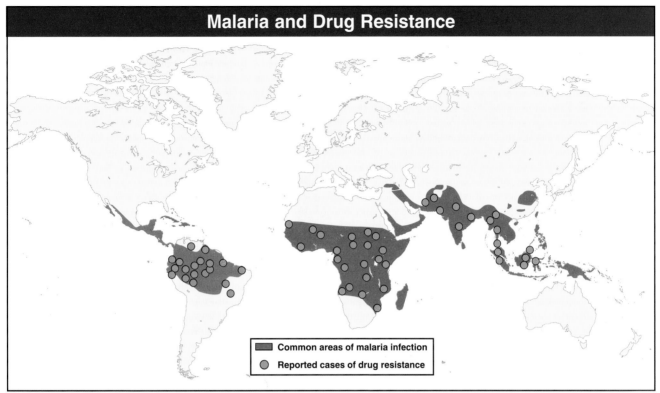

Malaria and Drug Resistance

Common areas of malaria infection
Reported cases of drug resistance

Drug resistance is a growing concern of health officials. As the map above illustrates, the effectiveness of current anti-malarial vaccines is declining.

netting, and treating cases with quinine, authorities prevented the spread of the disease during the construction of the Panama Canal in the early 1900s.

Because finding a VACCINE against plasmodia is far more challenging and costly than mosquito control, most health efforts in the twentieth century have focused on combating mosquitoes instead of the parasites they carry. Still, as late as 1934, over 125,000 annual malaria cases were reported worldwide. Before long, a new weapon was brought to bear against mosquitoes. Although the chemical compound DDT had been available since the 1870s, it was not until the 1940s that officials realized how effective it was against mosquitoes and other insects. Homes around the world were sprayed with DDT, and for the first time in history, new reports of malaria cases began falling rapidly. Following World War II, new, more effective medications such as chloroquine also became available. Other new malaria medicines followed. The progress seemed so dramatic that in 1955 the World Health Organization (WHO) declared that complete ERADICATION of malaria was within reach.

Malaria in the Twenty-first Century

Today, the promise of malaria eradication has slipped away. Following the 1962 release of Rachel Carson's environmental manifesto *Silent Spring,* society has been more aware of the dangers posed by highly toxic pesticides such as DDT. In 1972, the United States banned it. Many other nations have done the same.

Ironically, in poorer nations that cannot afford less harmful but more expensive pesticides, DDT has become less effective as mosquitoes have developed resistance to its effects. Malaria has returned with a vengeance, aided by global warming, as hurricanes and and other weather patterns have helped increase mosquito populations. Authorities are particularly alarmed that many new malaria infections are proving resistant to chloroquine and other drugs available for treatment.

As the twenty-first century opens, someone dies from malaria every fifteen seconds. The victims, more than two million each year, are mainly the elderly, those suffering from AIDS *(see page 38)* or other ailments, and young children. Most live in poverty in nations that lack the funds available to those in the developed world. Despite the alarming numbers, relatively little attention is currently being paid to malaria research. Perhaps this is because malaria is somewhat rare today in the United States, Europe, and other nations with the resources for medical research. As the number of new drug-resistant malaria cases grows, however, the risk to humanity grows, regardless of geography.

MEASLES

Global Distribution Measles can be found worldwide, but it is most common in countries that lack strong vaccination programs.

Causative Agent Measles is caused by a virus of the *Rubivirus* genus.

Transmission Measles, also called rubeola, is transmitted through airborne droplets from the nose or throat of an infected person.

Symptoms The first stage of measles is called the prodromal period. The symptoms include a runny nose, hacking cough, irritated eyes, and a fever which can run quite high. This period usually lasts three to four days before the rash appears. Once the rash appears the prodromal symptoms subside. Typically the rash first appears on the forehead and travels down the body until it hits the feet, a process that takes about three days. The rash is characterized by large red to brown blotches that sometimes flow together. When the rash fades it does so in the same order, forehead to feet. One unique indicator of measles before the rash appears is Koplik's spots. These are small, red spots with blue-white centers that are found inside the mouth a day or two before the rash begins.

Treatment It is necessary to see that the patient gets complete rest and lots of liquids to replenish the body water lost during the sweating episodes that accompany fever. The patient should be closely monitored for any changes in condition that might require medical attention, such as difficulty breathing or severe drowsiness.

Prevention and Control Measles can be prevented by a vaccine administered before exposure or within three days of exposure to the disease. Most children receive the vaccine at fifteen months and again at age eleven or twelve.

Worms are swarming in the streets and plazas,
and the walls are splattered with gore.
The water has turned red, as if it were dyed, and
when we drink it, it has the taste of brine.

–An anonymous Aztec poet, describing the aftermath of Tenochtitlán's destruction by the Spaniards. Based on the poet's description, it should not be surprising that disease spread rapidly after the Spanish conquest.

When messengers arrived at the court of Aztec emperor Montezuma in March 1519, they carried alarming news. They reported that bearded men with white skin were arriving on the coast in winged towers. Montezuma felt sure that these men were no ordinary visitors. Instead, he believed, they were accompanying the ancient god Quetzalcoatl, who, according Aztec legend, was due to return that very year to reclaim his kingdom.

Measles and the Conquest of Mexico

In truth, the visitors were Spanish conquistadores, led by Hernán Cortés. Cortés had sailed from Cuba, with six hundred men, sixteen horses, and a few cannons, on a mission to explore the mainland of North America. Little did they know it, but they were approaching the vast Aztec Empire of eleven million people.

Montezuma soon sent envoys to greet the newcomers. He also attempted to convince them to leave by sending Cortés gifts of silver and gold, including one enormous circle of gold representing the sun, and another made of silver representing the moon. Upon seeing these riches, Cortés determined not to turn around in peace. Instead he and his men would extract more riches from the Aztecs, even if they had to conquer them to do so. To prevent his men from turning back before victory was won, Cortés ordered that his ships be burned. He and his men then set off for the Aztec capital, Tenochtitlán. Aided by a Native American slave woman that Cortés had been given when he landed, and carrying with them steel weapons and armor unlike anything the Aztecs had seen, the Spaniards marched into Tenochtitlán the following November without encountering resistance. One of Cortés's soldiers, a man named Bernal Díaz del Castillo, wrote in his diary that some of the men, upon viewing the majestic city, had wondered if what they saw might not be a dream. Tenochtitlán's beauty was such that many others were reminded of the enchanting places depicted in Spanish legends. When the Aztecs first saw Cortés, they too were reminded of legends— but of impending death, destruction, and despair. They could not have been more accurate. Within the space of two years, Cortés and his small army had taken the capital, toppled the once proud Aztec Empire, and bore witness to the near complete annihilation of the Aztecs.

How were so few men able to conquer so many? Although Cortés had superior weaponry and was aided by Indian groups hostile to the Aztecs, he could never

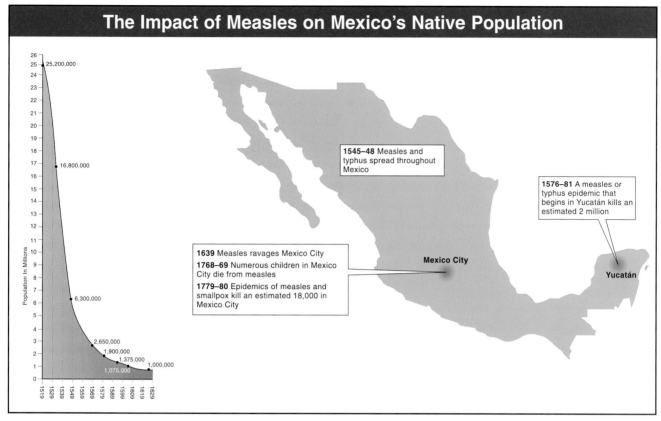

The Impact of Measles on Mexico's Native Population

Population In Millions

- 25,200,000
- 16,800,000
- 6,300,000
- 2,650,000
- 1,900,000
- 1,375,000
- 1,075,000
- 1,000,000

1545–48 Measles and typhus spread throughout Mexico

1576–81 A measles or typhus epidemic that begins in Yucatán kills an estimated 2 million

1639 Measles ravages Mexico City
1768–69 Numerous children in Mexico City die from measles
1779–80 Epidemics of measles and smallpox kill an estimated 18,000 in Mexico City

Mexico City

Yucatán

have won if he and his men had not unknowingly carried with them weapons far more powerful than any sword or cannon. In fact, it is likely that even before Cortés began his military siege on Tenochtitlán in 1521, several VIRUSES—causing smallpox (*see page 82*), measles, mumps, and other diseases—had already begun decimating the Indian population, preceding Cortés's troops like an invisible force of millions.

The Adaptable Measles Virus

To most present-day Americans, the thought that a childhood ailment like measles could contribute to the annihilation of an entire civilization seems difficult to comprehend. However, the measles virus is particularly contagious. It can replicate itself rapidly, spreading from one HOST to another in fluids from the nose, mouth, or breath, even before the initial host realizes that he or she is sick. Viruses, like all organisms, evolve mechanisms over time that allow them to overcome challenges. For instance, as contagious as measles is, those who contract it once acquire IMMUNITY from further INFECTION. For this reason, the measles virus needs a continual supply of healthy new hosts to survive. Initially, measles resembles nothing more than a common cold, beginning with a bad cough, low fever, and a sensitivity to light. It is not until the measles virus has

The arrival of Hernán Cortés (above) in Mexico had a dramatic impact. Although untold numbers of people would die in Spanish mines, or burn for refusing to convert to Catholicism, far more died of measles and other diseases. Several known epidemics are noted on the map (top). The plummeting native population of Mexico between 1519 and 1629 is shown on the graph at left.

already spread to others that about half of those infected develop large blotchy red or brown rashes which can spread from head to toe.

The Decimation of Mexico's Indigenous Population

Well before the first Aztecs developed rashes, the virus had spread, along with others causing smallpox, influenza, and other diseases, throughout Tenochtitlán. Passed easily along heavily traveled Aztec roads, these viruses reached many people in a short period of time, causing rapid, intense loss of life. The young, who had especially little protection, succumbed en mass. Even today, there is a 90 percent chance that a child under ten who has not been IMMUNIZED will contract measles after contact with an infected person. Further studies have shown a 47 percent fatality rate in fetuses if the virus is contracted during the early months of pregnancy.

Measles and Poverty

Since 1963, children in the United States and in much of the world have received routine VACCINATIONS against the disease. Despite this, measles continues to kill between one and two million people a year, most of whom are poor children in developing countries.

The Philippines: A Case Study

To see how poverty has contributed to measles outbreaks, one can examine the specific case of Manila, the capital of the Philippines. Much of Manila's population is impoverished. Unvaccinated and malnourished children are easy and plentiful targets for disease, as their weakened bodies produce too few ANTIBODIES to combat infections. In the case of measles, the real danger comes not from the virus itself, but from the fact that an infection can render a victim more susceptible to

Other Major Childhood Diseases

Chicken pox: Chicken pox is caused by a member of the herpes family, the varicella-zoster virus. The virus is transmitted through the air, through coughing and sneezing, or by touching the clothes or linens of an infected victim. Early symptoms include slight fever, headache, irritability, and loss of appetite. Within days, itchy, blister-like red bumps appear, first on the scalp, then on the back or stomach, and finally on the face and elsewhere. The bumps do not appear all at once, but surface in crops that take several days to form, break, and scab over. Chicken pox is a fairly mild disease in children, but can be more serious for adults. In 1994 a chicken pox vaccine was approved for use in the United States. The same virus can also cause herpes zoster, a painful infection that can affect people in midlife. Herpes zoster can damage nerve pathways leading to the eyes, but is generally nonrecurrent.

Mumps: Mumps is caused by a contagious viral infection. Symptoms include fever, swelling, and soreness in the neck glands. Rare complications can result in swelling of the brain and the meninges tissues covering the brain and spinal cord, as well as deafness. In adults, infection can be particularly severe, causing painful swelling of the testes and sterility in males. Mumps is passed through the saliva of an infected person and is most common in school-age children. Since 1967, a mumps vaccine has been available in the United States, where the annual number of mumps cases is now low. The disease is far more frequent in developing countries.

Scarlet fever: Scarlet fever is caused by *Streptococcus* bacteria and may occur in strep throat patients. Symptoms include sore throat, headache, fever, and sometimes vomiting. The bacteria can produce a TOXIN that causes the red rash and facial flush that gives scarlet fever its name. The rash lasts up to a week, typically beginning around the neck, underarms, or groin. The tongue may produce a white coating with swollen, red taste buds, known as "strawberry tongue." Today, scarlet fever is relatively rare, and can usually be prevented if strep throat is detected and treated early. Although it remains a serious illness that can lead to ear infections, rheumatic fever, or meningitis (*see page 64*), scarlet fever can be successfully treated with ANTIBIOTICS, generally penicillin.

Whooping cough: Whooping cough is caused by the bacteria *Bordetella pertussis* that are found in the mouth, nose, and throat of infected persons. Although whooping cough can infect people of any age, most patients are infants and children under school age. Symptoms may include runny nose, sneezing, slight fever, and cough, which may worsen over a two-week period into violent coughing fits known as cough paroxysm, noted for their characteristic "whooping" sound. Symptoms are usually much milder in adults and adolescents. Persons with whooping cough should be treated with a fourteen-day antibiotic treatment to cure the illness and prevent its spread. A combined whooping cough-diphtheria-tetanus vaccine is available in shot form.

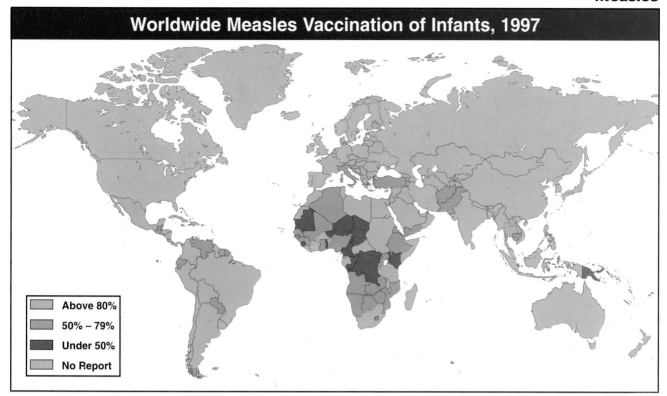

Worldwide Measles Vaccination of Infants, 1997

Above 80%

50% – 79%

Under 50%

No Report

secondary illnesses, such as pneumonia and encephalitis *(see page 12)*.

Unlike their counterparts in central Africa and elsewhere, where fewer than half of all children have received measles vaccinations, most Filipino children have been vaccinated. Nonetheless, a recent outbreak underscored the problem facing the Filipino government. In the first months of 1997 alone, Filipino health officials reported over a thousand measles cases—and forty-seven deaths. While the government initiated mass vaccination programs, it faced many hurdles. Homeless populations are particularly difficult to reach, and health officials admit that their campaigns may only reach only 30 percent of the most at-risk population. As overcrowding pushes large numbers of people into tighter and tighter spaces without access to sewerage, clean water, or health services, the government's ability to monitor, much less control, the spread of measles and other infectious diseases decreases markedly.

The measles EPIDEMIC in Manila was further complicated by global economics. The crisis coincided with an Asian recession that dramatically weakened the Filipino economy. As a result, Manila has had to rely on assistance from the international health community for its medicines. This in turn has placed the question of measles and other diseases into a political context instead of simply a medical one. Because measles is

According to the World Health Organization, although fewer than 50 percent of children in some nations received vaccination for measles, most children around the world were vaccinated against the once deadly disease. The Centers for Disease Control estimates that measles vaccination has saved over 24,600 lives in the United States alone in the last quarter century.

commonly perceived as a mild illness that rarely kills in the United States or Western Europe, measles eradication is not a high global priority.

Global Priorities and Measles Eradication

The Filipino epidemic provides just one example of the challenges measles poses. There may be reasons for optimism, however. In the 1980s, after the global eradication of smallpox, the World Health Organization (WHO) met to consider the global elimination of measles, but rejected the idea as unfeasible. At a 1996 conference, however, cosponsored by WHO, the Pan-American Health Organization, and the Centers for Disease Control, that ambitious goal gained renewed life as a new plan was developed, Measles, a disease that has killed millions, and altered the course of history, is targeted for global eradication between 2005 and 2010.

MENINGITIS

Global Distribution Cases of meningitis occur all over the world but most are concentrated in Africa.

Causative Agent Meningitis can be caused by viruses, but the type of meningitis discussed here (and the most severe form) is caused by the bacterium *Neisseria meningitidis.*

Transmission Transmission occurs through direct contact, including airborne droplets from the nose and throat of infected persons. Many who become infected, however, are symptomless carriers. Viral meningitis can be transmitted through sewage-polluted water.

Symptoms The two common forms of meningitis are bacterial and viral. Bacterial is the more serious of the two types, with major symptoms characterized by fever, sudden severe headache, stiff neck, vomiting, and irritability. Additional, more serious symptoms include speech impairment, altered consciousness, rapid breathing, chills, and sensitivity to light. Without treatment it can lead to seizures, coma, shock, and possibly death. Seizures occur in about one-third of persons infected with bacterial meningitis. Meningococcal meningitis is the only form of bacterial meningitis to cause epidemics. Viral meningitis is fairly common but is rarely serious. The symptoms include fever, headache, muscle aches, and sore throat followed by a stiff neck and back and vomiting. The symptoms typically last for three to seven days after onset.

Treatment Bacterial meningitis must be treated by a doctor as soon as possible and antibiotics should be prescribed. There is no specific treatment for viral meningitis.

Prevention and Control There is a vaccine for meningococcal meningitis, but it is only recommended for persons who live in highly susceptible areas, or travelers going for extended trips where meningitis is epidemic.

The word *meningitis* literally means "an inflammation of the meninges, or brain and spinal cord linings."

As long as African elders from the sub-Saharan region can remember, BACTERIAL meningitis has been killing their children and young adults. It was not long after Europeans began colonizing Africa in the late 1800s and early 1900s that the disease grew to EPIDEMIC proportions. Spreading along trade-route caravan trails established by the French, the disease quickly spread from Ethiopia and the Sudan in the east, to modern-day Nigeria, Burkina Faso, and Upper Volta in the west. Since then, thousands of deaths a year have been attributed to the disease.

The worst epidemic recorded occurred in 1936–37 in the French colony of Chad. In total, over three thousand Chadians died—so many that French authorities feared the economy would collapse. In fact, between 1943 and 1951, 4 percent of Chad's population died of the disease. Meanwhile the colony's total birthrate was only slightly higher, at 4.2 percent.

Bacterial meningitis is not restricted to Africa. It can, and has, made appearances worldwide, from India, Nepal, and Mongolia to Brazil and the United States. It is a seasonal disease that arrives during dry months in tropical climates and between January and May in more temperate regions.

A Dangerous Microbe

The word *meningitis* literally means "an inflammation of the meninges, or brain and spinal cord lining." Although mild meningitis cases can be caused by VIRUSES, it is the bacterial form of the disease that is far more dangerous. The most dangerous meningitis bacterium is *Neisseria meningitidis,* which after first infecting the respiratory passages will often then cause fever, severe headache, stiff neck, vomiting, and irritability. Other symptoms may include speech impairment, decreased or altered consciousness, rapid breathing, chills, and a sensitivity to light. If untreated, the infection can lead to seizures, shock, coma, and finally death. Not everyone exposed to meningitis bacteria will become ill. Approximately 10 percent of the world's population carries a bacterium that causes meningitis in the pharynges (upper throat) without developing the disease.

Unable to survive long in the air, meningitis bacteria require direct contact with an infected person via coughing, sneezing, or kissing to spread. For this reason, containing meningitis outbreaks is easier than containing outbreaks due to other types of bacteria. Since the 1940s, effective ANTIBIOTICS have been available, greatly decreasing the danger posed by the disease in the United States and other countries where access to appropriate health care is available. In the past, half of all those who contracted meningitis died. With early detection and immediate treatment, the U.S. death rate has fallen to 10 percent of those infected.

The Meningitis Belt

Despite this progress, not all the news has been good. Since 1980, large outbreaks that had previously occurred every eight to ten years have become more frequent. Meanwhile, the number of cases reported annually has risen, with the largest number of deaths occurring in sub-Saharan Africa, once again along the old east-west trade routes. Meningitis is so prevalent in the region that the area is now commonly called the "The Meningitis Belt."

One of the chief concerns of researchers has been that new cases of meningitis are now showing up in patients that had previously shown an immunity to the disease. One possible cause may be worldwide global warming. As holes in the earth's protective ozone layer have widened due to industrial pollution, surface temperatures have risen, leading to longer dry seasons, droughts, and dust storms, all of which extend the annual cycle of the meningitis bacterium's spread.

War, Poverty, and Vaccine Distribution

Trends such as this one underscore why the development and distribution of new VACCINES is a priority.

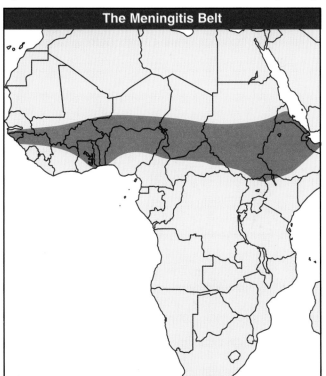

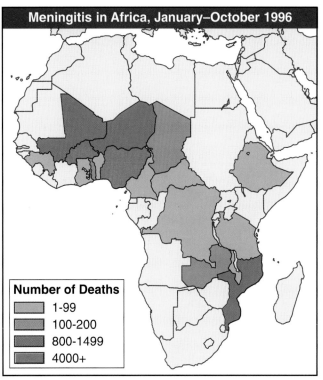

Bacterial meningitis is so common in sub-Saharan Africa, that the region has become known as "The Meningitis Belt." In 1996, a severe epidemic swept the region, killing over 16,000, including over 8,000 in Nigeria alone.

One of the greatest sources of frustration for health officials in the developing world is that although life-saving antibiotics exist, not all those who need them receive them. Distribution is complicated by ENDEMIC poverty and frequent wars. Violence continues to displace large populations, depriving them of what medical access is available and making the distribution of foreign aid a political and often dangerous undertaking.

The Will for Change

Even where funds do exist to treat populations effectively, not all governments have the will to do so. Oil-rich Nigeria, for instance, has no government health agency to oversee mass vaccinations or other preventive health care programs. In 1996, when a meningitis epidemic claimed over 16,800 victims across much of Africa, over eight thousand of those killed were Nigerians.

It is unsettling that the international community appears unwilling to commit resources needed to combat meningitis, and sovereign governments in the region seem unable to protect the health of their own citizens. Either way, victims continue to die needlessly from this curable disease.

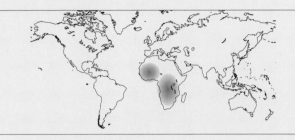

MONKEYPOX

Global Distribution Monkeypox is found in the rain forests of central and west Africa.

Causative Agent Monkeypox, like smallpox, is caused by an orthopoxvirus.

Transmission Monkeypox is most often transmitted to humans from squirrels and primates through contact with the animal's blood or through a bite.

Symptoms The characteristics of monkeypox are very similar to those of smallpox. The symptoms begin with a pustular rash, then fever, respiratory problems, and in some cases death. Because the smallpox vaccination became unnecessary after smallpox was eradicated, children born after 1980 are more vulnerable to monkeypox because they have never received the smallpox vaccine.

Treatment There is no treatment, although drugs are currently being tested.

Prevention and Control In high-risk areas, people are advised to limit contact with wild-caught animals, and to restrict such contact to a single person in the household, preferably an adult, as most children have not received a smallpox vaccine. There is consideration of using the smallpox vaccine in selected areas.

The eradication of smallpox has probably played a role in the spread of monkeypox. After smallpox was eradicated in 1979, smallpox vaccination programs, which had also been effective protection against the spread of the monkeypox virus from person-to-person, ended as well. Since then, the number of monkeypox cases caused by person-to-person transmission has increased dramatically.

When Joseph Conrad wrote his classic novel *The Heart of Darkness* about a white man's journey into the depths of the African jungle, he suggested that of all the dangers we face in life, it is what is inside us that we should fear most. While he was not referring to the human IMMUNE SYSTEM, his warning may have more literal implications than he realized. As war, hunger, and regional conflicts throughout central Africa have turned citizens into refugees and forced more and more people into previously uninhabited rain forests, humans are increasingly coming into contact with viral diseases for which they have no natural IMMUNITY.

Monkeypox, first identified in lab monkeys from Africa in 1958, is one such disease. Very similar to smallpox *(see page 82)*, it is believed to be contracted either through contact with infected squirrels and monkeys, or through contact with infected humans. Approximately one victim in ten who contract the disease will die, but all who become infected suffer scabby lesions, high fever, and severe respiratory problems. The disease is most fatal in the very young. Although scientists have theorized that monkeys acquired the VIRUS from squirrels, a recent study by the World Health Organization (WHO) revealed that of eighty-four squirrels examined, only one showed signs of carrying the virus.

The First Outbreak

In 1970, a group of boys from a village in the Democratic Republic of the Congo (DRC), then known as Zaire, became the first humans to contract monkeypox after hunting and eating small game. In the aftermath of these first cases, several minor outbreaks followed. Nonetheless, it appeared to officials from WHO that the number of secondary, person-to-person infections was fairly low. If that was the case, then the disease could be more easily contained to the isolated villages at the rain forest's edge, where the danger of primary infection was highest. When WHO personnel discovered that administering smallpox VACCINATIONS to villagers seemed to make them immune to monkeypox as well, fears of a wider epidemic began to shrink.

An Era of Confidence

In the late 1970s, health authorities announced a major victory. The deadly smallpox virus had been eradicated. The day in which all infectious disease could be eradicated seemed a real possibility.

With smallpox no longer a threat, mandatory vaccination programs in many industrialized nations came to an end.

Meanwhile, in Zaire, the end of the smallpox prevention campaign was followed by a high incidence of monkeypox in the mid-1980s. In 1986, 214 cases were confirmed. Again, the number of secondary INFECTIONS remained low, and the outbreak was limited to the forest edge.

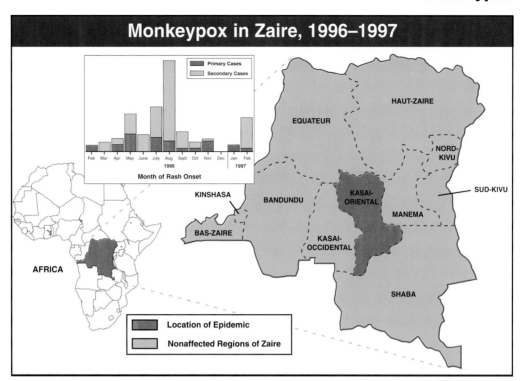

Between February 1996 and October 1997, over 500 people in the Kasai-Oriental Province of the Democratic Republic of the Congo (formerly Zaire) were stricken with monkeypox. Most cases were caused by secondary infections—spread from person to person. Prior to this outbreak, most monkeypox cases had been caused by scattered primary infections—from wildlife to humans. The graph above shows a month-by-month comparison of primary infections to secondary infections during the height of the epidemic.

Monkeypox Returns

In 1996, another monkeypox outbreak occurred in Zaire. This time, however, cases were far more widespread. More than five hundred cases were documented by the Zairian Ministry of Health and WHO between February 1996 and October 1997. (This was the same period when, following a civil war, Zaire became the DRC.) A single person in a single village of the Kasai-Oriental Province was reported to have infected eight members of his family.

Some have theorized that the end of smallpox vaccinations allowed monkeypox to spread more rapidly through secondary infections, although further research is needed before that theory can be proven. Only then can the potential danger of a large-scale monkeypox EPIDEMIC be determined.

The Price of War

Sadly, monkeypox research has been nearly impossible given the region's tumultuous political climate. The DRC and neighboring Rwanda have suffered from violent civil wars over the last decade. As of 1999, they were fighting each other in a conflict that threatened to engulf their neighbors. Villages have become battlefields, food transportation lines have been cut, and millions of refugees from both countries have been driven from their homes. Forced to choose between starvation and disease, many have taken to eating monkeys and other small game to survive.

When epidemics occur during times of war, caring for the sick becomes a political and economic decision as well as a public health concern. When more than a million refugees from Rwanda flooded into Zaire in 1994, an outbreak of cholera *(see page 16)* killed thirty thousand people in three weeks before it was contained.

If an outbreak of monkeypox were to occur not in scattered villages along the forest edge but within the heart of a refugee camp, the consequences could be equally dire. Even if definitive proof were found that smallpox vaccine can IMMUNIZE against monkeypox, administering vaccinations from WHO's remaining supply of some five hundred thousand doses of smallpox vaccine to those at risk would be difficult, to say the least.

Meanwhile, secondary monkeypox infections appear to be growing more virulent. As history has repeatedly shown, the more humans fight each other, the easier it is for disease to rise and wage its own war against humankind as well.

PLAGUE

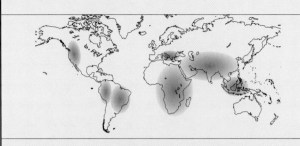

Global Distribution Plague is scattered throughout the world, mostly in southeastern Europe, much of the Middle East, China, southern and Southeast Asia, eastern Africa, and in South Africa. Plague is also found in the southwestern United States and the Pacific Coast states through British Columbia and Alberta, Canada. Two areas in South America struggle with plague: the northern Andean mountain area and Brazil.

Causative Agent Plague is caused by the bacterium *Yersinia pestis*.

Transmission Plague passes from infected animals to humans through the bite of an infected flea. Another but less common mode of transmission is by direct contact with infected tissues or fluids of an infected animal.

Symptoms There are three types of plague, each with different characteristics. Bubonic plague provokes swollen, tender lymph nodes, fever, and chills. Septicemic plague occurs when the bacteria has invaded the bloodstream, causing severe illness characterized by fever, chills, abdominal pain, and shock. Pneumonic plague is the most life-threatening, with symptoms of fever, chills, cough, and difficulty breathing. Rapid shock and death follow if not treated immediately.

Treatment Drug therapy should begin as early as possible with streptomycin or one of several other antibiotics.

Prevention and Control An active effort to eliminate or reduce rodent populations in rural and urban areas is important, but it is critical to reduce contact between infected rodents and house pets.

Ring a ring a rosie
A pocket full of posie
Atishoo, atishoo
We all fall down.

This well-known nursery rhyme originated as a description of bubonic plague's skin blemishes, efforts to fight off infection by carrying fragrant flowers, the wheezing failure of the respiratory system, and eventual death.

Between 1347 and 1351, twenty-five million people—fully one-third of Europe's population at the time—died in excruciating pain from a disease that can make human glands swell to the size of apples before they finally burst. Bubonic plague, the "Black Death," killed so many in such a short time in so many regions of the world that it altered human civilization forever.

The word *plague,* from the Latin *plaga,* meaning "to strike out violently with divine intent," underscores the popular belief that a pestilence so deadly could only be the work of an all-powerful and angry God.

Three Forms of Plague

Scientists now know that plague is caused by *Yersinia pestis,* a BACILLUS that thrives in the stomach of fleas that live on rodents. *Y. pestis* multiplies quickly until the flea's digestive tract is full of BACTERIA. When the flea finds a new HOST, it regurgitates the bacilli into the new host's body, causing an infection.

Bubonic plague is the most common form of plague. While it is most often acquired from infected fleas, it can also be spread through the skin, clothing, or fluids of an infected person. The most common symptoms are fever, headache, fatigue, and the telltale painful swelling of lymph nodes, or buboes, in the area that *Y. pestis* first entered the body.

If bubonic plague is left untreated and *Y. pestis* enters the bloodstream, it can progress to septicemic plague. Septicemic plague can also occur independently, without affecting the lymph nodes. This can be especially deadly since it is more difficult to diagnose.

The final form of plague is pneumonic plague. In cases of primary pneumonic plague, *Y. pestis* is inhaled after being expelled in the breath of an infected person or animal. Pneumonic plague patients are overcome with high fever, cough, bloody saliva, and chills.

The Earliest Plagues

The term *plague* has been used to describe numerous EPIDEMICS throughout history, from the plagues of Egypt mentioned in the Bible onwards. Although historians have long theorized as to what the true nature of these epidemics might have been, there seems little doubt that they were not necessarily the disease plague. Historians generally believe that plague first emerged from the Himalayan region bordering India and China, sometime between the third and sixth centuries C.E. Rats infested with plague-carrying fleas most likely traveled along trade routes to the Middle East and the Mediterranean.

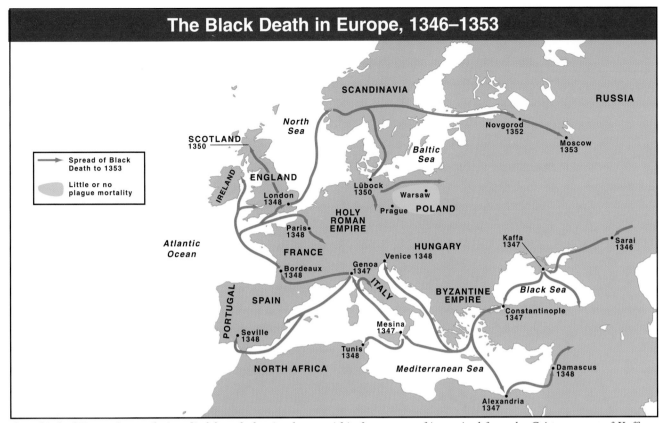

The Black Death in Europe, 1346–1353

Legend:
→ Spread of Black Death to 1353
Little or no plague mortality

One-third of Europe's population died from bubonic plague within four years of its arrival from the Crimean port of Kaffa.

The Plague of Justinian

For several hundred years prior to the first generally recognized outbreak of plague, the Roman Empire was decimated by epidemics, first between 165 and 180 C.E., and then again between 251 and 266. This second outbreak was accompanied by a period of civil war and invasion by outsiders. During the reign of the emperor Constantine the Great, from 306 to 337, the empire's capital was moved east to Constantinople, or present-day Istanbul. The empire was formally split in half in 395, with the eastern half becoming known as the Byzantine Empire. Meanwhile, the western region was almost entirely overrun by invaders.

During the reign of the emperor Justinian, who ruled from 527 to 565, the Roman Empire's fortunes revived, however briefly. In an attempt to reunite the two halves of the former empire, Justinian reconquered much of the empire's lost territory. Just when his goal seemed within reach, however, disaster struck.

The Plague of Justinian struck Constantinople between 542 and 543. Historian Procopius reported that at the epidemic's height, five to ten thousand people died each day in the city. Justinian himself was stricken, and although he survived, the devastation halted his

expansion, starved his empire by squelching trade, and helped bring about centuries of economic decline.

The Black Death

Many historians believe that the plague did not disappear from Europe after 543, and some evidence suggests it was only the first outbreak in a cycle that continued sporadically for the next few hundred years.

The plague's return in the fourteenth century is considered the second major cycle. It began in 1334, in the northeastern Chinese province of Hopei. Decimating 90 percent of Hopei's population, the outbreak eventually claimed two-thirds of the inhabitants in a wide swathe of China.

From China, the disease made its way west along trade routes to India and the Caucasus. In time, the Black Death reached Kaffa, a Genoese trading colony on the Crimean Peninsula of the Black Sea. The city, a key center of trade and cornerstone of Europe's defense against attack from the east, was at the time under siege by Mongol forces. Cut off from supplies, the city's inhabitants were suffering greatly. Then in 1347, the Mongols began dying in droves. Plague ravaged the invaders and forced an end to the siege. In a desperate last attack that marked perhaps the first instance of biological warfare, the Mongols catapulted the *Y. pestis*-riddled corpses of their dead over the city's walls. Plague immediately spread through the weakened port. When several Genoese ships fled Kaffa for Genoa, they carried the plague bacillus with them. From there, the disease began its second cycle of death throughout Europe.

An Age of Despair

When *Y. pestis* arrived in Europe, it found a climate ideally suited for it. The weather was dramatically colder than it had been in previous centuries. Particularly in northern Europe, winters were longer and colder, and crop failures were more common. Europe's population, which had been growing dramatically since about 900, found itself faced with increasing famine.

By 1347, France and England had already been engaged for a decade in what would become known as the Hundred Years' War. During the war, soldiers rampaged across France, looting villages and burning fields as they went. On Europe's eastern frontier, a civil war, begun in 1341, had left what remained of the Byzantine Empire in virtual collapse and vulnerable to the Ottoman Turks. Thus, even before those Genoese sailors fled Kaffa, trade with the East had been shrinking, and many European economies were on the brink of collapse.

The Social Impact of the Black Death

Whenever humans are weakened by famine and war, they are vulnerable to disease. It should be no surprise then that the arrival of *Y. pestis* in fourteenth-century Europe had disastrous consequences. Much of our understanding of Black Death in the fourteenth century comes from Giovanni Boccaccio's *Decameron,* a series of novellas documenting the plague's effects on those who lived through it. In describing the plague in Florence, Boccaccio wrote, "This tribulation struck such fear in the hearts of men and women that one brother abandoned another, uncles abandoned nephews, sisters abandoned brothers, often wives abandoned their husbands, and . . . fathers and mothers abandoned their children, as if they were not even theirs."

Some estimate that twenty-five million people, one-third of Europe's population, died between 1347 and 1352. Almost no region was spared and nearly all trade and commerce ceased. Royalty, magistrates, and clergymen all succumbed to the disease alongside their ser-vants. Societies centuries old dissolved into chaos, as political, religious, and community leaders, helpless to stop the disease and fearing for their lives, abandoned cities as if they were sinking ships.

The plague had a particularly profound impact on the Church, eventually helping to pave the way for the Protestant Reformation. The Catholic clergy's inability to stop the plague severely weakened its authority. So many priests died or fled from their posts that finding qualified replacements was difficult. Because of the important role priests played in blessing the sick, thousands of new, inexperienced, unreliable, and sometimes corrupt priests were ordained as replacements.

In this environment, popular resentment against the Church exploded. In Germany, the Flagellant movement gained popularity. This was a layperson-led sect noted for adherents who repeatedly beat themselves with whips as an act of penance. Flagellants and others saw the plague as a sign that the final battle between good and evil was near, and that Christ would come again to slay priests and others who oppressed the poor. This belief led some to seek out scapegoats, particularly Jews, who were accused of deliberately poisoning water. In several instances, Jews were burned alive. In Strasbourg, more than two thousand were hanged.

Scientific thinkers were also at a loss in dealing with the plague. In 1345, there had been both a solar and lunar eclipse followed by a conjunction of Saturn, Jupiter, and Mars. The Paris Consilium, a committee charged with explaining where the plague had come from, cited the Greek philosopher Aristotle, who had written that an alignment of Saturn and Jupiter would bring disaster. Others believed constellations brought changes in weather patterns that dispersed poisonous vapors. Although these ideas were based on superstitions, they did lead to some practical, though ultimately ineffective, measures. Quarantines were ordered for ships throughout Europe. (Quarantines, from the word Latin *quadraginta,* or forty, lasted forty days, reflecting the length of Noah's time at sea during the biblical flood.)

The Black Death and the Feudal System

Among the most dramatic effects of the Black Death was its impact on the relationship between economic classes. For centuries, the dominant economic structure in Europe was the feudal system, in which the peasant majority, or serfs, worked lands owned by wealthy lords. Serfs were responsible for supplying lords with all the food they desired, keeping what was left for themselves. Although serfs were not slaves, they could not leave the lords' lands, or manor, without permission. At the same time, they had little need to do so since the manor was a self-sustaining world. As long as serfs were available to harvest crops, the feudal system could be maintained.

As plague swept through Europe, this system began to collapse. In response, new laws were devised to address labor shortages that ensued. In 1351, for example, England passed the Ordinance of Laborers, freezing wages at their pre-plague levels. At the same time, so much land was abandoned by those fleeing the plague that lords were forced to lower rents charged to serfs in order to keep them on the manor.

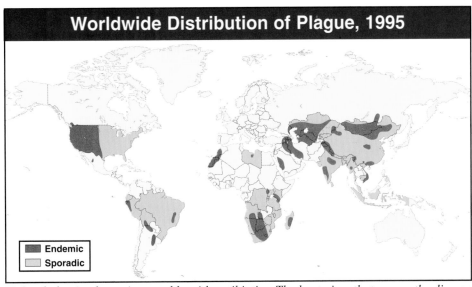

Worldwide Distribution of Plague, 1995

■ Endemic
□ Sporadic

Today, bubonic plague is treatable with antibiotics. The bacterium that causes the disease can still be found worldwide, however, including throughout the American West.

One of the most far-reaching effects of the Black Death was to force a rethinking of the relationship between lord and laborer. Throughout Europe, laborers rose up in rebellion. From the Jacquerie uprising in France in 1358 to Wat Tyler's 1381 rebellion in England, the plague helped shift the balance of power between Europe's wealthy and laboring classes, building an awareness of the rights of the individual.

The Great Plague

Although the worst years of the Black Death ended in about 1353, plague continued to circulate for several hundred years, just as it had after the Plague of Justinian a thousand years before. New outbreaks occurred in 1361, 1369, 1374, 1390, and periodically thereafter until the late seventeenth century. The worst of these occurred in London in 1665. The Great Plague, as it was known, spread rapidly, as flea and rodent populations flourished along the open sewage system that flowed through the city center. The first known victim, Margaret Porteous, was buried in April and by the end of the year, between 70,000 and 110,000 people had died. Not until the following year, when the so-called Great Fire of London destroyed most of the city, did the plague abate.

Plague Today

Although the last European plague epidemic occurred in the French port of Marseilles in 1720, others have broken out elsewhere since then. During the 1880s, an epidemic began in the interior of China, reaching the ports of Hong Kong and Canton by 1894, and two years later, Bombay, India.

During this era, scientists were making breakthrough after breakthrough in the study of epidemic disease. Shortly after the outbreaks in Canton and Hong Kong, Alexander Yersin of the Pasteur Institute in Paris became the first to identify the bacterium that now bears his name. Three years later, the British Sanitation Commission described the rat's important role in TRANSMISSION of plague.

Unfortunately, this new knowledge initially led to harsh measures being imposed on healthy people as often as it led to measures against rats. British authorities in India and American authorities in Honolulu and San Francisco burned down slums, and quarantined those suspected of being carriers.

Before the San Francisco epidemic of 1902, plague had been unknown in North America. Although the disease can now usually be cured with common ANTIBIOTICS, *Y. pestis* is now widespread throughout the western United States, principally among prairie dog populations. That prairie dogs carry *Y. pestis* provides those who would eliminate them with an excuse to do so, even though prairie dogs provide food for predators such as raptors and snakes—critical parts of the Southwest's ecosystem. Meanwhile, multidrug-resistant *Y. pestis* was isolated in 1995. While it seems unlikely that humankind will face a plague outbreak that rivals the Black Death anytime soon, a resistant STRAIN may be cause for concern.

Mapping Epidemics

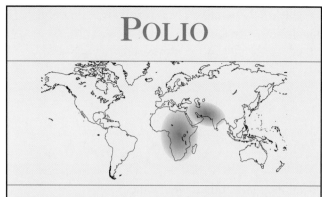

POLIO

Global Distribution Polio is found in Africa and Asia.

Causative Agent Any of three polio viruses can cause the disease.

Transmission The viruses that cause polio usually enter the body through the digestive tract, from which they then can spread to the central nervous system. A person may be infected through contact with infected fecal matter, either in trace amounts on food or on a previously infected individual. Unlike most diseases polio also occurs in societies where public health standards are high and where there is a sanitary public water supply.

Symptoms Polio symptoms begin with a fever and sore throat, and progress to a stiff neck and aching muscles. In very serious cases, polio paralyzes the muscles used for breathing and swallowing, causing death. While the symptoms typically begin seven to fourteen days after exposure, infected persons can transmit polio viruses as long as they remain in their throat (one week) or feces (six weeks).

Treatment There is no specific treatment for polio, but it is very important that a person with polio receive medical attention and supervision, especially at the beginning of the illness.

Prevention and Control There is a vaccine for polio that has drastically reduced the number of cases in areas where the vaccine is widely administered. In 1988, the World Health Organization launched a campaign to rid the entire world of the disease.

The National Foundation for Infantile Paralysis helped fund the work of Dr. Jonas Salk, who was the first to develop an effective polio vaccine. In 1954, his vaccine was administered to millions of schoolchildren, each of whom received the lapel button shown at right.

The emergence of new EPIDEMICS over the last few decades has tended to overshadow a great medical success story—the fight against poliomyelitis ("polio"). There has not been a new case of polio in the United States since the late 1970s, and fewer and fewer doctors have encountered the disease. Nonetheless, because polio has yet to be entirely eradicated, the struggle is not over. Until the disease is eradicated, it remains a threat to humankind.

The Fear of Polio

To anyone born prior to the 1960s, memories of polio's severity are haunting: three-year-olds on crutches, paralyzed and in pain; children doomed to spend the rest of their lives flat on their backs, encased in "iron lungs," unable even to breathe without such aid. Millions feared that any fever or sore throat could bring a lifetime of suffering or even painful death. In the United States alone, more than sixty thousand cases of polio were reported annually in the early 1950s. Then researchers found the key to beating back the disease. The story of how that happened is proof that with cooperation and adequate resources, many of the world's health problems can be solved.

A Modern Disease

Although some believe polio has been around since ancient Egypt, the first verifiable cases of "infantile paralysis," as it was also known, appeared in the late 1700s. After a small epidemic broke out in Sweden in 1887, however, further outbreaks occurred in France, Australia, and other developed nations. In 1909, Simon Flexner of the Rockefeller Institute proved that the disease was contagious by injecting a monkey with an emulsion made from the spinal cord of a polio victim, and then successfully transferring polio virus from that monkey to another.

Flexner's breakthrough would guide health officials in 1916 when the first large-scale epidemic broke out. From a few isolated reports in Brooklyn, New York, the disease spread rapidly. By the end of the year, more than 27,000 people were infected, 6,000 had died, and the nation was in a panic. The rate of fatalities per INFECTION was almost one in four. Adding to the panic was the fact that the disease primarily struck children—and struck them with incredible suffering.

The Campaign to Eradicate Polio, 1988–1998

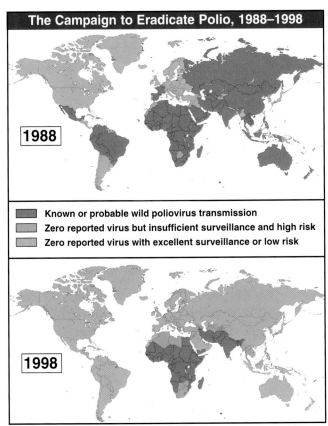

1988

■ Known or probable wild poliovirus transmission
■ Zero reported virus but insufficient surveillance and high risk
■ Zero reported virus with excellent surveillance or low risk

1998

These maps show recent progess toward eradicating polio.

The Search for Answers

Although officials knew that polio was contagious, and that any of three polio VIRUSES could cause the disease, they had no idea how it was being spread. One perception among the general public was that the disease was caused by the Jewish, Italian, and Slavic immigrants who had been arriving in New York since the 1890s. Commonly stereotyped as "unclean" because poverty forced them to live in segregated, overcrowded ghettos, these newcomers made easy scapegoats.

Without other leads, officials also looked to the slums. Since the source of previous major epidemics, such as cholera *(see page 16),* had been found in poor sanitation, this strategy seemed logical. New York and other cities soon acted on this hypothesis by embarking on massive disinfection programs.

Because outbreaks were concentrated during the summer, and since some felt the disease might be spread in water, public pools were closed. People were advised to avoid drinking fountains. Because others suggested the disease might be passed through the air, playgrounds were closed and parents were ordered to keep children from theaters, restaurants, and other public places.

Ironically, while, authorities focused on the poor, a much higher number of cases was to be found among other classes. During the 1916 epidemic, more children in Philadelphia's wealthy Main Line district became sick than in the slums of South Philadelphia. More cases cropped up on rural Staten Island, New York, than in crowded Manhattan. Nonetheless, attention remained fixed on the poor. In New York, the city government imposed quarantines on ghetto neighborhoods, and residents were required to obtain permits to travel, even from one neighborhood to another.

The Iron Lung

The public's fear was heightened by the visible ravages polio causes. After multiplying in a victim's intestines, the virus invades the spinal cord, causing paralysis and rapid muscle degeneration. Limbs become twisted and deformed, and in the most severe cases, muscles—including those controlling breathing and swallowing—are paralyzed. Worst of all, the disease leaves the body's nerve endings unharmed, ensuring that patients can feel this gradual, extremely painful process as it happens.

To fight this degeneration, most doctors relied on a common strategy. They immobilized stricken joints with splints and casts, in hope that this would prevent the disease from spreading to unaffected muscles. In the most severe cases, in which breathing and swallowing were impaired, little could be done.

Because polio can paralyze the muscles used to breathe, many polio patients spent their entire lives in iron lungs, devices that forced air in and out of their chests. This little girl, Regina Edwards, was photographed at age two years, five weeks, in the summer of 1952.

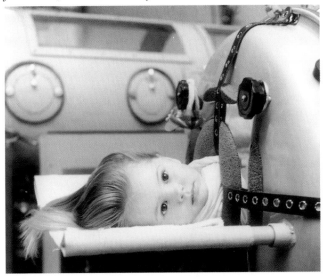

That changed in 1927, when Philip Drinker of Harvard University developed an airtight chamber that pushed air in and out of an immobilized polio patient's lungs. The following year, a young girl at Boston Children's Hospital became the first to use the iron lung. Although the device would prolong the lives of many desperately ill children, to be confined in one could be a terrifying and lonesome experience.

Roosevelt, Warm Springs, and the March of Dimes

The year that Drinker's machine was developed, the fight against polio acquired a formidable ally. The governor of New York, Franklin Delano Roosevelt, who had contracted the disease eleven years earlier, helped launch the Warm Springs Foundation in Georgia as a therapy center for polio patients. In 1934, two years after Roosevelt's election as president of the United States, the organization evolved into the National Foundation for Infantile Paralysis. The foundation was the first U.S. public health organization to rely on the general public for its funding. Its annual "March of Dimes" fund drives were highly successful, raising an estimated $630 million between 1938 and 1962.

The foundation's mission was "to lead, direct, and unify the fight against every aspect of the killing and crippling infection of poliomyelitis." Although some of the foundation's funds went into the development of a VACCINE (one of which contained a live virus that tragi-

cally killed several children), the majority of its money and time went to medical care for patients.

The Controversial Sister Kenny

While the use of splints and iron lungs was the accepted practice of most medical authorities, not everyone believed in it. In 1933, Elizabeth Kenny, a former nurse in the Australian army, opened her first clinic for the care of polio patients. ("Sister" was her military rank as a nurse, not a religious title.) Kenny believed the most serious problem facing polio victims was the spasms in their deteriorating muscles. To relieve them, she applied heat treatments and physical therapy. Doctors throughout the world condemned her for this practice, arguing that she was causing greater deformities by pulling on the damaged muscles.

The public felt otherwise, particularly after several of her patients had nearly miraculous recoveries. Although her methods have never been proven scientifically sound and were never endorsed by the National Foundation for Infantile Paralysis, she was invited to meet President Roosevelt and served as a guest lecturer at the University of Minnesota in 1943. When Sister Kenny died in 1952, a Gallup poll found her the most respected woman in America.

Towards a Vaccine

Sister Kenny did not live long enough to see a polio vaccine become available, but a number of breakthroughs were made during her lifetime. In 1936, Peter Olitski of the Rockefeller Institute IMMUNIZED mice

Sister Elizabeth Kenny, whose controversial treatment methods eventually gained popular support, if not always medical acceptance, is awarded the Legion of Merit.

against western equine encephalitis *(see page 12)* by using "killed" STRAINS of that virus instead of small amounts of live virus. An even greater breakthrough occurred in 1949, when John Enders, Thomas Weller, and their team at Harvard announced that they had successfully grown one of the polio viruses in test tube cultures of monkey kidney cells.

It was not a cure, but the benefits were many. Polio research had previously required live monkeys in which to grow the virus. By eliminating this time-consuming, costly, and difficult form of research, Enders and Weller opened the doors for much more experimentation. Further, by establishing that polio viruses grew in human intestines, Enders discovered the true path of its spread. The virus was not airborne, mosquito-borne, and certainly not immigrant-borne, but was spread through fecal-oral TRANSMISSION, or by unwashed hands infected with feces. This discovery eventually explained why polio infected children living in clean homes. In unsanitary environments, the virus was likely to be contracted earlier in life, allowing the body to develop IMMUNITY. The later in life the infection came, the less prepared the IMMUNE SYSTEM was to fight it.

As the 1950s began, polio's grip on the nation seemed stronger than ever. Not only were the number of cases increasing, but the typical age at which patients were acquiring it had risen from early in childhood to between fifteen and twenty-five years old. Ironically, because more and more Americans were living in cleaner conditions, moving away from inner cities to the suburbs that were sprouting up nationwide, fewer people had acquired immunity to diseases that previous generations had been exposed to at a young age.

Salk and Sabin

A disease that arises in conjunction with cleanliness was a new twist indeed. But this knowledge alone still did not stop the virus's spread. It would take Jonas Salk and Albert Sabin to do that. In 1953, Salk announced the development of a polio vaccine made of "killed virus" administered by injection. The following year, the National Foundation for Infantile Paralysis launched a mass INOCULATION program using the vaccine. Sabin followed in 1961 with an orally administered "live virus" vaccine. Although both won the Nobel Prize for their discoveries, Sabin's vaccine would eventually see wider use, since it was less expensive and easier to administer. In 1979, the United States registered its last new naturally-occurring polio case.

Post-Polio Syndrome

Since 1979, however, a disturbing trend has begun to appear. A number of polio survivors began experiencing muscle fatigue and other polio-like symptoms, what has now been termed post-polio syndrome (PPS). Although health authorities were initially skeptical about whether such a syndrome existed, and many insurance companies refused to pay for treatments relating to it, some doctors kept an open mind. Meanwhile, former polio patients who continue to experience PPS symptoms have used the Internet to create an increasingly large network of support groups to share resources and experiences.

Polio Around the Globe

The end of polio in the United States has not meant its end worldwide. India and China reported enormous infection rates until their governments, the Centers for Disease Control, and Rotary International joined forces to mobilize mass immunization drives. These efforts have been rewarded, reaching eighty-three million children in China in 1994 and 75 to 125 million children in India each year between 1995 and 1999.

After twenty years of effort, polio is in retreat. The number of cases worldwide has fallen from 400,000 in 1980 to just over 5,000 reported in 1997. The World Health Organization hopes to eradicate these viruses completely by the end of 2000, and reports that one polio virus has already been eliminated. Although most countries were on target as of mid-1999, some, such as the Democratic Republic of the Congo (DRC), were not.

In July 1998, the DRC's polio eradication campaign had to be halted due to the civil war there. During 1999, new immunization target dates were set in the DRC, but as of late 1999, those dates remained in doubt. Furthermore, the DRC's plan covered fewer than 10 percent of the country's children, not nearly sufficient for total polio elimination.

Health officials have been quick to point out that no nation can claim to be free of polio until all nations are free, and that if this potential victory is not seized upon, a renewed spread of the disease among unimmunized children is very possible, even likely. President Roosevelt was a strong believer that government had a responsibility for the health and welfare of its people. On the foundations of that belief, he was able to help eliminate a terrifying disease from America. Today, the world community stands on the brink of doing the same.

RABIES

Global Distribution Rabies is found in most countries worldwide.

Causative Agent Rabies is caused by a number of different strains of viruses in the *Lyssavirus* genus of the rhabdovirus family.

Transmission Rabies virus is usually transmitted to humans through the bite of an infected animal. All mammals can get rabies.

Symptoms Rabies begins with a prodromal period (symptoms that indicate the beginning of a disease) that last from one to four days. These symptoms include fever, headache, fatigue, muscle aches, sore throat, cough, and vomiting. More than half the time there is also a slight twitching feeling around the area of the bite. After the prodromal period, the symptoms progress to high fever, irritability, excessive agitation, confusion, hallucinations, aggressive behavior, muscle spasms, seizures, weakness or paralysis, increased production of saliva or tears, and sensitivity to bright lights, sounds, or touch. The late stages produce symptoms consistent with a deteriorating state of the nervous system, such as double vision, difficulty moving facial muscles, abnormal movement of the muscles that control breathing (including the diaphragm), and difficulty breathing. It is the combination of the excess saliva and the difficulty breathing that produce the "foaming at the mouth" appearance. Ultimately, an infected person can slip into a coma and die from the virus anywhere within four to twenty days after rabies symptoms begin. If rabies virus is left untreated it will always result in death.

Treatment The first step in treating a person who has been exposed to rabies virus is to immediately flush the wound with soap and water for approximately ten minutes, then seek medical attention. If a doctor believes a patient is at risk for rabies he or she will begin a series of intramuscular injections called human diploid cell vaccine and human rabies immune globulin, which will initiate an antirabies immunization. Patients who show signs of later symptoms should be tested for the disease and treated in a hospital, where they will need special life-support equipment.

Prevention and Control Although rabies can be prevented with vaccine, close contact with wild animals should be avoided, especially those that exhibit peculiar behavior. Pets should be vaccinated against the virus.

He was an average citizen who would not hurt a fly, until one night as he lay sleeping, a bat flew into his room and bit him on the neck. Now, two weeks later, they say he has gone mad. He can't stand the daylight, the smell of garlic, or the sight of himself in the mirror. He roams through the streets after dark attacking unsuspecting women and thirsting for blood. It is the stuff that Halloween legends are made of, but this may not be the beginning of a supernatural vampire tale. Instead, it may well be the equally frightening story of rabies.

Between Science and Superstition

For millennia, superstition and religion have helped shape society's view of rabies and of the animals that typically carry it. Rabies may have existed long before the domestication of animals. Legends among native peoples of the Pacific Northwest, for instance, tell of a rabies-like illness. The first written references to the disease come from 300 B.C.E. India, where the Sanskrit word *rabhas,* meaning "to do violence," gave its name to the disease.

Although details are sketchy, historians believe several other rabies outbreaks that may have started among animal populations further nurtured superstitions about the dark power of wild animals. Some even suggest that an EPIDEMIC in thirteenth-century France, possibly transmitted by wolves, may have helped inspire the werewolf legend. Stories circulated of madness among Spanish conquistadores in Latin America, caused by bites from vampire bats, but the first documented outbreak in what is now the United States occurred in California in 1703. Cases of rabies began appearing along the Atlantic seaboard during the late eighteenth century, and the number of cases grew after infected foxes and dogs were imported to the region for fox hunting.

Interestingly, recent studies have found surprising similarities between the mythology surrounding bats, dogs, and wolves and modern science's understanding of rabies. A vampire legend that originated in eighteenth-century Eastern Europe has been linked to the site of a major rabies outbreak in the 1720s. Further, rabies patients display many symptoms that coincide with the stories. Victims suffer from insomnia, a hypersensitivity to strong visual stimuli such as light and mirrors, and a heightened sensitivity to strong smells such as garlic. They also commonly exhibit aggressive sexual behavior, including telltale biting. They may even vomit blood. Rabies can also be TRANSMITTED through sex, the bite of an infected person, or perhaps even breathing air in a cave where infected bats live. Instead of the immortal life promised in stories, however, untreated rabies patients experience rapid neurological deterioration and invariably die. Yet even in death, rabies has its ties to vampire myths as the blood of infected victims is very slow to clot and a body exhumed days later can still appear lifelike and full of blood.

The Rabies Virus

Rabies VIRUS is transmitted primarily through direct contact with an infected animal. Dogs are generally considered the main carriers, but many other animals such as cats, raccoons, foxes, skunks, and, of course, bats can spread the disease just as effectively. Although the virus is most commonly

Rabies Carriers in the United States by Region

The map above illustrates where many of the most common carriers of rabies can be found. Bats, which can also carry the virus, can be found nationwide.

transmitted by the saliva of an infected animal, certain species of bats have recently been suspected of spreading rabies through indirect contact as well. In fact, the number and variety of ZOONOTIC reservoirs has increased over the years, thus illustrating that rabies is not at all a disease of the past, but an ongoing threat.

The Challenge to Researchers

For a number of reasons, rabies remains a puzzling illness. First, the large number of STRAINS of the virus that exist make it difficult for scientists to develop a "typical" model of how the disease is transmitted. Although most cases appear to be passed through bites or saliva, some victims have received no bites at all, apparently contracting the virus by an airborne route. Second, rabies has an unpredictable incubation period, ranging from as short as six days to as long as four years. In all cases, however, if an INFECTION is not detected and treated, the virus will begin attacking the central nervous system, leading to death.

In most cases, however, rabies is not fatal. When early detection is made, patients can be given a VACCINE. The first vaccine was developed in 1884 by Frenchman Louis Pasteur, using an inactive rabies virus he had grown in rabbit spinal cords. Although modified in the 1970s to make it safer, variations of Pasteur's vaccine are still in use today. The current vaccine is a live ATTENUATED one, grown in human CELL cultures.

Although the rabies vaccine only works before symptoms occur, human rabies deaths are very rare in the United States. During the past several decades, preventive vaccination programs and public education reduced the number of human rabies infections in the United States to only eighteen cases between 1986 and 1995.

On occasion, rabies scares do occur. When a rabid bear cub was found at an Iowa petting zoo in August 1999, officials scrambled to alert visitors. No cases of human infection were reported.

The Global Threat

Rabies is a much more constant threat worldwide, causing up to one hundred thousand deaths a year, mainly in Asia and Africa, where domestic animals often do not receive vaccinations. International health experts fear that unless a cohesive strategy is developed to address the problem, the number of deaths will increase. According to the World Health Organization, if rabies is not eliminated, the cost of preventing the disease in both humans and animals will probably increase dramatically in the developing world.

Due to a lack of resources, preventing zoonotic and other diseases in impoverished and politically unstable regions has always been difficult. That most of these deaths are potentially preventable only makes the crisis more tragic.

RIFT VALLEY FEVER

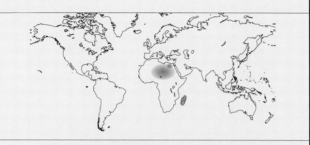

Global Distribution Rift Valley fever is found primarily sub-Saharan Africa, Egypt, and Madagascar.

Causative Agent Rift Valley fever virus is a member of the genus *Phlebovirus*, in the Bunyavirus family.

Transmission Rift Valley fever (RVF) virus is transmitted by mosquitoes that feed on infected livestock. Floods and heavy rainfall are a factor in the spread of the virus because mosquito populations grow so dramatically during these periods. RVF is also transmitted through airborne particles of infected blood during hemorrhage or slaughter.

Symptoms In livestock (primarily cattle, sheep, goats, and camels) RVF causes abortion of fetuses and death in young animals. The symptoms of human RVF include fever, headache, joint aches, and vomiting, at times progressing to bleeding of the gums and nose, and sometimes a deadly coma. If the later bleeding signs appear, death is likely to occur within twelve to twenty-four hours. Recent outbreaks of RVF have included severe bleeding.

Treatment Because there had not been serious human outbreaks of RVF until recently there is no established treatment of the infection. In the past, human cases were fairly mild, but now that hemorrhaging may be a factor in some cases immediate medical attention is necessary.

Prevention and Control Mosquito control, particularly during times of flooding, is needed to control future RVF outbreaks. If one is traveling to an area that has had a recent outbreak, insect repellent, long-sleeved shirts, and long pants should be worn at all times. Organizations such as the World Health Organization have called for a mass vaccination of all livestock, but this is still in the testing phase.

Changes to the environment—even those wrought by people—often play a direct role in the spread of disease. For instance, scientists suspect that the construction of the Aswan Dam on the Nile River in 1970 created new breeding grounds for mosquitoes carrying the Rift Valley fever virus.

Over ten thousand years ago, Earth's climate went through a dramatic change. Widespread drought stretched throughout the Med–iterranean world, killing off wild animals that provided food to the nomadic humans that populated the region. In order to survive, say historians, these nomads were forced to settle the land, and thereby launch the most important revolution in human history—the birth of agriculture. In about 8500 B.C.E., people in present-day Iraq became the first to domesticate sheep. In time, other animals followed, including goats (ca. 7500 B.C.E.), pigs (ca. 7000 B.C.E.), and cattle (6500 B.C.E.). By 5000 B.C.E., Egyptians began using irrigation to improve their farming, building dams along the Nile River to regulate the flow of water downstream to low-lying croplands from canals upstream. Animal domestication and sustained agriculture brought a population explosion that shaped history, as the world's population, just a few million in 8000 B.C.E., grew to one hundred million by 3000 B.C.E.

The Consequences of Agriculture

Changes of such magnitude do not come without consequences. Along with irrigation, animal domestication, and rapid population increases came an enormous increase in prevalence of diseases such as malaria *(see page 56)*, measles *(see page 60)*, and smallpox *(see page 82)*. Diseases that had evolved in animals found the growing population of humans to be hospitable HOSTS as well. At the same time, irrigation helped create ideal habitats for mosquitoes, which helped spread illness from animals to humans wherever they settled.

Today, Earth's climate is changing once again. Not only are we seeing the reemergence of mosquito populations carrying ancient diseases, but we also are seeing the appearance of new, increasingly deadly mosquito-borne diseases as well. Rift Valley fever is one such disease.

Rift Valley fever (RVF) VIRUS was first isolated in 1930 by veterinarians on a farm in Rift Valley, Kenya. The disease was first thought to infect only livestock, and was mainly confined to rural eastern and southern Africa. Nonetheless, it proved to be virulent where it struck. During a wave of outbreaks in 1950 and 1951, an estimated one hundred thousand sheep died from the disease in Kenya, causing severe hardship to farmers who relied on sheep for their living.

The first large RVF EPIDEMIC to involve humans occurred in Egypt in 1977. How the jump was made from livestock to humans is uncertain, although authorities believe the disease was probably transported to Egypt via infected cattle from Sudan, and was then passed to humans through *Aedes* mosquitoes, which are carriers of the RVF virus. Seven years earlier, the Egyptian government had finished an enormous dam on the Nile at Aswan. Scientists suspect that the dam's construction created new mosquito breeding grounds, causing an explosion in the mosquito population. In 1987, a second epidemic broke out along the Senegal River, leading to the death of two hundred people. Again, the outbreak had been preceded by the completion of a major dam.

The outbreak also coincided with floods. EPIDEMIOLOGISTS know that epidemics of RVF often occur after heavy rains or in recently flooded regions with high mosquito populations. That is one reason that rising global temperatures are raising alarms. In 1998, the heavy flooding resulting from tropical storms caused by El Niño led to dramatic increases in RVF and other diseases. For example, the main hospital in Kenya to which RVF victims were sent reported seeing as many as 115 new RVF patients a day during the fall of 1998.

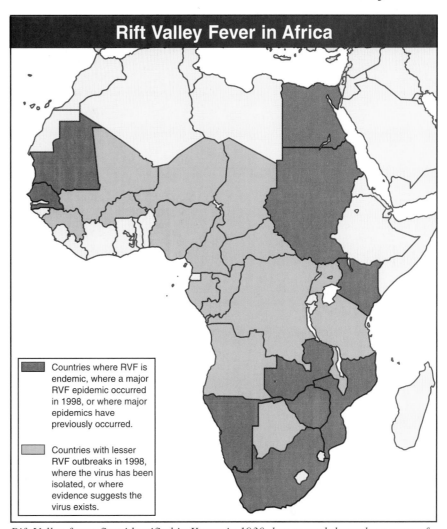

Rift Valley Fever in Africa

■ Countries where RVF is endemic, where a major RVF epidemic occurred in 1998, or where major epidemics have previously occurred.

▨ Countries with lesser RVF outbreaks in 1998, where the virus has been isolated, or where evidence suggests the virus exists.

Rift Valley fever, first identified in Kenya in 1930, has spread throughout most of Africa. The virus that carries it has been spread by Aedes *mosquitoes.*

A New, More Deadly RVF?

Prior to 1998, RVF symptoms typically included fevers and headaches, with full recovery after one to two weeks. Only occasionally did RVF INFECTION become acute in humans, causing retinitis (inflammation of the eye) or even encephalitis *(see page 12)*, which means "swelling of the brain." Historically, however, only about 1 percent of RVF patients died.

Unfortunately, that low death rate may be increasing. During the 1998 outbreak, a number of RVF patients began dying after hemorrhaging. Because many impoverished African nations lack the resources to carry out thorough disease surveillance programs, exactly how often this occurred is unknown. Nor can we be certain that historical data are entirely accurate.

African poverty presents a great challenge to local, regional, and international health officials. Since famine is commonplace throughout the areas most susceptible to RVF, researchers worry that many hungry Africans are acquiring RVF by eating meat infected with the virus. It seems an especially cruel twist of fate that RVF can be transmitted to people who are often already weak and malnourished becore becoming infected through the only food available to them.

Not all the news is bleak, however. A drug called ribavirin seems to effectively treat animals for RVF. While ribavirin had yet to be approved for human use as of early 1999, the drug is a step in the right direction.

Until a safe human VACCINE is devised and made widely available, however, there is no known prevention for RVF. Meanwhile, *Aedes* mosquito populations are expanding, not just in Africa but worldwide. Additional research is desperately needed.

SHIGELLA DYSENTERY

Global Distribution *Shigella dysenteriae* type 1, the most virulent cause of dysentery, has launched epidemics of dysentery throughout the world. Although sporadic outbreaks continue worldwide, since 1979, most epidemics have occurred in Africa.

Causative Agent There are two types of dysentery and each is distinguished by its causative agent. The first and more common form is caused by bacteria of the *Shigella* genus, and the second, amoebic dysentery, is caused by the protozoan *Endamoeba histolytica*.

Transmission Dysentery is most likely spread through person-to-person contact and contaminated water and food. Epidemics usually occur in impoverished areas.

Symptoms Symptoms include bloody diarrhea, abdominal cramps, and rectal pain. Rare cases result in complications that include seizures, renal failure, and hemolytic uremia syndrome.

Treatment Dysentery patients should receive an antibiotic and be rehydrated with salts or in severe cases with intravenous fluids.

Prevention and Control Early detection allows for proper care and control. Health education efforts should promote personal, domestic, and environmental hygiene.

Florence Nightingale, who was nicknamed the "Lady of the Lamp" for her tireless attention to caring for the sick and wounded during the Crimean War in the 1850s, was one of the first to focus attention on the connection between disease and poor sanitation in hospitals.

Clinically speaking, the word *dysentery* refers to any infectious disorder characterized by inflammation of the intestines. Because it has repeatedly affected soldiers during wartime, military historians have often referred to it as campaign fever. To those unfortunate enough to suffer from it, however, it is best described by its most notorious symptom—bloody diarrhea.

There are actually two types of dysentery, both of which have plagued humankind for centuries. The first, and more common, is bacillary dysentery, caused by the corkscrew shaped shigella BACTERIUM, or BACILLUS. The second form is amoebic dysentery, caused by a PROTOZOAN PARASITE, *Endamoeba histolytica*.

Because bacteria and amoebas that cause dysentery are spread in contaminated water (as well as by flies and in contaminated milk), any time unsanitary conditions exist, outbreaks are possible. Dysentery has trailed armies and shadowed the poor. In doing so, it has altered the course of history time and time again.

Dysentery and the Hundred Years' War

No one can be certain when the first dysentery cases occurred, but water-borne illnesses are among humankind's oldest. According to the ancient Egyptians, the god Horus, son of Isis and Osiris, suffered from it. The Greek historian Herodotus wrote that dysentery decimated the powerful Persian army after their surprising defeat by Spartan defenders at the Battle of Thermopylae in 480 B.C.E.

Events much later, during the Middle Ages, were also shaped by dysentery. England's King Edward I died of it in 1307. In 1346, troops under his grandson Edward III were so stricken with it at the Battle of Crécy that the French army ridiculed them as "the bare-bottomed army." Despite the taunt, the English won the battle—an early major engagement of the Hundred Years' War—and gained a hold on Normandy. Edward III's son, Edward, the Black Prince (nicknamed for his signature black armor) one of the greatest military commanders in English history, and the heir apparent to the throne, died of dysentery in 1376, a year before he could succeed his father.

In his stead, the Black Prince's ten-year-old son, Richard II, rose to the throne. The boy proved to be a weak leader, just when England needed a strong one. Since 1348, repeated waves of bubonic plague—the Black Death *(see page 68)*—had been decimating England, and as many as half of England's population had perished from it. As the nation's population fell, the centuries-old feudal system began to collapse as peasants demanded higher pay and new rights. Meanwhile, the French reclaimed much of the territory they had lost.

Richard II's reign came to an end in 1399, when he was deposed by his cousin, Henry Bolingbroke, who ruled as Henry IV. His son, Henry V, suceeded him in 1413, and renewed the war on France. Five years after a smashing victory at Agincourt in 1415 he forced France's Charles VI to name him heir to the French throne. The scene was set for England and France to unite, but the union was not to be. In 1422, Henry died before he could take the French throne—of dysentery.

Dysentery Through the Centuries

Dysentery's impact on English royalty is hardly unique. In every major war prior to the twentieth century, dysentery and other diseases claimed more soldiers than did actual wounds. For example, in 1792, twelve thousand Prussians died of dysentery during an effort to put down the revolutionary forces in France; and in one of the most stunning military setbacks in history, in 1812, eighty thousand soldiers in French emperor Napoleon I's Grande Armée fell sick from dysentery and other diseases at the beginning of a disastrous Russian campaign.

Florence Nightingale and Sanitation

Despite the shadow dysentery has cast on armies, it is not war itself that leads to the spread of this condition, but unsanitary environments. Temporary encampments were often filthy. Even by the nineteenth century, medical science had yet to fully understand the connection between disease and contamination.

During the Crimean War of 1854–56, ten times as many British soldiers died from dysentery as from disease. Nonetheless, the war marked a turning point in the medical community's understanding of sanitation. When Florence Nightingale, superintendent of a London hospital for invalid women, arrived with thirty-four nurses at the army hospital in Scutari (in present-day Turkey), she worked tirelessly in the face of horrid conditions and tremendous harassment from male doctors who dismissed her ideas. After Nightingale instituted thorough, new sanitary measures, the number of deaths from dysentery, cholera (see page 16) and typhus (see page 98) plummeted.

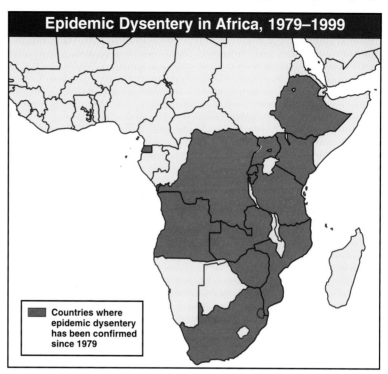

Epidemic Dysentery in Africa, 1979–1999

Countries where epidemic dysentery has been confirmed since 1979

Epidemic dysentery, caused by the bacterium Shigella dysenteriae *type 1, is most common in Africa. Since an outbreak in Zaire in 1979, further epidemics have occurred in fourteen other nations on the continent.*

Dysentery Today

Despite the advances made by Nightingale in the Crimea, it was not until the Russo-Japanese War of 1904–06 that fewer soldiers died from dysentery than war wounds. In 1904, Japanese bacteriologist Kiyoshi Shiga isolated the bacillus that now bears his name: *Shigella dysenteriae.* Discipline about water sanitation and systematic INOCULATION reduced dysentery deaths to a quarter of all combat fatalities.

While dysentery is now usually treatable with ANTIBIOTICS, outbreaks occur whenever conditions allow. The Milwaukee, Wisconsin, health department reported that through August 1999, more than two hundred local cases of shigellosis had been identified—more than double the normal amount. The primary cause: dirty diapers and unwashed hands.

In recent years, shigella has shown signs of developing resistance to antibiotics. In 1969 and 1970, for example, twelve thousand people died in Guatemala during a dysentery EPIDEMIC caused by a strain of drug-resistant shigella. The epidemic spread northward towards the United States before subsiding. If methods are not found to ensure the effectiveness of antibiotics, then dysentery and other water-borne diseases will continue to kill.

SMALLPOX

Global Distribution Smallpox no longer exists naturally.

Causative Agent Smallpox is caused by the viruses *Variola major* and, in a milder form, *Variola minor.*

Transmission Smallpox is spread through contact with pox pus, or through inhaling the breath of an infected person. The disease is highly contagious and spreads quickly because it has an incubation period of twelve days, during which time a person who exhibits no signs of the disease and feels no symptoms could still spread the virus.

Characteristics After the incubation period, high fever, head, back, and muscle aches quickly occur. After another two to five days raised bumps that develop into pustules cover the skin. In severe cases the pustules overlap, creating open sores with the possibility of a multitude of secondary infections. Typically, the fewer the number of pustules covering the body, the better the chance for survival. Even for those that survive, however, are often left pockmarked and sometimes deformed.

Treatment Until a vaccine was developed in the eighteenth century, there was no successful treatment or protection against infection.

Prevention and Control In 1979 smallpox was declared eradicated throughout the world.

Smallpox is one of the oldest diseases known to humankind. In this print, the twelfth-century Japanese shogun Minamoto Yoritomo expels the demon smallpox from Japan.

"I shall only say, that it behooves the whole race of Indians to beware, as the consequence will most certainly occasion measures to be taken, that, in the end will put a most effectual stop to their very being." So wrote Sir Jeffrey Amherst, commander of British forces in America, in 1763. Amherst was referring to a plan to distribute blankets that had been infected with the VIRUS that causes smallpox, one of the deadliest, most horrific diseases known to human history.

Today, smallpox is a disease of the past. The last outbreak occurred in 1977 and there has not been a single case anywhere in the world since then—a monumental scientific achievement. Yet before that date untold millions died in unimaginable pain after being exposed to the disease.

The smallpox virus, which can take the form of either *variola major* or the weaker *variola minor,* is spread through the air—often in the breath of victims. It can also be passed through contact with dead bodies, with their clothing, their bedsheets, or, as the British well knew, on blankets.

Smallpox is particularly dangerous because of its long INCUBATION period. Not until about nine days after a person is exposed to the virus does he or she begin suffering from headaches, fever, and chills, which then briefly subside. These symptoms are followed by the breakout of a rash of pus-filled sores, covering the face, arms, and legs. As the rash spreads, internal organs coincidentally become severely damaged. As the disease progresses further, the sores scab over, and skin begins to drop off. Approximately one quarter of all victims die, but those that survive are left horribly disfigured, and often blinded.

A Disease of the Ancients

No one knows exactly where smallpox came from, or when. Contemporary writings and circumstantial evidence have led some to suggest that the disease may be as old as humankind's first agricultural settlements. Remains of the Egyptian pharaoh Rameses V, dating to 1157 B.C.E., show signs of possible smallpox scarring, and manuscripts from India dating from the same time describe a disease marked by pus-filled sores. Many believe that the Greek historian Thucydides was describing a smallpox EPIDEMIC when he wrote the following about the Plague of Athens that killed hundreds, including the statesman Pericles, in 430 B.C.E.: "Many who were in perfect health . . . were with violent heats in the head and with redness and inflammation of the eyes . . . the breath became unnatural and fetid. The disorder . . . would move the stomach and bring on all the vomits of bile. [The body] was of a vivid color inclining to red, and breaking out in pustules and ulcers."

Smallpox may have also struck Rome during the reign of Emperor Marcus Aurelius Antonius, severely weakening Rome's influence in its territories while the disease raged. It is believed that the disease made its first appearance in China in about 48 C.E., reaching Korea and Japan in about 580 C.E.

While historians theorize on the nature of ancient diseases based on contemporary writing or circumstantial evidence, there is no way of knowing for sure whether these diseases were truly smallpox. In the ninth century, however, the disease was finally identified by the Persian physician Rhazes, who differentiated its symptoms from those of measles (*see page 60*), the childhood disease that causes similar rashes. Interestingly, his work, *The Treatise of Smallpox and Measles,* described smallpox as a common childhood disease in his region of the world. He also noted that survivors of smallpox were safe from contracting the disease again, thus becoming the first person to put forward the theory of acquired IMMUNITY. If smallpox was then no more than a routine childhood illness among his patients, that may have been because, after repeated exposure to the virus, they had developed immunity, allowing them to withstand it more successfully than they had in the past.

During this period, the disease also appears to have spread from the Near East to western and northern Europe, probably along trade routes. How deadly the disease was to Europeans during this time is also conjecture, but little evidence—circumstantial or otherwise—supports the idea that smallpox caused large-scale death in Europe until the sixteenth century. Perhaps Europeans too had begun to develop immunity.

Smallpox the Conquistador

Repeated exposure may have granted Europeans some resistance to the disease during the Middle Ages, but whenever the virus reached a region where it had never been before, it proved catastrophic. Such was the case when the Spanish conquistadores crossed the Atlantic in the sixteenth century. Within a few short years, smallpox, as well as measles and several other diseases, wreaked havoc on the populations of Central and South America. Historians estimate that disease reduced the Native American population from fifty million to one million in two hundred years.

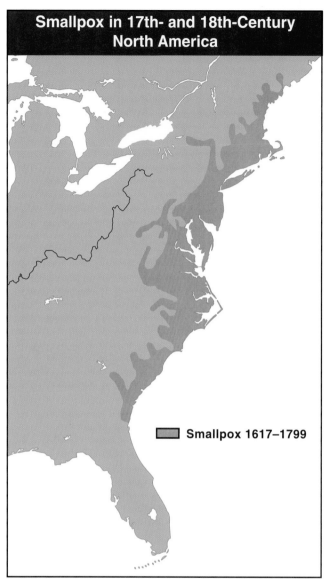

Smallpox in 17th- and 18th-Century North America

◻ Smallpox 1617–1799

Smallpox first arrived in North America in the early 17th century. It may have spread northward from Spanish settlements in Florida or the Caribbean, but there is no conclusive evidence of its spread there before 1800.

A More Deadly Strain?

In 1617, a century after the Spanish arrived in America and the Caribbean, smallpox swept through Native Americans in New England, killing nine out of every ten people. The virus was not spread by the Pilgrim settlers, who landed on Plymouth Rock three years *later*. Nor did it arrive in North America with the first shipload of African slaves to arrive at the Jamestown, Virginia, colony to the south, since that boat did not arrive until 1619. It may well, however, have spread northward from Spanish colonies in Florida or the Caribbean.

Mapping Epidemics

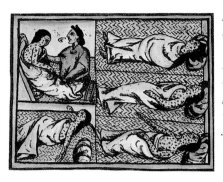

After Europeans arrived in the New World, millions of Native Americans died from smallpox, measles, and other diseases from which they had no immunity.

Interestingly, the sixteenth century marks a turning point in the history of smallpox. Not only did the virus reach the New World during that century, but in Europe it appears to have resurrected itself in a deadlier form. Some have theorized that the virus may have MUTATED during this era, perhaps in the Americas, after contact with Native Americans. Others suggest that a deadlier strain emerged from Africa, and was brought to America, and then back to Europe during the slave trade. In any case, beginning in the sixteenth century, the disease began killing at an alarming rate, preying upon all segments of society. Among those stricken with the disease were Queen Elizabeth I of England (she survived) and William II, prince of Orange (he did not).

Lady Montagu, Cotton Mather, and Variolation

As European doctors grew increasingly frustrated by the disease, a number of increasingly bizarre treatments emerged. Some claimed smallpox's red pus-filled sores could be countered by drinking red wine and placing red curtains and blankets in a room. Other remedies included bloodletting rituals and chewing powdered horse manure. While quarantines were also practiced, they often proved ineffective, since the virus can remain infectious for long periods, particularly in dried scabs.

In Africa and Asia, the search for a cure had been more fruitful, thanks to a method of prevention called variolation. Variolation is the practice of scratching the skin of a healthy person with pus from an actively sick case, thereby causing only a mild INFECTION that killed fewer than 5 percent of those infected—a considerable decrease from the 25 to 30 percent mortality rate among those not treated with variolation.

Variolation was first brought to Europe's attention by Lady Mary Wortly Montagu, wife of the British consul in Constantinople. In the Americas, Puritan minister Cotton Mather learned about the technique from one of his African slaves. When Mather's son Samuel rushed home from college after his roommate died of smallpox during an outbreak in 1721, Mather recruited a Boston doctor named Zabdiel Boylston to use variolation on his son. Although Samuel Mather was saved, the experiment incensed most Bostonians, and one of them proceeded to firebomb the Mathers' house. Nonetheless, 287 Bostonians volunteered for variolation. When the epidemic ended, 2 percent of those variolated had died, compared to 15 percent of those who were not.

In time, variolation grew to be accepted by more and more Europeans and Americans. The French, however, remained opposed to the controversial method until smallpox took the life of King Louis XV in 1774, ending his fifty-nine-year reign. Historians have long suggested that French resistance to variolation may have dramatically affected events to come. Five years after Louis XV's death, a French plan to invade England with help from Spain was foiled when smallpox broke out on French ships, killing eight thousand troops.

Edward Jenner and Cowpox

While variolation proved that it could save the lives of those who dared try it, the fact remained that some people died from the process—either as a direct result of the INOCULATION or in an epidemic that variolation launched artificially. In 1796, Edward Jenner, an English country doctor, noticed that milkmaids who were coming down with a milder cousin of smallpox, known as cowpox, were not coming down with even mild smallpox symptoms. Somehow, acquiring cowpox made these women immune to smallpox. Jenner made one of medical science's greatest breakthroughs when he inoculated a local boy not by smallpox variolation, but with pus taken from a cowpox pustule on the hand of an infected milkmaid. A week later the boy developed a mild reaction, but soon recovered. A few months later, Jenner inoculated the boy again—this time with pus from a smallpox victim. The boy remained perfectly healthy. Jenner had shown that immunity from smallpox could be acquired by prior cowpox inoculation.

Philadelphians receive smallpox vaccination in the late nineteenth century.

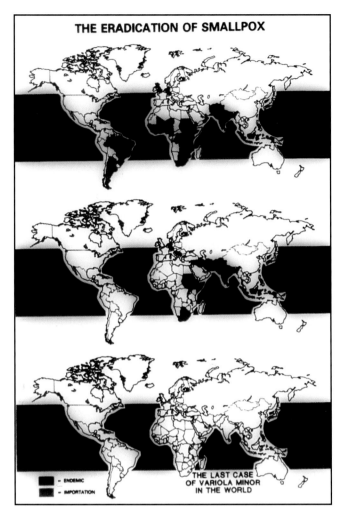

THE ERADICATION OF SMALLPOX

= ENDEMIC

= IMPORTATION

THE LAST CASE
OF VARIOLA MINOR
IN THE WORLD

The successful international effort to eradicate smallpox is documented on the maps at far left. At near left, smallpox vaccine is administered to a child in Bangladesh following the world's last smallpox outbreak.

Jenner named the process VACCINATION, from the Latin word *vacca,* or cow. In 1798, Jenner's findings were presented to the world. The counterattack on smallpox had begun.

The Global Eradication Campaign

The key to eliminating smallpox virus lay in the fact that smallpox, unlike other viruses, can only be TRANSMITTED from human to human. Therefore, the more people that were vaccinated against it, the fewer opportunities the virus would have to spread, particularly since a single vaccination gives life-long immunity. By 1900, smallpox had been virtually ERADICATED from North America and Europe.

The existence of a vaccine, however, does not ensure that it will be distributed to all who need it. Millions of people in the developing world, particularly children, continued to die from the disease. In 1967, the World Health Organization (WHO) formed the Global Commission for the Eradication of Smallpox, with the goal of locating each new outbreak, isolating those

infected, and vaccinating all who came in contact with those victims. Thanks to a massive organizational effort, by 1972 smallpox had been eradicated from South America. Two years later, the few remaining cases were reported in Somalia, Ethiopia, and India. The last *V. major* infection occurred in Bangladesh in 1975 and the *V. minor* in Somalia in 1977. In 1979, WHO announced that smallpox, the disease that had killed countless millions over thousands of years, had been eradicated throughout the world.

The Debate over Smallpox Destruction

While the last smallpox case occurred in 1977, that does not mean that the smallpox virus has entirely disappeared. Nor has it been made harmless. In 1978, after the virus was accidentally released into the air in a laboratory at the University of Birmingham, a researcher died from the disease, and the professor that had allowed the accidental release committed suicide.

During the last few decades, a debate has developed on whether to destroy the last remaining vials of smallpox virus still being held in laboratories. Those in favor of destroying the last samples have argued that as long the virus exists in any quantity, the potential exists for it to be used by governments or terrorists as a biological weapon. Others support this argument by claiming that since the virus's DNA structure has been almost entirely mapped, little further scientific benefit can be gained from keeping the virus alive.

Those opposed to destroying the samples argue that the biological weapons danger is not merely a potential risk. North Korea, Iraq, Russia, and possibly China are suspected of experimenting with the smallpox for military purposes, and therefore, destroying the last openly-stored samples weakens the scientific community's ability to protect those who might be targeted for attack. In addition, the virus's potential in the fight against diseases such as AIDS *(see page 38)* and monkeypox *(see page 66)* is also cited. Some have argued that if cowpox had been eradicated based solely on the harm that it caused, it would not have been available in the fight against smallpox. In 1999, a final decision on eradication was delayed for further consideration.

SYPHILIS

Global Distribution Syphilis is found worldwide.

Causative Agent Syphilis is caused by the bacterium *Treponema pallidum.*

Transmission Syphilis is spread sexually, but it can be passed through contact with a lesion or from mother to fetus.

Characteristics Symptoms appear in three phases, beginning with genital sores, usually at the site of entry. These lesions heal, and several weeks later a rash appears, often accompanied by a fever, achy body, and general tiredness. The third phase, which is less common now, includes abscesses all over the body. These may eat away at the face bones and internal organs. If untreated, death often follows after a long period of pain and suffering.

Treatment Syphilis is treated with the antibiotic penicillin.

Prevention and Control Syphilis can be prevented by using a condom during sexual intercourse or by abstinence.

This woodcut, entitled The Syphilitic, *by Albrecht Dürer, clearly illustrates the disfiguring symptoms of syphilis in the sixteenth century.*

"I tasted the delights of paradise and they produced these torments of hell," cried Dr. Pangloss in Voltaire's eighteenth-century satire *Candide.* Pangloss was describing the symptoms of syphilis, a disease he believed had spread to Europe from the Americas. Voltaire's comic character is known for his ceaseless optimism, and not even a bout with a disfiguring disease could change that. For most real-life syphilis sufferers, however, such optimism is harder to come by. For at least five hundred years, the disease has marked its victims with painful physical degeneration, heart disease, blindness, paralysis, insanity, and death, while also scarring their names and reputations with the stigma of sin.

Syphilis is known as a venereal disease (from Venus, the goddess of love), since the BACTERIUM that causes it, *Treponema pallidum,* is spread by sexual intercourse between humans. Syphilis is one of several related bacterial diseases—the others being yaws, pinta, and bejel—known as treponematoses. Syphilis is the only one of the four that has spread across the globe.

The Origins of Syphilis: A Continuing Debate

Where and when syphilis first emerged has been a subject of ongoing, and sometimes heated, debate. The first known outbreak occurred in Naples, Italy, in 1493. In that year fifty thousand mercenaries in the employ of France's Charles VIII laid siege to the Italian city. Although the French were defeated—thanks largely to an epidemic of typhus *(see page 98)*—when they retreated they carried syphilis with them through Europe.

Contemporary accounts of the disease make clear its gruesome nature. According to one, "Some are covered from head to knee with a rough scabies dotted with black and hideous lumps. They had become so filthy and repugnant that, left on the battlefield, they hoped to die. Some moaned and wept and uttered heart-rending cries because of the ulceration of their male organ."

Almost immediately after the siege ended, a theory began circulating about the disease's origins. Because the disease had broken out shortly after Christopher Columbus and his men had returned from the New World, it seemed logical that the disease had come from the Americas. This view was widely held at the time, and continues to have many supporters to this day, particularly since there is no mention of the disease at any earlier date in Europe.

Others have suggested that the New World origins theory—or the Columbian theory, as it has become

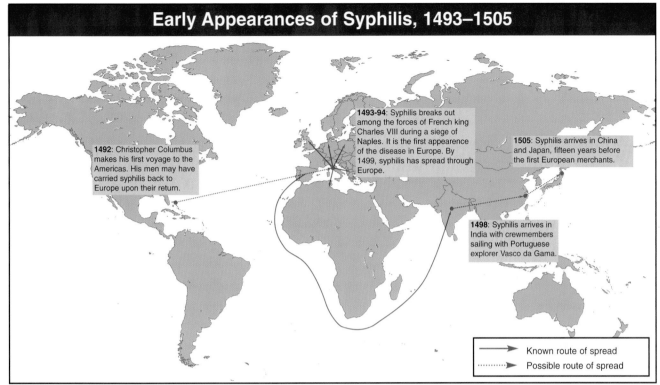

Early Appearances of Syphilis, 1493–1505

1492: Christopher Columbus makes his first voyage to the Americas. His men may have carried syphilis back to Europe upon their return.

1493-94: Syphilis breaks out among the forces of French king Charles VIII during a siege of Naples. It is the first appearence of the disease in Europe. By 1499, syphilis has spread through Europe.

1505: Syphilis arrives in China and Japan, fifteen years before the first European merchants.

1498: Syphilis arrives in India with crewmembers sailing with Portuguese explorer Vasco da Gama.

→ Known route of spread
⋯⋯▸ Possible route of spread

The origin of syphilis has long been debated. Since the early sixteenth century, the most widely accepted theory has been that it arrived in Europe when crewmen sailing with Christopher Columbus brought it from the New World.

known—reflects cultural biases more than scientific evidence. Some argue that syphilis may very well have existed prior to the late fifteenth century, but was not recognized. The key to this theory lies in the fact that syphilis is virtually indistinguishable from pinta, bejel, and yaws, and therefore that all four varieties may be one species, whose effects have varied depending on the climate and the way that each is transmitted. In fact, the treponemes are so closely related that people infected with pinta will often test positive for syphilis. According to this theory, then, the bacterium that causes syphilis may have existed in a different form on many continents before MUTATING into its present form in the fifteenth century.

The Unspeakable Disease

Regardless of how syphilis first got there, fifteenth- and sixteenth-century Europeans were sure that someone else was to blame for its spread. Although it was widely known as "*Morbus Gallicus*" or "French pox," the French referred to it as "Italian pox." On the other hand, the Russians called it "Polish pox," while the Poles called it "German pox."

Although a few recognized that syphilis was spread though sexual contact, most failed to make the connection. Instead they saw the symptoms not as the result of infection, but as punishment from God for generally sinful, though not necessarily sexual, behavior. When the epidemic began, Holy Roman Emperor Maximillian I issued a series of edicts in 1495 banning gambling, cursing, blasphemy, and other vices, but to little effect. There may have been some understanding that the disease was contagious: when clergymen began acquiring the disease, other means of TRANSMISSION, such as breathing the air of an infected person, were also accepted.

The Stigma of Sin

Because syphilis was viewed as God's punishment, curing its victims was not a high priority. When treatments were administered, they often caused more harm than good. Among them were injections of poisonous arsenic compounds, massages with mercury, and even infection with malaria *(see page 56)*. The misery caused by these treatments was seen as just punishment. And when medical authorities began to accept after about 1520 that the disease was sexually transmitted, the stigma associated with the disease only increased.

It was not until the eighteenth century that true medical progress began to be made. In 1736,

Mapping Epidemics

Frenchman Jean Astruc wrote that syphilis was caused by a particular VIRUS that could be identified and categorized. Although the cause of syphilis is not a virus but a bacterium, Astruc was on the right track.

Syphilis in the Victorian Era

By the nineteenth century, syphilis had lost little of its social stigma. In the name of family honor, people bribed examiners to keep it off death certificates. Frequently, women became scapegoats for the disease.

Prostitutes were persecuted ruthlessly, and those even suspected of prostitution were targeted.

In 1866, a law called the Contagious Disease Act was drafted in England targeting prostitutes for forced medical examinations. Under the act, a policeman who suspected a woman of being a syphilitic prostitute could bring her in for three compulsory examinations and up to five days detention. The act was repealed in 1883, when its unfairness became apparent to lawmakers.

Other Sexually Transmitted Diseases

Sexually transmitted diseases, or STDs, as they are known, have been on the rise since the late 1960s. This group of diseases widely range from bacterial infections to incurable viruses, some have been around for centuries while others have mysteriously appeared in the last twenty years. Most STDs are difficult to detect, but without treatment they can lead to serious health problems such as sterility, cervical cancer, blindness, heart disease, and even death. The best way to prevent STDs is by abstaining from sexual relations, practicing safe sex through the use of a condom, or limiting oneself to one partner who is disease-free. Syphilis, AIDS, and hepatitis are all covered in this book; four other major STDs are discussed below.

Chlamydia: The most common bacterial STD in the United States, chlamydia is known as the "silent epidemic" since 75 percent of infected women and 50 percent of men show or feel no symptoms. Those that do may experience discharge from the vagina or penis and a burning feeling when urinating. Women may experience lower abdominal pain, discomfort during sexual intercourse, and bleeding between menstrual periods. Additional symptoms for men may include burning and itching around the opening of the penis or pain and swelling in the testicles. When detected, chlamydia is one of the easiest STDs to treat, either with a single dose of azithromycin or a week-long regimen of doxycycline. If undetected, chlamydia can lead to pelvic inflammatory disease (PID), an infection of a woman's pelvic area and sexual organs. PID is the leading cause of infertility, tubal (ectopic) pregnancies, and, when left untreated, painful scarring that can only be treated with a hysterectomy.

Gonorrhea: *Neisseria gonorrheae,* a bacterium that multiplies in moist warm areas of the body such as the mouth, reproductive tract, and rectum, causes the STD gonorrhea. Because early symptoms are mild or nonexistent, the disease can go undetected for some time. Early symptoms that may occur are a burning sensation when urinating or vaginal discharge that is discolored or bloody. Later symptoms in women, which indicate progression to PID, are abdominal pain, bleeding between menstrual periods, vomiting, or fever. Men also experience discharge, and the burning sensation during urination is often more severe. Symptoms of rectal infection include discharge, itching, and painful bowel movements. Because a penicillin-resistant strain of gonorrhea has developed, other antibiotics are used to treat most infected patients. One of the most effective is ceftriaxone, administered in single-dose injection. Cefixime, ciprofloxacin, or ofloxacin are effective antibiotics patients take orally.

Herpes: Herpes simplex virus (HSV) occurs in two types. HSV-1 is usually found on the lips, while HSV-2 is most commonly found on the genitalia. HSV-2 affects the vulva, vagina, and cervix in women. In men it causes sores on the penis. Herpes lesions, however, are not always present, and people with herpes may remain symptomless for extended periods, possibly passing the virus unknowingly, regardless of the presence of sores. Once a person is infected, he or she is infected for life. Although herpes can be treated, it cannot be cured. The antiviral drug acyclovir can reduce the number and duration of sores.

Genital warts: Human papillomaviruses (HPV) are a group of more than eighty viruses that cause warts. (Warts are tiny noncancerous tumors.) Of the many types of HPV, more than thirty can affect the genital tract. In women the virus can infect the skin around the vulva and anus, the vagina, and the cervix. Men can develop warts around the entrance to the urethra, on the shaft of the penis, and around the anus. Not everyone who is infected with HPV will develop warts; however, he or she will probably always carry the virus and will be able to spread it whenever warts are visible, and possibly even none are detectable. Topical medicines are applied directly on the warts and rinsed off six to eight hours later. The medicine is reapplied until the warts disappear. Laser treatment, burning, freezing, and surgery are other ways to remove certain kinds of warts. In women genital warts have been linked to cervical cancer. If a woman contracts warts she should be sure to have an annual Pap smear to detect any precancerous symptoms.

The Syphilis Bacterium Is Discovered

In Berlin in 1905, German microbiologists Fritz Schaudin and Erich Hoffman discovered the bacterium responsible for syphilis and dubbed it *Treponema pallidum* for its pale, twisted, thread-like appearance. Then, in 1928, Alexander Fleming, a British bacteriologist, found a treatment for the disease when he discovered the ANTIBIOTIC penicillin.

Penicillin could not have come at a better time. Between 1914 and 1945, syphilis killed over two million people in America. With the onset of World War I in 1914, the rate of infection rose dramatically. Prostitutes were again called for compulsory registration and examinations, but the infections continued.

During World War II, which ended in 1945, military planners took aggressive steps to protect their forces. The Germans established and maintained state-run brothels, with doctors on hand, and condoms required. This exclusive focus on prostitutes as the cause of the disease's spread guaranteed the plan to fail. Nothing prevented soldiers from spreading the INFECTION themselves when they engaged in sexual activity with women other than prostitutes.

The Tuskegee Program

Despite the difficulty faced by authorities trying to contain syphilis during wartime, penicillin had a dramatic impact. Following World War II, the number of syphilis cases began falling, thanks largely to the new wonder drug. Today, penicillin remains the only effective medication for treating the disease.

That penicillin has been successfully curing syphilis and many other diseases since the 1920s makes the story of the Tuskegee Program all the more tragic. Beginning in 1932 and ending forty years later, 399 African-American men were involved—without their knowledge—in a U.S. Public Health Service study of syphilis in Tuskegee, Alabama. The men had all contracted the disease but were told they were being treated for "bad blood." Denied treatment for forty years, the men were unaware that they might be spreading the disease to their wives or passing infection to their children. When the men got sick, they were discouraged from seeking help elsewhere. All the men received in exchange for participation in the study was free meals, medical examinations, and burial insurance.

The Syphilis-HIV Connection

Shortly after AIDS *(see page 38)* emerged in 1981, researchers began taking a closer look at syphilis. Both

During World War II, the U.S. government printed educational posters such as this one, warning soldiers of the dangers of sexually transmitted disease. As had been true for centuries, "promiscuous" women were blamed for the disease's spread, while men were seen as innocent victims.

diseases are transmitted during sex, but can also be transmitted from mother to child and through blood transfusions. Both have long dormant periods, during which patients show no symptoms. Like AIDS, syphilis is a chameleon. In 1947, Joseph Earle Moore wrote in the *American Journal of Syphilis*, "The patient who contracts syphilis is faced with a triple hazard: an unfavorable outcome of his infection, the possibility of a fatal reaction to treatment, and lowered resistance to other diseases. To what extent does death directly from syphilis masquerade under other diagnoses, or to what extent is syphilis an indirect cause of death from other conditions? Is it justifiable to assume that syphilis actually ranks first, instead of its apparent tenth, among killing infections?"

This is the most troubling aspect for researchers. It has long been known that syphilis victims are more likely to acquire and transmit AIDS, yet there might be an even more direct relationship. One study has suggested that AIDS might be more deadly when syphilis is involved. More studies are needed to answer this question, but syphilis research has been declining. In the meantime, twelve million new cases are reported annually.

TRYPANOSOMIASIS

Global Distribution Trypanosomiasis is found in many countries in sub-Saharan Africa and Latin America.

Causative Agent The three kinds of sleeping sicknesses—East African, West African, and American trypanosomiasis—are very similar, though caused by different protozoan parasites. The West African version is caused by *Trypanosoma brucei gambiense* and the East African by *Trypanosoma brucei rhodesiense*. The American version, called Chagas disease, is caused by *Trypanosoma cruzi*.

Transmission African trypanosomiasis is transmitted through the bite of an infected tsetse fly; American trypanosomiasis is passed through the excrement of an infected reduviid bug. A person will become infected by scratching a bug bite or rubbing the eyes, nose, or mouth with fingers that have been exposed to the excrement. In rare cases, the disease is passed from an infected pregnant mother to her unborn child, or through blood transfusions or organ transplants.

Symptoms The first sign of the African disease is a chancre (sore) next to the insect bite. In the case of Chagas disease, swelling occurs at the point of infection. Fever, severe headaches, extreme fatigue, aching muscles and joints, and a rash follow in all three varieties. As illness progresses, irritability, slurred speech, confused thoughts, difficulty walking and talking, and seizures occur. Symptoms typically appear within one to four weeks after infection with East African trypanosomiasis and within several months with West African trypanosomiasis. The American version may be slightly milder, but some people will not develop symptoms for ten to twenty years after infection, at which point serious damage to the heart and intestinal tract has already occurred.

Treatment The treatment is the same for the three diseases. Medication is available, but treatment is prolonged. Hospitalization is required during treatment, and periodic follow-up exams, including a spinal tap, are necessary for two years.

Prevention and Control No vaccine or drug exists to prevent any type of trypanosomiasis. When traveling in at-risk regions, people are advised to wear protective clothing, including long-sleeved shirts and long pants. Because the tsetse fly is attracted to bright and dark colors, drab, light-colored clothing is recommended. People should also use insect repellent and bed nets, avoid riding in open air vehicles, and avoid low vegetation.

"As man suffers from the same physical evils as lower animals, he has no right to expect IMMUNITY from the evils of consequence in his struggle for existence. Man is liable to receive from the lower animals, and to communicate to them certain diseases." So wrote Charles Darwin in *The Descent of Man*. Darwin himself seems to have been suffering from the disease trypanosomiasis when he wrote those words in 1868.

If Darwin did have trypanosomiasis, his was the variety known as Chagas disease. Chagas is transmitted by reduviid bugs in South and Central America, where Darwin did much of his work. The other forms of trypanosomiasis, known as sleeping sickness, are found in Africa, where they are spread by the tsetse fly. In all cases, the illness is caused by PROTOZOAN PARASITES known as trypanosomes. In its struggle to survive, the trypanosome alters its outer MEMBRANE, allowing it to move more freely from animals to humans.

The Origins of Sleeping Sickness

Many historians believe that sleeping sickness has its origins in fourteenth-century Africa. It was first spread—along with malaria *(see page 56)* and other diseases—during the period of European colonial expansion that began after the mid-sixteenth century, traveling through the Congo region along trade routes and river tributaries. Over the next three centuries, as Portuguese, French, British, and other European powers began attempting to transport metals and slaves from central Africa to the western port cities, their route was constantly slowed by sleeping-sickness outbreaks. Eventually, as routes were cleared from central Africa to the western coast, the tsetse fly emerged where it had not been before, carrying disease with it. From there, the disease made its way to Europe, and across the Atlantic to the Caribbean and South America with Spanish, French, and English colonists.

Three strains of African trypanosomiasis have been identified, two of which infect humans and one that infects livestock. East African sleeping sickness has a rapid cycle of INFECTION; West African sleeping sickness can take years to kill its victims. Though the IMMUNE SYSTEM responds quickly to sleeping sickness infections, the parasite's ability to MUTATE within a HOST usually allows it to overcome the body's defenses, move on to attack the organs and nervous system, and eventually kill its host. The only early symptoms of either human form of infection are swollen lymph glands, which are common to many diseases. Therefore proper diagnoses are difficult to make without blood tests.

During the early years of the twentieth century, sleeping sickness raged virtually without pause in Africa, killing over half a million people. Following a massive, fifty-year international effort involving a number of regional and international health organizations, the disease was effectively contained by the 1960s. Nonetheless, the disease is steadily returning across the continent. Currently, conservative estimates put the number of people becoming infected each year at more than three hundred thousand.

During the 1990s, sleeping sickness reached epidemic proportions in the Sudan, Angola, and Zaire—now the Democratic Republic of the Congo. The disease is nearing critical levels in other nations as well. While increased global travel has played a part in this spread, the real culprit today is ENDEMIC poverty and war. A 1992 EPIDEMIC coincided with ethnic genocide in Rwanda that pushed millions of refugees into Zaire. World Health Organization (WHO) officials estimate that in some rural areas of the Congo, sleeping sickness has infected 50 percent of the population and is the leading or number two cause of death in many countries. Civil wars in Sudan and Angola, have left millions more vulnerable and without access to medical aid.

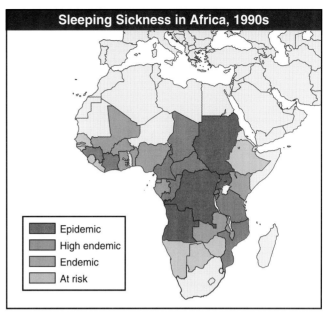

The spread of sleeping sickness in Africa has been facilitated by wars in countries like Sudan, the Democratic Republic of the Congo, and Angola.

Chagas Disease

Meanwhile, across the Atlantic, the number of Chagas disease cases has also been rising. Named for Carlos Chagas, a Brazilian physician who first described it in 1909, Chagas disease manifests symptoms similar to those of sleeping sickness, except that it is TRANSMITTED by a different VECTOR, a reduviid bug, or, as Darwin called it, "the great black bug of the Pampas." The reduviid bug feeds on human blood and thrives in the mud brick walls of thatched roof housing in rural communities.

During the 1970s and 1980s, Chagas's traditional EPIDEMIOLOGICAL pattern changed. Cases began appearing in cities when unscreened blood transfusions created a new means of transmission.

There are no known cures for either sleeping sickness or Chagas disease. Control efforts have focused on killing off tsetse flies and reduviid bugs as well as destroying their habitats when they are in proximity to humans. However, these efforts have been hampered by the extreme poverty of the affected regions. Using what is termed "vector-symbiont intervention," however, Guatemalan and American researchers are exploring new ways to vaccinate not humans but the insects themselves. Their idea is to use genetically engineered bacteria to destroy the PATHOGEN while it is still inside the insect. This remarkable approach may be used someday to help diminish the need for insecticides.

Chagas disease, passed through the excrement of the reduviid bug, has been found thoughout Latin America.

TUBERCULOSIS

Global Distribution Tuberculosis (TB) is found worldwide.

Causative Agent TB is caused by two species of bacteria, *Mycobacterium tuberculosis* and *Mycobacterium bovis*.

Transmission Tuberculosis spreads through the air. If even a single bacillus of *Mycobacterium tuberculosis* is inhaled when an infected person sneezes, coughs, or talks, it can infect someone with the disease.

Symptoms In the early stages of tuberculosis, patients may experience very mild symptoms, or even none at all. As the disease progresses, it typically leads to a lack of appetite, weight loss, chest pain, low fever, a constant cough with mucus and sometimes blood, and night sweats.

Treatment Tuberculosis is usually treated with a multidrug therapy which lasts five to twelve months. Because the drug therapy is long, many do not finish the full term necessary for full recovery. In order to combat this problem the World Health Organization has launched a program in which a health worker monitors and ensures that all TB patients finish their required course of treatment. Unless treated, patients infected with tuberculosis will eventually die from the effects of the disease.

Prevention and Control Infected persons should seek medical attention immediately and begin proper treatment, and should stay home from school or work until successful treatment is concluded.

Robert Koch was the first to identify the tuberculosis bacterium. He is shown here on a "Benefactors of Humanity" advertising card for a chocolate product.

"I have been sick as a dog for the last two weeks; I caught cold in spite of 18 degrees C. of heat, roses, oranges, palms, figs, and three most famous doctors on the island. One sniffed at what I spat up, the second tapped where I spat it from, the third poked about and listened how I spat it. One said I had died, the second that I am dying, the third that I shall die. . . . All this has affected the 'Preludes' and God knows when you will get them."

Thus wrote the great composer Frédéric Chopin, shortly before his death in 1849 at age thirty-nine from what was then known as consumption. Today, consumption is better known as tuberculosis, or TB, and although medical science recently thought that TB had been relegated to the past, the disease has reemerged in the last decade as deadly as ever. Today, nearly one-third of the world's population—1.7 billion people—is infected with TB, leading to nearly four million deaths a year. And most frightening of all is that treatments that have been used for over forty years to cure the disease are losing their effectiveness.

Mycobacterium Tuberculosis

TB is caused by two species of BACTERIA. The first, known as *Mycobacterium bovis,* is TRANSMITTED to humans through the milk of infected cows. The second, and more common, is *Mycobacterium tuberculosis,* spread through the air when breathed out by INFECTED individuals. *M. tuberculosis* may remain in the air for hours, contained in tiny respiratory droplets that are then breathed in by someone else. These droplets, small enough to pass through the defenses of the upper respiratory system, then settle in tiny sacs in the lungs called alveoli. Once there, the bacteria are ingested by WHITE BLOOD CELLS called MACROPHAGES. Some bacteria are killed. Others may multiply and, in victims with already weakened IMMUNE SYSTEMS, spread to other parts of the body.

In the two to eight weeks that follow the infection of a person who was previously healthy, white blood cells known as T CELLS begin to defend against the intruding bacteria by releasing a series of chemical signals. One signal activates specialized CELLS to kill bacteria while walling-off infected macrophages in tiny growths in the lungs called tubercules. At this point, the infection can remain inactive for years, as the BACILLI remain trapped within the tubercules. In fact, only about 10 to 15 percent of those infected with TB ever become sick. This happens when bacteria spread through the bloodstream from the alveoli to other parts of the lungs and elsewhere. If this happens, the body's immune system begins to kill off not only TB bacteria, but healthy tissue as well. These dead cells and tissues form an inflamed mass called a GRAN-ULOMA. Victims may then suffer dramatic weight loss, night sweats, and high fever. As the disease progresses,

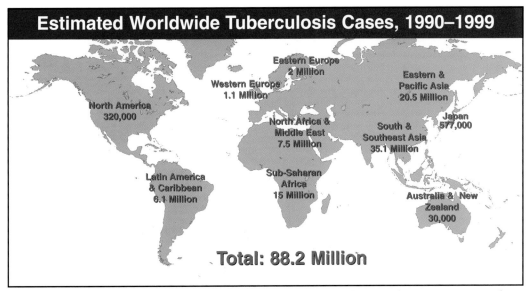

Estimated Worldwide Tuberculosis Cases, 1990–1999

North America
320,000

Western Europe
1.1 Million

Eastern Europe
2 Million

Eastern &
Pacific Asia
20.5 Million

Japan
577,000

North Africa &
Middle East
7.5 Million

South &
Southeast Asia
35.1 Million

Latin America
& Caribbean
6.1 Million

Sub-Saharan
Africa
15 Million

Australia & New
Zealand
30,000

Total: 88.2 Million

Nearly one-third of the world's population now carries the tuberculosis bacterium. In most cases, the infection has not progressed to full-blown illness. However, the number of active cases is expected to top one hundred million worldwide early in the twenty-first century.

cavities form in the lungs. These can break into the lung's large airways, which are called bronchi, allowing larger quantities of bacteria to spread when a victim coughs. Eventually, granulomas begin to liquefy, causing victims to cough up of one of TB's most notorious symptoms—bloody sputum.

The Impact of Industrialization

It is not clear when the first cases of TB occurred, although Egyptian mummies from 2400 B.C.E. show signs that may have been caused by the disease. The number of TB cases in Europe may have risen after 1346, just as the devastating Black Death of bubonic plague *(see page 68)* was reaching Europe. Perhaps the bacterium gained new opportunity to spread during the unusually cold winters of the fourteenth century, when people huddled close together for warmth. Perhaps it increased as more and more people moved from rural farms to towns.

By the seventeenth century, however, scientists had gained a degree of certainty about various aspects of TB. In 1679, the Prussian anatomist Franciscus Sylvius identified tubercules as a verifiable sign that could be found in all TB victims. Soon thereafter, the contagious nature of the disease appears to have been recognized. In 1699, the Italian Republic of Lucca (in present-day Tuscany) issued an edict stating, "Henceforth, human health should no longer be endangered by objects remaining after the death of a consumptive. The names of the diseased should be reported to authorities and measures undertaken for disinfection."

By the nineteenth century, the number of TB cases began to increase dramatically. Rapid industrialization,

the movement of rural populations into the cities, particularly into the working-class slums, all created close contact among people and helped the TB bacteria spread from HOST to host. The poor were more susceptible to the disease because they were more likely to be malnourished, more likely to have weakened immune systems, and therefore less capable of battling infection. By 1815, the "Great White Plague," as consumption was also called, accounted for one quarter of all deaths in England.

The Romance of Consumption

Not all consumption victims were poor. All members of society, whether destitute laborers or well-known composers like Chopin, were susceptible to the disease. The virtuoso violinist Niccolò Paganini; poet John Keats; novelists Charlotte, Anne, and Emily Brontë (and their brother, Branford); and novelist Robert Louis Stevenson all fell to the disease.

Although in previous generations relatives of the dead had sometimes paid doctors to keep the word *consumption* off death certificates, by the early decades of the nineteenth century, the image of the victim, thin and frail, stricken in the prime of youth, coughing into an ever-present handkerchief, actually made acquiring the disease fashionable. So alluring was the image that girls throughout Europe starved themselves and abandoned rouge for whitening face powder to obtain a more consumptive look. Men and women alike feigned symptoms of consumption by carrying handkerchiefs and coughing into them frequently for effect. According to novelist Alexandre Dumas, and only partly in jest, spitting blood and "dying before the age of thirty" were considered "good form."

The Progress of Science

One reason that the ailing consumptive was able to capture the public imagination in the nineteenth century has to do with the chronic nature of the disease. TB is a slow killer that leads to a gradual withering of the body over time. It is not, like cholera *(see page 16)*, diphtheria *(see page 24),* and some of the other great EPIDEMIC illnesses of the day, a sudden killer with symptoms so outwardly debilitating that they could not possibly be romanticized.

Regardless of TB's status as a fashionable disease, scientists recognized that the disease was not to be taken lightly. In Paris, doctors closely monitored the city's poor for common signs and symptoms that might help them understand the disease. After many impoverished citizens were found to have irregular breathing patterns, a doctor named René Laënnec invented the stethoscope, a device to magnify the sound of those patterns. The stethoscope allowed physicians to diagnose the various stages of TB's progress, and new terms, such as emphysema and pleurisy, soon entered the medical lexicon to describe various stages of tubercular disease.

Despite this progress, most doctors still believed that each individual was born with an inherited susceptibility to TB, and depending on environmental factors such as diet or exposure to cold or damp weather, one would or would not come down with the disease.

Other doctors disagreed. They felt that answers might be found within the tubercules that Sylvius had identified in the seventeenth century. In 1865, Jean-Antoine Villemin implanted a tubercule under the skin of a rabbit, and when the rabbit developed lesions, he knew that Sylvius had been right.

The late nineteenth century was a time of enormous progress in scientific understanding, and two of the greatest giants of the era would both help alter the understanding of TB. The same year that Villemin conducted his experiment, Louis Pasteur perfected a method of purifying milk and other liquids by heating them, killing bacteria in the process. Pasteur's method, known as PASTEURIZATION, led to a drop in the number of TB cases caused by *Mycobacterium bovis*. Then, in 1882, German bacteriologist Robert Koch announced that he had identified the *M. tuberculosis* bacterium as the cause of TB. Eight years later, Koch produced a substance called tuberculin, which he argued would cure TB. Although this was later discovered not to be the case, tuberculin is still used today to diagnose the disease. A drop of tuberculin under the skin will stimulate the production of an ANTIBODY in those with TB.

In 1920, two doctors at the Pasteur Institute created a vaccine using a strain of the *M. bovis* bacterium. The VACCINE, known as BCG, or Bacillus Calmette Guérin, after their names, was not entirely effective, but was used extensively in Europe and Canada, and continues to be used in parts of Europe and in the developing world.

The American Sanatorium Movement

Two years after Koch identified the TB bacterium, an American named Edward Trudeau founded the Adirondack Cottage Sanatorium at Saranac Lake, New York. Trudeau had come down with the disease a decade earlier and had sought out fresh mountain air for relief. In time, sanitoria became popular—among those wealthy enough to afford them—throughout the United States and in Europe. In addition to fresh air, patients were put on strict diets, heavy with dairy products, and received plenty of bed rest. Although these measures did not in and of themselves cure TB, they did assist the healing process. What's more, they also served to isolate TB patients, and thus the TB bacteria from the public at large.

Waksman and TB Chemotherapy

In 1939, Selman Waksman of the University of California discovered that certain fungi could inhibit the growth of bacteria. In 1943, he and his fellow researchers isolated an ANTIBIOTIC from a fungus called *Streptomyces griseus*. In 1944, a new drug, streptomycin, was given to a TB patient for the first time. Almost immediately, the patient's disease was halted, the bacteria disappeared from his sputum, and he recovered. Waxman had found a way to rid the body of *M. tuberculosis.*

Following the introduction of streptomycin, health officials in the United States launched a massive campaign to further reduce the number of TB cases. Together with an expansion of the number of sanitoria and the creation of a new array of TB antibiotics, the number of cases in the United States fell from almost 130,000 per year in 1944 to 24,400 in 1989.

After the introduction of antibiotics in the 1940s, health officials were optimistic that tuberculosis could be eradicated. This American Red Cross poster illustrates that confidence.

The battle against TB not only succeeded in the United States but also in many other nations. Public health authorities were so optimistic that during the 1980s, the World Health Organization (WHO) launched a campaign to eradicate TB entirely, as it had done with smallpox *(see page 82)* a few years earlier.

The Return of TB

The English poet John Keats, a consumption victim who died in 1821, at age twenty-seven, wrote, "Land and sea, weakness and decline are great separators, but death is the great divorcer for ever." In many ways, Keats might have been writing about TB.

Since 1990, there has been a dramatic rise in the number of TB cases worldwide, with the vast majority of new infections occurring in a relative handful of countries. Many developed countries, particularly the United States, have also seen rapid increases in the number of TB cases. New York City, home to one of the world's largest immigrant populations, underwent a full-blown TB emergency during the early 1990s. The disease struck New York's poorer neighborhoods hardest, confirming once again that people living in poverty are most at risk for disease.

The global pandemic of AIDS *(see page 38)* has also been a key to the rise in TB, since by destroying the body's immune system, AIDS makes its victims more vulnerable to TB. According to the National Institute of Allergy and Infectious Diseases, the death rate from TB infection among AIDS patients is 80 percent.

Drug-Resistant TB

Perhaps the most frightening trend in the fight against TB has been the appearance of STRAINS that are resistant to all known antibiotics. Drug resistance has come about as TB patients have incorrectly or inconsistently followed prescribed treatments. These new drug-resistant strains are not only incurable but difficult to contain, especially in countries with weak or ineffective health care systems.

WHO's strategy has been to recommend that all countries follow a program of case detection and monitoring called DOTS (Directly Observed Treatment, Short course). Health workers have been mobilized to observe and document patients for six to eight months while they take their anti-TB medicines. In some of the world's poorest nations, the DOTS program has recorded a 95 percent cure rate and has established an affordable ($11 per person) way to prevent new infections and multidrug-resistant TB strains.

Unfortunately, not all nations are successfully following the program. The sixteen countries that WHO cites as "trouble spots" account for more than 80 percent of all TB cases worldwide. Half are countries that lack the funding to control the disease. The other eight countries include Brazil, the Philippines, and Russia, which have the resources, but have yet to take effective action. In Russia, patients in overcrowded TB hospitals are being released every day even though they remain as infectious to others as they were the day they entered the facilities. These patients then return home, putting their families, friends, and neighbors at risk as well.

Worldwide, someone becomes infected with TB every second. The longer TB is allowed to spread, the harder it will be to contain. Some estimate that unless authorities make prolonged efforts to stop this airborne bacterium's spread, by 2020 as many as seventy million people will die and two hundred million will be made sick by a MICROBE that just a few years ago seemed headed for eradication.

TYPHOID

Global Distribution Typhoid occurs worldwide, although it is most common in the developing world.

Causative Agent Typhoid is caused by the bacterium *Salmonella typhi.*

Transmission *Salmonella typhi* are found in the stools of infected individuals, who sometimes pass the infection to others by handling their food or beverages. Typhoid is also often passed through water contaminated with sewage. Flies can also pass the bacteria on to food, particularly in areas where there is not a good sanitation system for the disposal of garbage and feces.

Symptoms The symptoms include fever, headache, fatigue, constipation, loss of appetite, and rose-colored spots on the body. The symptoms range from mild to severe and begin one to three weeks after infection.

Treatment Antibiotics are effective against typhoid.

Prevention and Control There is a vaccine for the disease, but it is not recommended for the general population. Vaccination is reserved for those living with known carriers of typhoid and for people traveling to, or living in, developing countries where typhoid is endemic. Experts advise that people carefully wash their hands after using the bathroom, particularly before preparing food or drinks; not consume raw shellfish, unpasteurized milk, or other dairy products; and not drink from any untreated water systems (streams, ponds, lakes) before boiling or chemically treating the water to kill bacteria and other microorganisms.

In U.S.A. (across the brook)
There lives, unless the papers err,
A very curious Irish cook
In whom the strangest things occur:
Beneath her outside's healthy gloze
Masses of microbes seethe and wallow
And everywhere that MARY goes
Infernal epidemics follow.

—Anonymous poem published in the British humor magazine Punch, *in 1909, about Mary Mallon, an infamous carrier of typhoid.*

For New York City's wealthiest families at the turn of the twentieth century, spending the summer months at country estates on nearby Long Island was a welcome respite from the hustle and bustle of urban life. Each family was waited on by an array of servants—butlers, maids, nannies, gardeners and cooks—all of whom worked to make their employers' lives as carefree as possible. For one Long Island family, however, the summer of 1905 was far from carefree. Several members of the house fell seriously ill with typhoid, a disease caused by INFECTION by a BACTERIUM called *Salmonella typhi*. Its victims often experience fever, blinding headaches, fatigue, either constipation or diarrhea, loss of appetite, and rose-colored spots on the body.

In order to find out what—or who—was spreading the potentially deadly disease around their estate, the family hired a sanitary engineer named George Soper to investigate. Soper learned that the family cook, an Irish immigrant named Mary Mallon, had left her job shortly after the typhoid outbreak began in the home. Soper quickly tracked the cook down, and found her at work in another family's kitchen. When Soper asked the cook for a stool sample for testing, she angrily refused to comply, denying that she had ever had typhoid herself.

Soper then traced Mallon's work history and found that typhoid outbreaks had occurred in several homes in which she had worked. Armed with a court order, Soper had Mallon jailed so that she could be examined. Her stools were found to be swarming with *Salmonella typhi*. Despite the tests, Mallon insisted that she was not carrying the bacterium in her system. In fact, when she had her own test done, none was evident. (Scientists now know that typhoid carriers only periodically shed the bacterium.)

Mallon's incarceration spurred a public outcry as her defenders argued that she was the victim of anti-Irish prejudice. Public pressure led to her release in 1907, but she was required to keep in touch with public health authorities and never to work again as a cook. Upon her release, however, Mallon disappeared. Five years later, she was found working under an assumed name, as a cook in a hospital. She was sent back to prison, and died there in 1938. Mallon, who was responsible for at least forty-seven cases of typhoid (and possibly far more than one hundred), including three deaths, is now better known in history as "Typhoid Mary."

Early Appearances of Typhoid

While "Typhoid Mary" demonstrated how one infected carrier could pass on a deadly disease, *Salmonella typhi* had been making people sick for centuries before she

Countries With Less Than 50 Percent Sanitation Coverage, 1990–1994

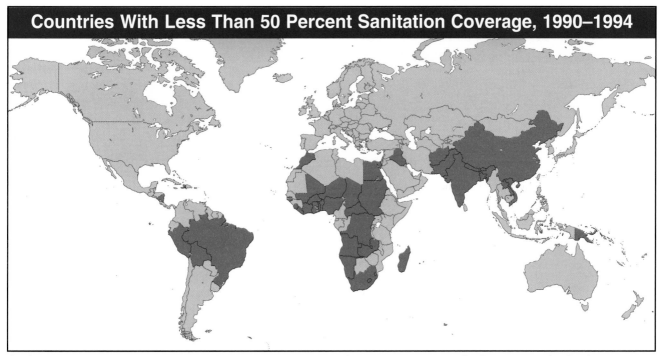

Typhoid is most common in countries where sanintation is poor due to poverty, war, or both. For example, the disease became widespread in Iraq following that nation's defeat in the Gulf War of 1991.

arrived on the scene. Although typhoid shares many symptoms with other diseases (which makes it difficult to pinpoint its first appearance), the Roman emperor Augustus may have had it in the first century C.E.

One reason historians believe typhoid bacteria have circulated for so long is that there are so many ways they can be passed along. In addition to person-to-person TRANSMISSION, the disease can be spread by flies or in drinking water that has been contaminated by human feces. Any time unsanitary conditions exist, typhoid outbreaks are a danger. For this reason, typhoid has likely existed ever since humans ended their nomadic lifestyle, settled in communities along the banks of rivers, and ingested water that had been contaminated upstream.

Typhoid and War

Wherever proper sanitation is lacking, typhoid threatens. Not surprisingly then, typhoid has had a long relationship to warfare. During the American Civil War, for example, more than eighty thousand soldiers in the Union Army died from either typhoid or dysentery *(see page 80)*, a similar ailment. During the Spanish-American War, only 289 Americans died in battle while 1,580 died of typhoid. So many troops fell sick that the army itself was seriously weakened by the illness.

During the Boer War (1899–1901) between Great Britain and the Boer colonists in South Africa, sewage

flowed into the rivers where drinking water was obtained. Toilets were located near eating areas and flies swarmed throughout the camps. Typhoid struck hard.

A Continuing Crisis

Even with careful hygiene, feces can make its way onto food and into the water. Public education and higher standards of sanitation have reduced the incidence of typhoid in the United States and in other developed nations. Still, even today, the disease ravages poor and overpopulated communities worldwide, causing up to sixteen million infections a year and close to a million deaths. In 1996, the central Asian country of Tajikistan reported 16,500 cases in a single year. (By contrast, fewer than five hundred cases are reported annually in the entire United States—70 percent of these in travelers.)

Since the 1940s, effective VACCINES have existed that can prevent the onset of typhoid. Those who are infected can be treated with ANTIBIOTICS. Even so, people in undeveloped countries and communities often lack the resources to provide such care. In Israel, Arab citizens are forty times more likely than Jewish citizens to contract the disease—a direct result of poverty and poor sanitation in Arab villages. As long as impoverished communities without access to clean water, proper sewage systems, and other sanitation devices exist, so too does the risk of typhoid.

Mapping Epidemics

TYPHUS

Global Distribution Typhus is prevalent globally, but is more common in countries with unsanitary conditions.

Causative Agent Typhus is caused by any microbe of the genus *Rickettsia*.

Transmission Typhus is transmitted to humans by insects under the following classifications: epidemic (louse-borne) typhus; murine, or endemic (flea-borne) typhus; scrub (mite-borne) typhus; and tick-borne typhus. In the case of epidemic typhus the infected body louse does not pass the infection through its bite, but rather defecates on the victim, who then scratches the feces into his or her own skin, thereby causing infection.

Characteristics All of the various types of typhus are characterized by a sudden, severe headache, chills, fever, an achy body, and a rash which typically appears on the third to fifth day after infection.

Treatment Antibiotics such as tetracycline and chloramphenicol are effective if given early enough. If typhus goes untreated it can lead to kidney failure or pneumonia, and death.

Prevention and Control Good hygiene and sanitation are the best ways to prevent typhus. Throughout history typhus was usually found in jails, in concentration camps, on ships, and generally in conditions where people were crowded together in dirt, cold, and poverty. For people who live in areas where there is constant risk of infection there is a vaccine which must be administered every several months.

Typhus was first described in 1546 by the "father of epidemiology," Girolamo Fracastoro. In his work *De contagione et contagiosis morbis,* he became the first to suggest that infections spread when tiny bodies he called *seminaria contagionum* were passed from person to person.

The French writer Antoine de Saint-Exupéry once wrote, "War is not a true adventure. . . . It is a disease. It is like typhus." Not a single disease, but the name for related diseases caused by rickettsiae, typhus has altered history more often than any army has done. EPIDEMIC typhus, the most deadly form, is transmitted by lice that nest in unwashed hair and clothes—conditions often found among battle-weary sailors and soldiers. Taken from the Greek word *typhos,* or fever-induced stupor, typhus causes fever and rashes lasting several weeks, and in some victims, coma and death.

Typhus and the Holy Roman Empire

The first known appearance of typhus was in 1489 and 1490, when an outbreak killed 17,000 Spaniards in the final stages of their 800-year effort to expel the Moors from the Iberian peninsula. Historians believe the Spanish brought the disease home from battles in Cyprus. While this epidemic delayed the expulsion of the Moors from Spain by a few years (the Spanish reclaimed their territory in 1492), the next epidemic helped her achieve an unexpected victory. For decades, Spain had battled France for control of Naples. In 1528, France laid siege to Naples, and seemed poised for victory. Then typhus swept Italy, killing 21,000 in July alone. By the end of August, France's force of 25,000 had been reduced to just 4,000. The siege ended.

King Charles I of Spain was also, and more importantly, the Holy Roman Emperor Charles V. When he was not battling other Catholic kings, Charles fought to maintain Catholic supremacy in his empire, contending with Turks, clamping down on Protestants, and conquering newly discovered lands in the Americas. Charles repeatedly found his efforts hampered by typhus. In 1542, thirty thousand of his German troops died of typhus while attacking Turks in Hungary. In 1552, after ten thousand of his troops were felled by typhus while laying siege to the city of Metz, Charles was forced to withdraw. His men then promptly spread the disease to their homes throughout the empire. In 1556, exhausted from maintaining his far-flung lands, Charles abdicated his throne.

Typhus in Spanish America

Although it is not known exactly when typhus crossed the Atlantic, it is clear that Spaniards carried it there. In 1545, hundreds of thousands of people died throughout the Spanish colony of New Spain, including, according to some estimates, as many as 250,000 in Cuba, 150,000 in Tlascala, Mexico, and another 100,000 at Cholula, Mexico. Even as further epidemics broke out

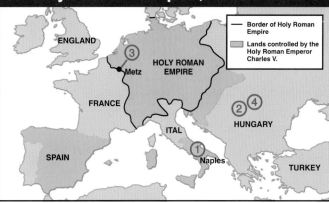

Selected Typhus Outbreaks and the Holy Roman Empire, 1529–1564

① An epidemic in Italy decimates French invaders, allowing the forces of Holy Roman Emperor Charles V to hold Naples (1528).

② Thirty thousand Germans die of typhus while preparing to attack Turks in Hungary (1542).

③ Ten thousand imperial troops are killed by typhus during the siege of Metz, forcing them to withdraw (1552).

④ Typhus kills 80,000 imperial troops in Hungary during another unsuccessful campaign against the Turks (1564).

Typhus struck European armies often in the 1500s.

in 1551, 1573, 1576, and 1595, the Spanish survived while those around them died. Their years of suffering may have won them some resistance to the disease.

Misery Through the Centuries

By the early 1600s, Spain's power was waning. Europe's great religious and political battles would be fought by others. In 1618, Maximilian I, the duke of Bavaria, sent troops to Bohemia to put down a Protestant revolt, launching the Thirty Years' War. Typhus that had struck Württemberg, the Tyrol, and Magdeburg five years earlier ravaged both sides of the conflict. Several years before that war ended, civil war broke out in England. In 1643, typhus struck both the forces of England's Catholic King Charles I and the Puritan army that had deposed him, forcing the king to abandon plans to attack London.

In 1741, a French-Bavarian force seized Prague as 30,000 Austrian defenders fell to the disease. In 1812, typhus was the first enemy that Napoleon's Grande Armée met in its invasion of Russia. The eighteenth and nineteenth centuries also saw a number typhus epidemics that sprang from famine. The worst occurred in Ireland in 1848, after the country's potato crop failed. As food dwindled, typhus raged through the country-side. As many as 700,000 died of disease and starvation.

A New Understanding

In 1909, Frenchman Charles Nicole identified lice as the VECTOR responsible for spreading typhus. The next year, American Howard Taylor Ricketts identified the PATHOGEN the lice were spreading, earning rickettsi-ae their name.

Identifying rickettsiae did not end its trail of death. Ricketts himself died of typhus, as did 150,000 men in the first months of World War I alone. In 1917, typhus

was so rampant in Russia that Bolshevik leader Vladimir Lenin exclaimed, "Either socialism will defeat the louse, or the louse will defeat socialism!"

In 1937, scientists reproduced *rickettsiae* for the first time, and during World War II, a VACCINE was administered to Allied soldiers. While this did not prevent the disease, it did weaken its virulence. Meanwhile, researchers found that the pesticide DDT was an effective weapon against lice.

Despite these advances, typhus remained a threat. The disease was particularly rife in Nazi concentration camps, and epidemics were noted each time Allies liberated a camp. Anne Frank, the diarist who spent most of her short life in exile and hiding, died of typhus at Belsen at age sixteen.

The Evolution of Rickettsia

Today, the developed world is relatively lice-free. That is not the case worldwide, and lice-borne typhus threatens wherever unsanitary conditions exist. Even if humans rid the world of lice, that would not be enough. Like all MICROBES, rickettsiae adapt to survive. In 1951, researchers discovered milder typhus symptoms returning to those who had survived earlier bouts with the disease. While surviving INFECTION often means IMMUNITY from reinfection—as might have been the case with the Spanish conquistadores—this new syndrome, known as Brill-Zinsser disease, contradicts that pattern.

The emergence of murine typhus (from fleas), Rocky Mountain spotted fever (ticks), and tsutsugamushi disease (mites) illustrates yet another means by which rickettsiae have adapted. Louse control has not killed off rickettsiae; it has only made the louse a less efficient HOST

YELLOW FEVER

Global Distribution Yellow fever is found in South America and Africa.

Causative Agent It is caused by yellow fever virus.

Transmission Yellow fever is transmitted through the bite of an infected *Aedes aegypti* mosquito.

Symptoms The symptoms of yellow fever range from mild to fatal. They usually begin three to six days after infection and are characterized by fever, chills, vomiting, and aching muscles, head, and back. If the infection progresses to a severe state, the pulse slows and the gums and nose bleed, with blood in the urine as well. The skin yellows (due to effects on the liver) and bloody, black vomit may occur.

Treatment There is no really effective treatment for yellow fever except rest, fluid replacement, supportive care, and reduction of fever.

Prevention and Control Mosquito control is necessary in the prevention and control of yellow fever. The second best prevention against the virus is a live virus vaccine available to those who live or travel in areas where yellow fever virus is endemic.

Walter Reed headed the U.S. Army Yellow Fever Commission at the turn of the twentieth century.

"New Orleans has been built upon a site that only madness of commercial lust could have tempted men to occupy." So wrote the *London Illustrated News* in the summer of 1853 about an EPIDEMIC of yellow fever in the city. Before it was over, the fever would kill twelve thousand of the city's residents. Nonetheless, in early July, after the first two hundred people had died, the *Orleanian,* a local newspaper, pronounced, "We know of no prevalent diseases, nor do epidemics exist among us. The deaths are fewer in number than in any other city of similar population in the Union." By the end of July, so many people had died that not enough gravediggers could be found to bury them all.

"Go-Aways" and "Can't Get Aways"

Despite the press's refusal to acknowledge any serious health threats in their city, by 1853, longtime residents of New Orleans had dealt with epidemics many times before. Yellow fever, malaria *(see page 56),* cholera *(see page 16),* and other diseases had regularly ravaged the city, particularly during summer. For this reason, any New Orleans family that could afford to leave the city did just that from May to October. The wealthy would travel to northern resorts such as White Sulphur Springs, Virginia (now West Virginia), or Newport, Rhode Island, while middle-class families would head to the Gulf Coast or to the northern side of nearby Lake Pontchartrain. The poor, however, could rarely afford to leave the city. So ingrained was this practice that New Orleans society had long divided up the city's population into "go-aways" and "can't get aways."

Black Vomit and Yellowed Skin

During the epidemic of 1853, New Orleans' "can't get aways" risked contracting a disease whose gruesome symptoms were well known to them, but whose cause remained a mystery. Although doctors did not know it at the time, yellow fever attacks the liver, the kidneys, and the digestive system, causing fever and jaundice. Jaundice, the yellowing of the eyes or skin, is a sign of the disease's rapid progression. As the liver deteriorates further, internal bleeding begins, followed by the vomiting of black blood, the appearance of which has been compared to coffee grounds. According to some estimates, half of those INFECTED are dead within two weeks. Those victims lucky enough to survive are doubly fortunate: they are IMMUNE from further attacks.

Yellow fever survivors often had to suffer through treatments that were only slightly less dangerous than the disease itself. One English traveler to New Orleans in 1843 was actually grateful to his doctor after having blood drained by eighty leeches applied to his throat—a treatment, he claimed, that had saved his life.

The Origin of Yellow Fever

Bloodsucking leeches, of course, do nothing to cure yellow fever. In fact, no real progress was made against the disease until scientists understood where the malady came from in the first place. We now know that yellow fever is caused by a VIRUS that is TRANSMITTED through the bite of an infected female mosquito. By biting an infected person or animal, and then biting a healthy person, the mosquito acts as a conduit for the virus.

None of this was understood in 1853. Instead, some argued that MIASMA, or fumes from buried animal and human corpses, were more likely causes. Others argued that the disease was spread through contagion, or contact between a victim and other people. One New Orleans doctor argued that the CAUSATIVE AGENT was a "wingless animalcula," a germ that was spread by hot weather. And finally, as the local newspapers had done, some blamed the victims themselves for their plight.

Many of the victims were recent Irish immigrants who lived in the waterfront slums, usually in miserably unsanitary conditions. Many worked in construction, digging canals in steaming hot weather, standing in stagnant water. And because much of New Orleans is actually situated below sea level, such work usually was performed amid swarms of mosquitoes.

Because their work and their waterfront neighborhoods exposed them more frequently to mosquitoes carrying the yellow fever virus, the New Orleans' immigrants were blamed for spreading the disease. According to the *Orleanian,* the Irish were falling ill only because they were "poor—reckless and indifferent . . . less cautious and careful of themselves than those that are habituated to our summers." Some lifelong residents of the city argued that New Orleans would have no diseases if outsiders had just stayed away.

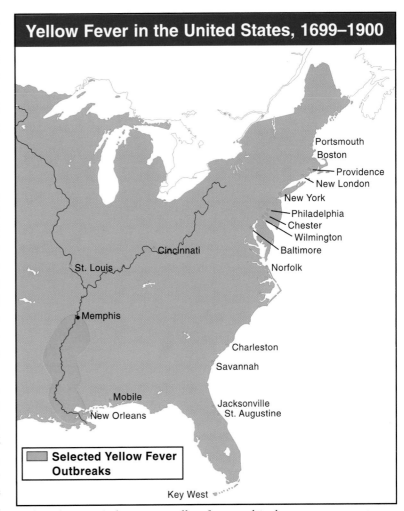

Yellow Fever in the United States, 1699–1900

Portsmouth
Boston
Providence
New London
New York
Philadelphia
Chester
Wilmington
Baltimore
Norfolk
Cincinnati
St. Louis
Memphis
Charleston
Savannah
Mobile
Jacksonville
St. Augustine
New Orleans
Key West

Selected Yellow Fever Outbreaks

Before the twentieth century, yellow fever outbreaks were a constant threat to port cities on the Atlantic, and particularly along the lower Mississippi River, where quarantines were common from New Orleans to Memphis.

Africa's Best Defense

Ironically, it probably *was* outsiders who caused yellow fever's spread—just not outsiders to New Orleans. Instead, the outsiders were Europeans who arrived on the west coast of Africa beginning in the fifteenth century. It is now believed that the virus causing yellow fever emerged from the central African rain forest, and that the people of that region lived with it for centuries before the first whites arrived on the continent's coast. What is more, over those centuries, Africans appear to have developed a degree of resistance to the virus that usually relegated yellow fever to the status of a mild childhood illness. European slave traders arriving in Africa during the sixteenth and seventeenth centuries had no such immunity, and for centuries, white settlement in Africa was limited to a few coastal trading posts, all of which saw almost constant outbreaks of yellow fever and other diseases.

Yellow Fever in the Caribbean

After two centuries of outbreaks among the Slave Coast trading posts, yellow fever made its first appearance in the New World when it broke out in Barbados in 1647. The next year, outbreaks occurred both in Cuba and on the Yucatan Peninsula. The reason the virus took so long to reach the Americas has to do with the mosquito that carries it. The *Aedes aegypti* mosquito only breeds in small bodies of stagnant water, often avoiding natural bodies of water with sandy or muddy bottoms. Water containers such as those transported aboard slave ships bound for the Americas made perfect breeding grounds.

Nonetheless, conditions still have to be just right in order for the yellow fever virus to spread. The *A. aegypti* must bite an infected monkey or human, and then survive long enough to allow the virus to mature within its gut before passing the progeny to a new victim.

Once the virus arrived in the Caribbean, it did so with a vengeance that would alter the course of colonial history in the region. Seven years after the first outbreaks in Cuba and the Yucatan, France sent 1,500 soldiers to conquer the tiny island of St. Lucia. Yellow fever decimated the force within weeks—leaving only 89 survivors. In 1741, when English Admiral Edward Vernon led nineteen thousand men in an attack on the Spanish colonial city of Cartegena in northwest Colombia, half of those men died of yellow fever. And nowhere was yellow fever's impact greater than in Haiti, now the western half of Hispaniola. The island had passed from Spanish to English to French hands during the 1790s, largely due to the high cost of battling rebellions among the African slave population. By 1803, the French army, one of the most powerful forces in the world, had been ravaged by yellow fever in Haiti. Napoleon Bonaparte—soon to crown himself emperor of France—was more interested in expanding his empire closer to home. He withdrew his forces, and the newly independent island was renamed Haiti.

Napoleon had viewed Haiti as the key to France's power in the Americas. It was to be a springboard to greater conquests. Once it was lost he decided to abandon the Americas almost completely. Shortly after losing Haiti, he signed an agreement with President Thomas Jefferson of the United States in which Napoleon agreed to sell France's Louisiana Territory to the United States. That one treaty, signed as a direct result of the ravages of yellow fever in Haiti, doubled the size of the United States overnight.

"Yellow Jack"

Among the French possessions sold to the United States was New Orleans. Situated at the mouth of the Mississippi River, New Orleans was perhaps the busiest port on the Gulf of Mexico. Before the international slave trade was outlawed in the United States in 1808, it was also one of the busiest slave-trading centers in the United States, receiving a steady stream of slave ships at its docks. Also carried in those ships were mosquitoes, some of them infected with yellow fever.

New Orleans was not the only American port to experience yellow fever outbreaks. In fact, ports all along the Atlantic coast began seeing outbreaks shortly after the first cases cases erupted in the Caribbean. Outbreaks occurred as far north as New England. In the 1830s and 1840s, Florida had its statehood delayed because of widespread outbreaks. Still, nowhere in the the United States was yellow fever more prevalent than along the Mississippi, where the disease traveled from New Orleans to points inland. In 1878 and 1879, Memphis, Tennessee, was practically abandoned after two years of epidemics.

The constant onslaught of yellow fever led to dramatic measures. Quarantines were ordered all along the U.S. coastline. Ships from the Caribbean carrying infected passengers were ordered to fly a "Yellow Jack" or yellow flag and were denied permission to land for forty days. Entire cities were quarantined under yellow-jack flags as well, and people caught trying to escape were often shot by police and vigilantes. The quarantines were of marginal effect, however, since they did little to prevent mosquitoes from moving from one place to another.

The U.S. Army Yellow Fever Commission

Health officials remained helpless against yellow fever until the aftermath of the Spanish-American War. During that war, the U.S. Army lost more men to the disease than to enemy fire. Because an occupying force of fifty thousand soldiers remained in Cuba after the war, the U.S. government launched an aggressive effort to find the cause of the disease. Walter Reed, who had previously conducted work on typhoid *(see page 96)*, was appointed head of the U.S. Army Yellow Fever Commission. The commission was particularly interested in a breakthrough in malaria research made in 1897 by Ronald Ross, a British scientist who had proved that mosquitoes are the carriers of the PARASITES that cause malaria. Reed also knew the work of a Cuban doctor named Carlos Finlay, who had correctly surmised in the 1880s that mosquitoes passed yellow fever, although he misidentified the species of mosquito and argued that the causative agent was a BACTERIUM and not a virus.

To test the mosquito theory, Reed enlisted two groups of volunteers. The first wore vomit-stained clothing of yellow fever patients but were housed in quarters completely screened from mosquitoes. The second lived in spotless quarters, where they were exposed to mosquitoes that had bitten yellow fever patients. Only the second group came down with the disease. Reed had proven mosquitoes to be the VECTOR responsible for yellow fever transmission. His commission also proved that the disease was caused by a virus by passing yellow fever SERUM through a filter with pores small enough to block bacteria. Doing so meant that the causative agent was smaller than a bacterium.

Yellow Fever and the Panama Canal

By identifying mosquitoes as the cause of yellow fever's spread, Reed provided the information needed to combat the disease. William Crawford Gorgas, a former army sanitation officer and Reed's successor in Cuba, was chosen to take on the daunting task of ridding the Panama Canal Zone of mosquito-borne diseases during the decade-long canal construction from 1903 to 1913. Gorgas had himself contracted and recovered from yellow fever, which gave him the necessary immunity to face the job. Beginning in 1904, Gorgas waged war on the *Aedes aegypti* mosquito. He built sewer systems and hospitals, cut down jungles, and drained lakes, ponds, ditches, and swamps. He poured oil over the waters he could not drain, to kill mosquito eggs and larvae. He had screens put on every door and window, ordered all water vessels covered, and implemented numerous other rodent-, insect-, and flea-control measures. Within two years, yellow fever had disappeared from the canal zone.

Yellow Fever Today

During the 1930s, the first effective yellow fever VACCINE was developed by Max Theiler of the Rockefeller Institute in New York. Today, researchers are experimenting with ways of vaccinating infected mosquito populations. The hope is that those mosquitoes, when released to breed with other mosquitoes, will eventually pass on resistance to yellow fever to succeeding generations. Because such techniques have yet to be perfected, reducing mosquito populations is still the most effective (and least costly) way to fight the disease.

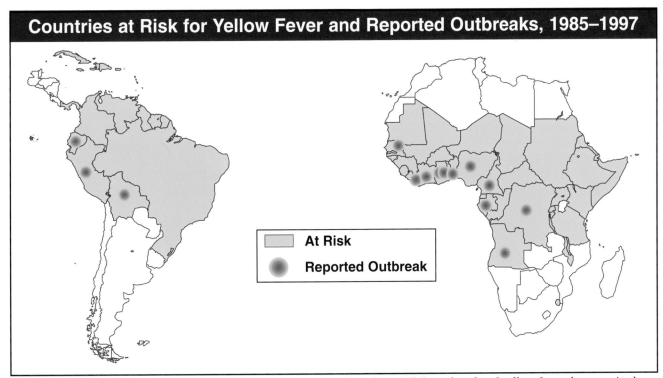

Countries at Risk for Yellow Fever and Reported Outbreaks, 1985–1997

At Risk

Reported Outbreak

These maps show the countries that continue to be at risk for yellow fever. While outbreaks of yellow fever do occur in the Americas, they are rare. In Africa, however, they are more common.

A Chronology of Infectious Disease

The chronology below illustrates selected epidemics and medical breakthroughs throughout history. Major events in world history are also listed to illustrate the interplay between disease and the events of the day. Dates of events related to epidemics and medical discovery are highlighted in red, while dates of all other events are in black.

8500 B.C.E. People in present-day Iraq become the first to domesticate sheep. By 6500 B.C.E. other animals, including goats, pigs, and cattle, will follow.

5000 B.C.E. Egyptians begin to use irrigation to improve their farming.

3000 B.C.E. The world population reaches 100 million.

2700 B.C.E. Malaria-like symptoms are described in the *Nie Ching*, a Chinese medical text.

c. 2400 B.C.E. A Hindu poem warns against lepers with the words, "Let us drive him from our villages with stones."

2400 B.C.E. The remains of Egyptian mummies show signs of possible tuberculosis.

1173 B.C.E. The remains of Pharaoh Rameses V show signs of possible smallpox scarring.

1100–500 B.C.E. The Phoenicians set up trading colonies in the Mediterranean, opening up trading all along the Mediterranean coasts of Europe and Africa.

480 B.C.E. The Plague of Xerxes—probably dysentery—hits the Persian army, contributing to its defeat by Greece. The outbreak, described by the historian Herodotus, becomes the first epidemic to be described at length.

430 B.C.E. Writing about "the Great Plague of Athens," the historian Thucydides describes an outbreak thought to be smallpox, typhus, bubonic plague, or scarlet fever. The disease seriously debilitated the Athenian army, thereby prolonging the Peloponnesian War.

c. 400 B.C.E. Descriptions of a cholera-like disease appear in ancient Indian manuscripts.

c. 400 B.C.E. Greek physician Hippocrates describes the first known cases of jaundice. His studies of environmental factors and their relationship to illness will become cornerstones of medicine.

c. 400 B.C.E. Leprosy is described in Indian and Chinese medical texts.

336 B.C.E. Alexander the Great of Macedonia conquers Asia Minor, Egypt, Mesopotamia, and Persia.

323 B.C.E. Alexander the Great develops a high fever, probably malaria, and dies.

300 B.C.E. Indian manuscripts mention rabies for the first time.

94–74 B.C.E. China opens trade with the West along the "Silk Road."

48 C.E. Smallpox first appears in China.

165–180 The Plague of Galen, probably smallpox or measles, is carried to Rome from the Middle East. Emperors Lucius Verus and Marcus Aurelius Antoninus both die from it.

250–900 Mayan civilization flourishes in southern Mexico and Central America.

395 Malaria has become so prevelant in Rome that farmlands are taken out of cultivation.

410 Alaric, a Teutonic chieftain, dies of malaria after capturing Rome.

542–543 The Plague of Justinian, a pandemic of bubonic plague, sweeps the Mediterranean.

580 Smallpox reaches Korea and Japan.

735–736 Many members of Japan's ruling Fujiwara family fall to smallpox, paving the way for a blossoming of religious fervor that fosters the spread of Buddhism.

900–1300 The Aztecs invade the valley of Mexico, triumphing over other tribes and establishing a highly developed civilization.

1000–1200 European towns grow larger and richer as trade is revived. Western Europe's population grows from 30 million to 42 million in 200 years.

1081 Typhoid fever, dysentery, or malaria strikes the army of Holy Roman Emperor Henry IV during its attack on Rome.

1179 Pope Alexander III orders that lepers wear oversized tunics emblazoned with the letter "L," bans them from touching or looking at non-lepers, and forces them to carry bells or wooden clappers to warn others of their approach.

1300s The Incas begin building their empire on the Pacific coast of South America.

1307 Edward I of England dies of dysentery.

1320 King Phillip V of France accuses lepers of plotting with Jews and Muslims to destroy Christianity by poisoning water wells.

1337 The Hundred Years' War between France and England begins. The war will last until 1453.

1346 English troops are so sick with dysentery at the Battle of Crécy in France that the enemy taunts them with the nickname "the bare-bottomed army."

1347 History's worst bubonic plague pandemic, the Black Death, reaches Europe from Asia. It spreads through the Mediterranean, carried by merchants. One-third of Europe's population and countless millions elsewhere will die from the disease within four years.

1351 To combat growing demands for higher wages by laborers who have survived the Black Death, the English government passes the Ordinance of Laborers, freezing wages at their pre-plague levels.

1358 A peasant revolt known as the Jacquerie uprising takes place in France.

1376 Edward, the Black Prince, and heir to the English throne, dies of dysentery.

1381 Wat Tyler's Rebellion, a peasant revolt, takes place in England.

1415 Henry V of England smashes French forces at the Battle of Agincourt.

1422 Having been declared heir to the French throne, England's Henry V dies of dysentery before he can unite the two nations.

1441 The Portuguese become the first Europeans to explore the west coast of Africa, returning with African slaves.

1489–90 An epidemic of typhus kills 17,000 Spaniards.

1492 Christopher Columbus makes his first attempt to sail to the East Indies, landing instead on an island in the Caribbean and "discovering" the New World.

1493–94 Syphilis appears in Europe for the first time, striking French soldiers in Naples.

1503 Spain begins importing African slave labor to the Americas.

1519 Spanish conquistador Hernán Cortés reaches Mexico. Within two years, his army will seize the Aztec capital at Tenochtitlán.

1520 The Spanish introduce smallpox and measles to the Americas.

1525–27 Two hundred thousand Incas, including ruler Huayna Capac, die of smallpox.

1528 French forces laying siege to Naples are decimated as typhus sweeps through Italy.

1552 Holy Roman Emperor Charles V loses 10,000 men to typhus at the Battle of Metz.

1558 Elizabeth I, the second daughter of Henry VIII, becomes queen of England; her forty-five-year reign will see England emerge as a world power.

1562–98 French Protestants, or Huguenots, clash with Catholics in France.

1576 Diphtheria sweeps through Paris and other European cities, spread by Catholic soldiers quartered in Paris.

1583–1618 Diphtheria ravages Seville for 35 years.

1607 The Jamestown colony becomes the first permanent English settlement in the Americas.

1617–19 Smallpox kills 90 percent of the Indians around Massachusetts Bay.

1618 The Thirty Years' War begins when Maximillian I, the duke of Bavaria, sends troops to Bohemia to put down a Protestant revolt.

1619 The first African slaves arrive in Jamestown, Virginia.

1620 English Pilgrims arrive on Cape Cod, where they settle the Plymouth Colony.

1642 The English Civil War begins.

1643 Both the forces of English king Charles II and the Puritan army that deposed him are struck with typhus, forcing the king to abandon plans to retake London by force.

1647 Yellow fever kills more than 5,000 people in Barbados.

1652 The Dutch found Cape Colony on the southern tip of Africa.

1658 English Puritan Oliver Cromwell dies of malaria.

1662 Spanish doctor Pedro Barba administers a chinchona bark extract to a patient, a treatment taught to Jesuit priests by Indians in the Americas. Quinine, the active ingredient in the bark, will remain the primary treatment for malaria until the 20th century.

1665–66 The Great Plague of London kills at least 20 percent of the population.

1666 The London Fire destroys more than 13,000 houses and leaves 100,000 Londoners homeless, but ends the plague.

1668 Perhaps the earliest recorded epidemic of yellow fever in non-tropical America hits New York.

1679 Prussian Franciscus Sylvius identifies tubercules as a verifiable sign that is common to all tuberculosis patients.

1695 Boston clergyman Cotton Mather describes diphtheria as "a malady of the windpipe."

1703 The first documented case of rabies in the present-day United States occurs in Spanish California.

1710 The first well-documented influenza begins in Russia.

1720 An outbreak of plague in Marseilles kills one-third of the population.

1721–22 A smallpox epidemic in and around Boston results in the first use of inoculation against the disease in the Americas.

1735–40 Diphtheria and scarlet fever spread through parts of New England, killing hundreds, mostly children.

1741 French and Bavarian forces seize Prague as 30,000 Austrian defenders fall to typhus.

1763 The British army distributes to Native Americans blankets intentionally contaminated by smallpox virus.

1774 King Louis XV of France dies from smallpox.

1775–83 The American Revolutionary War takes place, ending in independence for the United States of America.

1780 Dengue fever is identified by Philadelphia doctor Benjamin Rush, who calls the disease "breakbone fever."

1789 The French Revolution begins.

1792 Twelve thousand Prussian troops die of dysentery during an effort to put down the French Revolution.

1798 Edward Jenner announces his discovery of a smallpox vaccine.

1803 French troops in present-day Haiti, on the island of Hispaniola, are decimated by yellow fever, forcing France to cede control of the island to African slaves who had rebelled against them. Emperor Napoleon I decides to withdraw from the Americas.

1803 President Thomas Jefferson purchases the Louisiana Territory from France, doubling U.S. territory.

1812 Napoleon launches an ill-fated attack on Russia.

1812–13 Typhus and dysentery (and hunger and cold) strike Napoleon's army during its Russian campaign. Only 30,000 out of 600,000 soldiers survive.

1815 Tuberculosis accounts for one quarter of all deaths in England this year.

Mapping Epidemics

1817–23 A cholera pandemic originates in India and spreads throughout Asia, the Middle East, and Russia.

1826–28 Dengue fever spreads from Savannah, Georgia, to other cities along the Atlantic seaboard.

1826–37 A second cholera pandemic begins in India and spreads through Asia to Russia and Ottoman Turkey, and then to Europe and the Americas.

1827–28 Russia invades the Ottoman Empire in support of Serbian nationalists.

1848 Typhus sweeps Ireland after the country's potato crop fails. Some 700,000 people starve or die of disease.

1853 Yellow fever kills 12,000 people in New Orleans.

1854–56 After Russia invades the Ottoman Empire, Great Britain and France enter the Crimean War on the side of the Turks. Russia is defeated.

1854 Florence Nightingale arrives in Scutari, Turkey, and institutes sanitation measures that lead to a rapid decline in deaths from dysentery, cholera, and other diseases.

1853 A diphtheria pandemic begins in Great Britain, spreading worldwide by 1856.

1854 John Snow, an English physician, proves that cholera is spread through contaminated water.

1861–65 During the American Civil War, three times as many soldiers die from disease as die from combat wounds.

1863–66 A cholera pandemic begins in India in 1863, and spreads to Europe and the United States.

1865 A leper colony is founded on Molokai, Hawaii. Eight years later, Belgian missionary Damien de Veuster arrives on the island to care for the sick.

1866 The British Parliament passes the Contagious Disease Act, allowing police to forcibly examine women suspected of prostitution for signs of syphilis.

1871 The virus that causes Japanese encephalitis (JE) is identified in Japan.

1873 G. Armauer Hansen isolates the bacterium that causes leprosy after scratching a women's eye with pus from a leper's lesion.

1876 Robert Koch discovers that anthrax is caused by the bacterium *Bacillus anthracis*. This discovery leads to a revolution in medicine, illustrating for the first time that specific diseases can be caused by specific microorganisms.

1878 Queen Victoria of England loses both a daughter and granddaughter to diphtheria.

1878–79 Memphis, Tennessee, is virtually abandoned during a severe yellow fever epidemic.

1881–96 A fifth cholera pandemic begins again in India and spreads both to the east and west. Because of improved sanitation many European and American cities are spared.

1882 Robert Koch identifies the bacterium that causes tuberculosis.

1883 German pathologist Edwin Klebs isolates the bacterium that causes diphtheria.

1884 Robert Koch confirms John Snow's discovery that cholera is spread in contaminated water, on soiled clothing, and unwashed hands.

1884 Louis Pasteur develops the first rabies vaccine.

1890s–1900s A third plague epidemic that began in China in the 1850s now reaches pandemic proportions, striking Hawaii, South America, India, Egypt, and North Africa particularly hard

1894 French researcher Emile Roux announces a cure for diphtheria.

1898 Over 1,500 American soldiers die of typhoid fever during the Spanish-American War. Only 289 die of battle wounds.

1898 The United States annexes Puerto Rico and the Philippines from Spain after winning the Spanish-American War.

1898 British doctor Ronald Ross confirms that mosquitoes spread malaria from bird to bird.

1899–1901 Britain defeats Dutch settlers known as Boers to gain full control of South Africa.

1900 The U.S. Army Yellow Fever Commission effectively rids Havana, Cuba, of yellow fever by eliminating its mosquito population.

1902 Two British physicians working in Gambia identify the parasite that causes chronic West African sleeping sickness.

1903 The United States begins building the Panama Canal.

1905 Mary Mallon, known as "Typhoid Mary," is forcibly detained after being linked to numerous typhoid outbreaks.

1909 Simon Flexner proves that polio is contagious.

1914–18 World War I takes place, pitting Germany, the Austro-Hungarian Empire, and the Ottoman Empire against the Allied forces of France, Britain, Italy, Russia and eventually the United States.

1916 The first widespread polio outbreak occurs in the United States, killing approximately 7,000.

1917–19 The most devastating influenza pandemic ever kills as many as 30 million worldwide.

1917 Bolshevik revolutionaries, led by V.I. Lenin, seize control of Russia.

1917 As typhus rages through Russia, Bolshevik leader V.I. Lenin exclaims, "Either socialism will defeat the louse or the louse will defeat socialism!"

1925 A diphtheria epidemic in Nome, Alaska, ends when dogsleds are used to carry antitoxin serum 600 miles through a blizzard.

1927 Philip Drinker introduces the first iron lung, a chamber that forces air in and out of the lungs of polio patients.

1929 Alexander Fleming introduces penicillin.

1930 Western equine encephalitis is found for the first time, in the brain of a horse.

1930 Rift Valley fever is discovered in Kenya.

1932 The U.S. Public Heath Service begins a forty-year syphilis study on 399 African-American men. The subjects are never told that they are infected with syphilis, nor are they treated for it.

1933 St. Louis encephalitis is discovered in the United States.

1933 Sister Elizabeth Kenny opens her first polio clinic.

1934 The Warm Springs Foundation, founded by polio patient Franklin D. Roosevelt, becomes the National Foundation for Infantile Paralysis two years after Roosevelt, who was stricken with the disease as an adult, assumes the presidency of the United States.

1936–37 Over 3,000 people die from meningitis in Chad.

1939–45 World War II engulfs Europe and Asia, eventually ending in the defeat of the Axis powers—Germany, Italy, and Japan.

1944 A year after Selman Waksman of the University of California isolates an antibiotic from a fungus, streptomycin, an effective treatment for tuberculosis, is given to a patient.

1950 The world's first known case of Dengue hemorrhagic fever occurs in the Philippines.

1950–99 The world's population grows from around 2.5 billion to 6 billion.

1950–53 United Nations forces intervene in the Korean War after North Korea invades South Korea.

1950–53 About 3,000 U.S. and other UN troops stationed in Korea become infected with Hantaan virus, and develop hemorrhagic fever with renal syndrome (HFRS).

1953 Argentine hemorrhagic fever erupts for the first time.

1955 Dr. Jonas Salk's killed-virus polio vaccine is introduced to the general public.

1957–58 An "Asian Flu" pandemic spreads worldwide from China. The virus will infect as many as 35 percent of the world's population.

1958 Monkeypox is identified in lab monkeys from Africa.

1959 Bolivian hemorrhagic fever is identified in the Beni province in Bolivia.

1962 Rachel Carson publishes *Silent Spring*. The environmental manifesto eventually leads the United States and other countries to ban the pesticide DDT.

1963 LaCrosse encephilitis is discovered in Wisconsin.

1963 Vaccination for measles becomes routine in the United States.

1964–75 U.S. forces assist the South Vietnamese army in a failed effort to prevent North Vietnam's takeover of South Vietnam.

1967 Laboratory workers in Marburg, Germany, die after becoming infected with Marburg virus.

1969 Scientists isolate Lassa fever virus in West Africa.

1970 A group of boys in Zaire become the first humans to contract monkeypox.

1975 The first cases of Lyme disease are discovered in Old Lyme, Connecticut.

1976 Ebola hemorrhagic fever is reported for the first time in Nzara, Sudan. Over 250 people die.

1976 Several members of the American Legion die during and after a convention at the Bellevue-Stratford Hotel in Philadelphia. Scientists discover the cause of the disease is bacteria in the hotel's water cooler.

1977 Smallpox is eradicated worldwide.

1977 The first Rift Valley fever epidemic to involve humans occurs in Egypt.

1979 An outbreak of anthrax follows an explosion at a plant in the Soviet Union. In 1992, Russian president Boris Yeltsin admits that anthrax biological-warfare research has been conducted at the site.

1980 The first cases of HIV infection are reported in San Francisco, Los Angeles, and New York.

1981–85 Dengue hemorrhagic fever spreads through Latin America, first reaching the United States in 1985.

1986 The first cases of bovine spongiform encephalopathy, or mad cow disease, are found in British cattle.

1989 A mysterious form of hepatitis known as non-A, non-B (NANB) is finally identified as hepatitis C.

1989 Laboratory monkeys in Reston, Virginia, begin dying from an Ebola-like hemorrhagic fever. The virus that causes the deaths proves harmless to humans.

1991 Following revolutions in Eastern Europe, the Soviet Union collapses.

1991 United Nations weapons inspectors discover that Iraq grew large quantities of anthrax during the Gulf War

1992 African sleeping sickness strikes Rwandan refugee camps in the Democratic Republic of the Congo.

1993 Hantavirus pulmonary syndrome (HPS) is identified in the Southwestern United States.

1993 Five hundred people are infected with *E. coli* O157:57 bacteria after eating contaminated meat at a chain of fast food restaurants.

1994 Bolivian hemorrhagic fever resurfaces, killing six in Magdelena, Bolivia.

1995 Over 300 die in Kikwit, Zaire, from Ebola hemorrhagic fever.

1996 The U.S. Food and Drug Administration approves the use of protease inhibitors to treat HIV infection.

1996 Bacterial meningitis kills over 17,000 in Africa this year.

1996 Over 500 people in Zaire become infected with the virus that causes monkeypox.

1997–98 The El Niño phenomenon causes unusual weather patterns worldwide.

1998 The United States begins vaccinating its military personnel against anthrax due to an increased threat of its use as a biological weapon.

1998 Reseachers introduce a Lyme disease vaccine to the market for the first time.

1999 Scientists announce that the chimpanzee *Pan troglodytes troglodytes* is the source of the HIV-1 virus.

1999 In what may have been its first appearance in North America, West Nile virus kills six people in metropolitan New York.

Index

For Further Reading/Internet Resources

Books

Biddle, Wayne. *A Field Guide to Germs*. New York: Doubleday and Company, 1995.

Bordley, James III, and A. McGehee Harvey, M.D. *Two Centuries of American Medicine: 1776–1976*. Philadelphia: W.B. Saunders Co., 1976.

Cartwright, Frederick F., and Michael D. Biddiss. *Disease and History*. New York: Dorset Press, 1972.

De Kruif, Paul. *The Microbe Hunters*. New York: Harcourt Brace and Company, 1926.

Diamond, Jared. *Guns, Germs, and Steel: The Fates of Human Societies*. New York and London: W.W. Norton Company, 1999.

Dixon, Bernard. *The Power Unseen: How Microbes Rule the World*. Oxford and New York: W.H. Freeman, 1994.

Garrett, Laurie. *The Coming Plague: Newly Emerging Diseases in A World Out of Balance*. New York: Penguin Books, 1994.

Goodfield, June. *Quest for the Killers*. Boston: Birkhauser, 1985.

Hays, J.N. *The Burdens of Disease: Epidemics and Human Response in Western History*. New Brunswick, NJ, and London: Rutgers University Press, 1998.

Helman, Cecil G. *Culture, Health and Illness*. Oxford: Butterworth-Heineman, 1994.

Karlen, Arno. *Man and Microbes: Disease and Plagues in History and Modern Times*. New York: G.P. Putnam & Sons, 1995.

Kiple, Kenneth F., ed. *Plague, Pox and Pestilence*. New York: Barnes and Noble Books, 1997.

Lappé, Marc. *Breakout: The Evolving Threat of Drug-Resistant Disease*. San Francisco: Sierra Club, 1995.

Leavitt, Judith Waltzer. *Typhoid Mary: Captive to the Public Health*. Boston: Beacon Press, 1997.

Lederberg, Joshua, Robert E. Shope, and Stanley C. Oaks, Jr. *Emerging Infections. Microbial Threats to Health in the United States*. Washington, D.C.: National Academy Press, 1992.

McNeill, William H. *Plagues and Peoples*. New York: Anchor Books, 1989.

Preston, Richard. *The Hot Zone*. New York: Anchor Books, 1994.

Rosenberg Charles E. *The Cholera Years: The United States in 1832, 1849, and 1866*. Chicago: The University of Chicago Press, 1962.

Roueché, Berton. *The Medical Detectives*. New York: Times Books, 1980.

———. *The Medical Detectives*, Vol. II. New York: E.P. Dutton, 1984.

Ryan, Frank, M.D. *The Forgotten Plague: How the Battle against Tuberculosis Was Won—and Lost*. Boston: Little Brown and Company, 1992.

———.*Virus X: Tracking the New Killer Plagues*. Boston: Little Brown and Company, 1997.

Schmeck, Harold M., Jr. "Medical Detective Story: A Polio Virus Tracked Down." In Keylon, Arleen, ed. *Science of the Times 4: A New York Times Survey*. New York: Arno Press, 1981.

Shilts, Randy. *And the Band Played On: Politics, People, and the AIDS Epidemic*. New York: St. Martin's Press, 1987.

Wilkins, Robert. *The Fireside Book of Deadly Diseases*. London: Robert Hale Ltd., 1994.

Wills, Christopher. *Yellow Fever, Black Goddess: The Coevolution of People and Plagues*. Reading, MA: Addison-Wesley, 1996.

Zinsser, Hans. *Rats, Lice and History*. Boston: Little Brown and Company, 1935.

Zimmerman, Barry E., and David J. Zimmerman. *Killer Germs. Microbes and Diseases that Threaten Humanity*. Chicago: Contemporary Books, 1996.

Ziporyn, Terry. *Disease in the Popular American Press: The Case of Diphtheria, Typhoid Fever, and Syphilis, 1870–1920*. New York: Greenwood Press, 1988.

The Internet

The Internet is playing an increasingly important role in the fight against infectious disease. In tracking the outbreak and spread of disease, epidemiologists and other health professionals are able to share information more rapidly than ever before. The websites listed below are a small but representative sample of those that provide useful additional information on infectious disease and epidemics. To begin your further research, we recommend starting with federal and international organizations, particularly the Centers for Disease Control (CDC) and the World Health Organization. Information on all diseases covered in this book can be found on the websites run by these organizations. We found all of the websites listed below both useful and informative, but neither the authors nor the publisher of this book are responsible for the specific content of any of the websites:

Federal and International Public Health Websites

Centers for Disease Control. http://cdc.gov/

MEDLINE: National Library of Medicine. http://www.nlm.nih.gov/databases/freemedl.html

National Institute of Allergies and Infectious Diseases. http://www.niaid.nih.gov/

Pan-American Health Organization. http://www.paho.org/

For Further Reading

U.S. Department of State, Early Warning and Surveillance of Infectious Disease
        http://www.state.gov/www/global/oes/health/task_force/early.html
U.S. Global Change Research Information Office–Climate, Ecology and Human Health.
        http://www.gcrio.org/CONSEQUENCES/vol3no2/climhealth.html
Walter Reed Army Medical Center–Infectious Disease Service.
        http://www.wramc.amedd.army.mil/departments/medicine/infdis/id_home.htm
World Health Organization. http://www.who.int/

Non-Governmental Internet Resources
The Alliance for the Prudent Use of Antibiotics. http://www.healthsci.tufts.edu/apua/apua.html
American Society of Tropical Medicine and Hygeine. http://www.astmh.org/
Anatomy of an Epidemic. http://library.advanced.org/11170/
The Association of State and Territorial Directors of Health Promotion and Public Health Education.
        http://www.astdhpphe.org/
Brown University–Development of Vaccines to Infectious Disease. http://www.brown.edu/Courses/Bio_160/
CELLS alive! http://www.cellsalive.com/
The DNA Vaccine Web. http://www.genweb.com/Dnavax/dnavax.html
Emerging Infectious Diseases Journal Homepage. http://www.cdc.gov/ncidod/EID/
Emerging Infections Information Network, Department of Epidemiology and Public Health, Yale University School of Medicine.
        http://info.med.yale.edu/EIINet/
Epidemic: The World of Infectious Disease. http://www.amnh.org/exhibitions/epidemic/
Frontline–Endemic Infectious Disease. http://www.pbs.org/wgbh/pages/frontline/shows/syndrome/analysis/diseases.html
Harvard School of Public Health. http://www.hsph.harvard.edu/
Indiana University–Resources for School Health Educators K-12. http://www.indiana.edu/~aphs/hlthk-12.html
Infectious Disease News. http://www.slackinc.com/general/idn/idncurr.htm
Infectious Disease News. http://206.1.96.2/general/idn/199606/crisis.htm
Michigan State University–The Microbe Zoo. http://commtechlab.msu.edu/sites/dlc-me/zoo/
The Mining Company–Antibiotics: The Basics. http://pharmacology.miningco.com/library/weekly/aa970514.htm
Outbreak. http://www.outbreak.org/cgi-unreg/dynaserve.exe/index.html
New York State Department of Health Communicable Disease Fact Sheets. http://www.health.state.ny.us/nysdoh/consumer/commun.htm
Panafrican News Agency–Science and Health. http://www.africanews.org/PANA/science/
The Plumber–Plagues and Epidemics. http://www.theplumber.com/plague.html
Photo Gallery of Pathogenic Bacteria. http://www.geocities.com/CapeCanaveral/3504/gallery.htm
PROMed: Emerging Infectious Disease Reports. http://www.healthnet.org/programs/promed.html
Tulane University School of Public Health and Tropical Medicine. http://www.sph.tulane.edu/
University of Arizona–Biology Project. http://www.biology.arizona.edu/immunology/immunology.html
University of Cape Town–Principles of Virus Architecture. http://www.uct.ac.za/depts/mmi/stannard/virarch.html
University of Minnesota–The Pathophysiology of Infectious Diseases. http://www.courses.ahc.umn.edu/medical-!school/IDis/class.html
University of Utah–Image Photo Gallery. http://medstat.med.utah.edu/parasitology/
University of Wisconsin–Antimicrobial Agents. http://www.bact.wisc.edu/Bact330/lectureama
University of Wisconsin–Climate and Infectious Disease. http://rainforest.meteor.wisc.edu/Clim_Inf_D.html
University of Wisconsin–Information about Microbiology for the Public. http://www.bact.wisc.edu/GenInfo.html

Useful Infectious Disease Links Pages
The websites listed below are among those that provide numerous links to other sites on the World Wide Web:
All the Virology on the WWW. http://www.virology.net/garryfavweb.html
Eutopia: Epidemiology and Medical Geography. http://ihs2.unn.ac.uk:8080/epidem.htm
Infectious Disease Weblink. http://pages.prodigy.net/pdeziel/
Infectious Diseases–Suite101.com. http://www.suite101.com/linkcategory.cfm/microbiology/244
Just Another Medical Geography Page. http://members.xoom.com/mgdigest/medical_geography.html
The Karolinska Institute–History of Diseases. http://www.mic.ki.se/HistDis.html
The Wonderful World of Diseases. http://www.diseaseworld.com/disease.htm